No Minor Accomplishment

No Minor Accomplishment

The Revival of New Jersey
Professional Baseball

BOB GOLON

Rivergate Books, an imprint of Rutgers University Press
New Brunswick, New Jersey, and London

Library of Congress Cataloging-in-Publication Data

Golon, Bob.
  No minor accomplishment: the revival of New Jersey professional
baseball / Bob Golon.
    p. cm.
  Includes bibliographical references and index.
  ISBN 978-0-8135-4274-4 (pbk. : alk. paper)
  1. Minor league baseball—New Jersey—History.   2. Baseball teams—New Jersey—
History.   I. Title.
  GV875.A1G65 2008
  796.357'6409749—dc22

                                                                        2007024984

A British Cataloging-in-Publication record for this book is available from
the British Library.

Visit our Web site: http://rutgerspress.rutgers.edu
Manufactured in the United States of America

To Jill, Jay, and Janet,
John, Olga, Jim, and Marie,
I hope I've done enough.

Contents

Acknowledgments

Since August 2004, I've depended on many people for the help and support necessary to finish this project, and I would like to acknowledge them now, and sincerely hope that I do not leave anybody out.

First, I'd like to thank my former employer, the Bernards Township Library in Basking Ridge, under the direction of Anne Meany, and my supervisor, Ruth Lufkin, for their early encouragement of this project. I would especially like to thank the head children's librarian, Antonette D'Orazio, for drafting me to do a presentation on New Jersey baseball for the kids of Bernards Township, which led to the idea of this book. I would also like to thank my current employers, the Special Collections and University Archives, Rutgers University Libraries; and in particular the head of Special Collections, Ronald Becker; the university archivist Tom Frusciano; and all of my coworkers for their continued patience and encouragement as I have moved through this process. The materials contained in the New Jersey Room at Special Collection, as well as the online resources available via the Rutgers University Libraries Web site were a great source of historical information for me.

I'd like to acknowledge Robert Mulcahy, athletic director of Rutgers University, for giving me insight into his days with the New Jersey Sports and Exposition Authority and their efforts to bring baseball to the Meadowlands Sports Complex in the 1980s. Also, Helene Lynch, the local history librarian, and Rina Banerjee, the adult reference librarian, at the Mercer County Library, Lawrenceville branch, for assisting me in researching the early days of the Trenton Thunder and Waterfront Park via their vertical clippings files. Tony Torre and Herm Sorcher, the former general manager and assistant general manager of the New Jersey Cardinals, provided me with insight into the operation of the Sussex County club prior to its move to Pennsylvania, as did the use of the microfilm facilities at the Sussex County Library, Newton branch.

Brad Taylor and his fantastic staff at the Trenton Thunder gave me continuing access during my research. In particular, I would also like to thank Dan Loney for arranging my initial visit to Trenton, as well as Eric Lipsman, Bill Cook, and Greg Coleman in the front office and former general manager Rick Brenner for sharing their insights into the organization with me. Former head groundskeeper, Nicole Sherry, was gracious enough to sit for an interview prior to her leaving for the head groundskeeper job with the Baltimore Orioles. I'd also like to thank the former Thunder and current New York Mets broadcaster, Tom McCarthy, for sharing his recollections of his days with the Thunder with me.

I owe a debt of gratitude to Bob Wirz, the publisher of the *Weekly Independent Baseball Insider*, for spending four hours with me at his home in Connecticut, teaching me all about the ins and outs of independent professional baseball. Also, Frank Boulton, the founder and chief executive officer of the Atlantic League, sat for a lengthy interview that enabled me to better understand the origins and continued successful operation of the league. Joe Klein, the executive director of the Atlantic League, met with me twice in his office in Camden to explain to me the detailed inner workings of player-procurement issues and procedures of the Atlantic League; and Adam Gladstone, one of the chief talent scouts of the league, gave me great detail on what he looks for in an Atlantic League player. Mike Ashmore, who writes a successful Atlantic League daily column, also helped me understand the operation of the league.

My initial team visit was with the Somerset Patriots back in July 2005, and I would like to thank the vice president of public relations, Marc Russinoff, for arranging interviews and otherwise facilitating my visit there. Steve Kalafer took an ample amount of time out of his busy schedule to sit with me that evening, providing me insight into his ownership of the club. I'd also like to give a big thanks to general manager, Patrick McVerry, and front-office staffers Matt Rothenberg, Chris Bryan, and Dave Marek for information on the Patriots operation. The Patriots chapter also received considerable contributions from the shortstop and team captain Emiliano Escandon; broadcaster Brian Bender;

Geoff Mosher of the *Courier News*; and, of course, the biggest Somerset Patriot fan that I know, Yvonne Selander, the reference librarian at the Somerset County Library, Bridgewater branch. Somerset County Freeholder Denise Coyle, graciously met with me to explain the workings of the ballpark-financing deal that made the park in Bridgewater possible.

The chapters on the Camden Riversharks and Newark Bears were helped immeasurably by John Brandt, the current General Manager of the Bears and former GM of the Riversharks. John was "lucky" enough to have to deal with me twice in my information gathering on both clubs. Jeff Dean, the athletic director of Rutgers University–Camden, shared his insights into the Rutgers–Riversharks relationship. Jim Cerny and Mike Collazo of the Bears' front office were particularly helpful in gaining me access to aspects of the Bears operation. Professors Clement Alexander Price and Kim Holton of Rutgers-Newark, gave me their expert insights into the culture and history of Newark. Rick Cerone, the original Newark Bears owner and an Atlantic League pioneer, shared with me his recollections on getting the Bears started in the 1990s.

Up in Montclair, the New Jersey Jackals owner Floyd Hall and president Greg Lockard generously gave their time to be interviewed, as did the general manager, Ben Wittkowski. Joe Ameruoso, the talented young Jackals broadcaster, provided me access to the Jackals operation and helped facilitate my day of interviews there. Zach Smithlin, Kevin Dattola, and manager Joe Calfapietra spent time with me on the field before a game to give me an insight into a player's and manager's role with an independent professional club. I would also like to thank Dave Kaplan, the director of the Yogi Berra Museum and Learning Center, for his assistance with this project.

Chuck Betson, the former director of marketing and media for the Atlantic City Surf, spent considerable time with me at the Sandcastle in 2005, and John Kiphorn and Frank Dougherty of the Surf front office gave me their insights into the operation. Pete Thompson, the sports director at television station WMGM in Atlantic City, was extremely helpful in explaining to me the Atlantic City and southern New Jersey sports scene.

Ben Wagner, the former media and public relations manager and broadcaster for the Lakewood BlueClaws, gets a huge debt of gratitude from me for arranging a whirlwind afternoon of interviews that included general manager Geoff Brown and numerous members of his front-office staff including Hal Hansen, Joe Scalise, Brandon Marano, Mike Ryan, Jon Clark, Nelson Constantino, and Jim DeAngelis. Wagner recently moved to Buffalo to become the new play-by-play voice of the Triple-A Buffalo Bisons, and I congratulate him. The Bronx is next, Ben!

Economics has never been my strong point, so I'd like to thank two experts for taking the time to explain the economics of ballpark building and naming rights to me. Dr. Michael Leeds of Temple University and Dr. Larry McCarthy of Seton Hall University, well noted and published in their field, gave me valuable insight and understanding into this aspect of the game. The noted sports business columnist Evan Weiner also has given me the benefit of his knowledge and insight on the economics of sport.

When I began this project, I had no idea how to proceed, as I had never written a book before. I needed someone with the patience to guide me through the process and with the understanding not to get frustrated with my repeated questions. I was lucky enough to find the ideal person in Beth Kressel, assistant editor at Rutgers University Press in New Brunswick, New Jersey. Beth was with me from the beginning to end, and without her, I probably would never have gotten past the proposal stage. Thank you, Beth, for all of the expertise and assistance. I could not have done this without you.

Finally, I'd like to thank my wife Jill, who for the past three years has had to put up with living not only with me but with this project as well. It truly amazes me that after all of the heartburn that I've given her over the years, that she is still my biggest fan and the person in this world who believes in me the most. I certainly don't deserve her, and I owe everything I have to her patience and understanding.

Chronology

New Jersey minor league and independent professional clubs, in the order that they appear in the chapters:

Trenton Thunder
Mercer County Waterfront
Park
One Thunder Road
Trenton, NJ 08611

Somerset Patriots
Commerce Bank Ball Park
One Patriots Park
Bridgewater, NJ 08807

Newark Bears
Bears and Eagles Riverfront
Stadium
450 Broad Street
Newark, NJ 07102

Camden Riversharks
Campbell's Field
401 North Delaware Avenue
Camden, NJ 08102

Atlantic City Surf
Bernie Robbins Stadium
545 North Albany Avenue
Atlantic City, NJ 08401

New Jersey Jackals
Yogi Berra Stadium
One Hall Drive
Little Falls, NJ 07424

Sussex Skyhawks
Skylands Park
94 Championship Place
Suite 11
Augusta, NJ 07822

Lakewood BlueClaws
FirstEnergy Park
2 Stadium Way
Lakewood, NJ 08701

No Minor Accomplishment

Introduction

L ike many New Jersey residents, I have been a frequent attendee at the minor league and unaffiliated independent professional baseball parks in New Jersey since their introduction to the state in 1994. I never really gave much thought as to why I've come to enjoy the experience of spending summer afternoons and evenings in this way. I wrote it off to my being a baseball junkie, and the fact of having professional baseball so close to home and accessible made it easy for me to

Sparkee, General Admission, and friends. Commerce Bank Ballpark, Bridgewater. Photograph by Bob Golon, 2005.

attend. As the years have passed, I've noticed that the crowds at these games are much different from those at Yankee Stadium, Shea Stadium, or the Phillies' ballpark in Philadelphia. There were more kids, more young families, and more young couples in attendance. But the full impact of what was taking place in New Jersey did not occur to me until I had a firsthand experience with the baseball clubs of the state.

In the spring of 2004, while I was an adult reference librarian at the Bernards Township Library in Basking Ridge, New Jersey, our children's librarian, Antonette D'Orazio, asked me if I would put together a presentation about baseball for children. Given my interest and previous work with baseball research and history, this seemed like a fun idea. But, she added a requirement: it would have to have a New Jersey flavor and slant, as our children's librarians were interested in teaching the young boys and girls more about our state.

I said, "Sure, no problem," then walked away, scratching my head. What would I do? Most of my baseball research and the presentations that I had done at the Baseball Hall of Fame in Cooperstown dealt with New York City and major league events. These stories, although entertaining, would not fit the criteria. The research presentation on the 1915 Federal League Newark Peppers and Harrison Field that I first did for the Society for American Baseball Research in 1996 would certainly fit, but it also would have reduced a room full of eight- to twelve-year-olds to tears of boredom! I fondly remember when, in the late 1950s, my father would drive me past the abandoned Ruppert Stadium in Newark. He would stop the car and tell me stories about when he would sit in the bleachers and root for the great Newark Bears in the 1930s. The Bears were, after all, a Yankees farm club. Nice memories, but I doubt the kids in Bernards Township would care that Tommy "Old Reliable" Henrich and Charlie "King Kong" Keller played for the Bears.

The story and presentation needed to be something new and fresh that the kids could identify with. It had to emphasize fun with the game instead of performance statistics and the pressure of wins and losses. But most of all, it had to be about New Jersey. It finally dawned on me that we have no fewer than eight minor league and independent professional teams currently playing in New Jersey. We could draw a big map of the state, place stars over where the teams are located, and do a presentation about our New Jersey baseball clubs, emphasizing pictures of their mascots, logos, and stadiums. I could certainly do that, but it needed to have a little something extra. I needed something fun to give to the kids.

I decided to sit down and write letters to all eight of the franchises, describing what I was doing, and I asked for their help and support. I asked if they could send something; a hat, a ball, a stuffed animal, a pennant, anything that I could use as a giveaway, in return for my mentioning their generosity to the parents who would also be sitting there. As I sent out these letters, I fully expected to get what I will call "major-leagued."

What does it mean to get 'major-leagued'?" Getting "major-leagued" means getting the distinct feeling of fan-unfriendliness that has developed around big-league baseball ever since the contracts got larger, the advertising became more expensive and intense, the games got longer, and the postseason got a lot later at night for those of us on the East Coast. It's the attitude of the typical player when asked for an autograph without receiving a fee at signing table or a card show. Getting "major-leagued" means only being able to afford having your family of four sit in the upper deck or the bleachers while the better seats in the lower deck are occupied by the corporate guys with the expense accounts. Getting "major-leagued" means traffic jams, screaming video screens, $20 parking fees and $4.50 bottles of water. And, it's having innocent, non-income-generating requests for help—like mine for the library kids—ignored because, after all, you're "small potatoes." That's getting "major-leagued."

What took place next astounded me. One by one, our New Jersey clubs responded. The Trenton Thunder sent a beautiful autographed yearbook. The Camden Riversharks, New Jersey Cardinals, Atlantic City Surf, Newark Bears, and Lakewood BlueClaws each sent four free tickets to any remaining game in the 2004 season. Being the local club for Bernards Township, the Somerset Patriots truly outdid themselves. They sent their mascot, Sparkee, to crash our August 2004 presentation. And, Sparkee came bearing gifts: free tickets, autographed baseballs, caps, pens, refrigerator magnets, trading cards, and bobble-head dolls. The look on the children's faces when Sparkee came into that room was absolutely priceless. And I thought, "There's a story here. This is different from what I've grown used to."

What follows is that story, the story of minor league and independent professional baseball in New Jersey since 1994, when baseball returned to New Jersey in a big way. It's a story of dedicated owners and front-office people providing inexpensive family fun and entertainment in a safe and clean environment. It's about players being fan-friendly and community-minded. It's about big enjoyment and small egos. It also examines the state of the baseball industry in New Jersey, analyzing via industry experts the success of some franchises and the struggle of some others.

Most of all, this book is about the people of New Jersey—rich and poor, owner and employee, player and fan—who have put this game on our New Jersey map once again, hopefully to never leave.

1

Baseball's Early Roots in New Jersey

It was April 1946, and New Jersey paused for a deep breath. During this particular spring, the sun seemed warmer and brighter, the air smelled fresher, the smiles were broader, and the laughter returned. Optimism replaced pessimism, and relaxation regained its rightful place in life alongside of work. World War II was over, after four long years, and it was time to have fun again.

Servicemen and servicewomen lucky enough to have survived the war returned home to their loved ones. Families were reunited. Baseball, which did its best during the war to provide New Jersey and the rest of

Harrison Field, home of the Newark Peppers of the Federal League, 1915.
Photo courtesy of the Town of Harrison, New Jersey.

the nation with a diversion from the daily news of the war overseas, was becoming whole again. Baseball clubs were being reassembled to their prewar status as players returned from the military. At Griffith Stadium in Washington, President Truman limbered up his left arm and delivered the ceremonial first pitch of the baseball season to a group of waiting Washington Senators players, the first presidential ball to be tossed since Franklin D. Roosevelt abandoned the practice during the war. Baseball was reestablishing its rightful place in the American psyche, which craved relaxation and recreation. The editorial in the *New York Times* on April 17 summed up the feeling of much of America: "The war is over. We can settle down at last and give more attention to the box scores."

New Jersey experienced the same relief as the rest of the country, especially in the industrial cities. The war placed a burden on the people of these cities by increasing demand for their industrial output for the war effort. As New Jersey's professional baseball teams in Newark, Jersey City, and Trenton began their 1946 seasons, the future of the game in New Jersey seemed brighter than ever as fans crowded back to their ballparks to celebrate the return of the prewar ritual of the opening of another baseball season. In Jersey City in particular, the political drums were beating, urging residents to welcome the boys back to the playing field.

Years before Bruce Springsteen acquired the moniker, "the Boss" in New Jersey could only mean mayor Frank Hague of Jersey City, who ruled with his own particular brand of political favoritism and entitlement. The Boss ran Jersey City with an iron fist from 1917 through 1947, his thirty-year tyrannical control a testament to the power of the political organization that he created. Nothing was beyond Hague's will or influence, including driving the attendance at Jersey City Giants games. On April 16, 1946, a full-page "proclamation" from Mayor Hague ran on page 15 of the *Jersey Journal,* urging residents to "join in carrying out the purpose of this resolution to lend their aid, support and assistance in making the attendance at this opening game of the league season at Roosevelt Stadium a memorable occasion." In other words, you had better be there! So eager were the residents and businesspeople of Jersey City to please Boss Hague that he, through his city employees, was able to sell in excess of 50,000 tickets for opening day at Roosevelt Stadium, even though the concrete-and-steel Works Progress Administration structure at the lower end of Danforth Avenue and Route 440 could only seat half that number. Opening day in Jersey City was no different in this respect, but

April 18, 1946, was destined to become a milestone in American social history as well as baseball history. The Montreal Royals, the Triple-A affiliate of the Brooklyn Dodgers, opposed the Giants on this day. The game took on the flavor of the major-league rivalry that constantly took place across the river at the Polo Grounds and Ebbets Field. As the 25,000-plus fans settled into their seats at Roosevelt Stadium, they were met by a sight that they had never seen in International League baseball—or in any white professional baseball game, for that matter. The Royals' second baseman, Jackie Robinson, took the field to become the first black player since the late nineteenth century to play in a regular-season game, integrating a sport that had been off-limits to blacks up until this time. Robinson punctuated the occasion by leading the Royals to a 14-1 rout of the Giants, hitting a home run, scoring four runs, batting in four, and stealing two bases.

Across Newark Bay, 12,928 Newarkers filed into Ruppert Stadium in the Ironbound section of the city to see the Newark Bears open their season with an 8-7 loss to the Buffalo Bisons. The Bears, the Triple-A affiliate of the mighty New York Yankees, played alongside the Jersey City Giants in the International League and typically held the upper hand over their cross-bay rivals in the standings. Both clubs struggled in 1946, with the Bears barely breaking a .500 record and the Giants finishing dead last. Little did it matter to the devotees of the Newark Bay rivalry: big-time baseball was back and ready to resume its place as a northern New Jersey summertime staple. White fans in northern New Jersey weren't the only citizens enjoying the revitalized game in 1946. Black fans, especially those in Newark, also had a reason to follow the game on a daily basis.

Despite the introduction of Jackie Robinson to white baseball in 1946, the game remained basically segregated that season, with only five blacks under contract to play minor-league ball for major-league organizations. This situation would remain the same for the next two years. Other talented black ballplayers, unable to display their skills in the major and minor leagues, were forced to compete against each other in what was known as the Negro Leagues, where some of the greatest baseball of the 1930s and 1940s was played for devoted audiences of black fans. Newark had a club of its own in the Negro National League, the Newark Eagles, owned by an ex–Camden numbers entrepreneur and his wife, Abe and Effa Manley. In 1946, the Eagles opened their season at Ruppert Stadium with the future Baseball Hall of Famer Leon Day pitching a no-hitter against the Philadelphia Stars. It was the first of many big days in 1946 for the Eagles as they rolled to the Negro National League Championship in front of big, enthusiastic crowds. Even though the integration of organized baseball would have a serious negative effect on the Negro Leagues by 1950, black Newarkers in 1946 felt that they would have their Eagles to root for forever. The fans of the Trenton Little Giants, in New Jersey's capital city, felt pretty much the same.

Trentonians spent April anxiously awaiting the Giants' opening game against the Sundbury (Pa.) Yankees, scheduled to take place on May 1. That evening, 4,712 fans jammed the wooden stands at Dunn Field, which had a listed capacity of 3,500. Even though the Giants were a lower-level, class B minor-league team, Trenton embraced the club and was rewarded one year later when the New York Giants affiliate won the Interstate League championship.

Baseball was solidly entrenched in Jersey City, Newark, and Trenton in 1946. Unbelievably, just five short years later—by the end of the 1950 season—all four clubs disappeared from New Jersey, leaving the state without a professional baseball team, for the most part, for the next forty-four years. What made this absence even harder to understand was the fact that New Jersey's rich baseball legacy stretched back to the beginning of the modern game itself.

With apologies to the loyalists in Cooperstown, New York, home of the National Baseball Hall of Fame and Museum and the supposed birthplace of baseball in 1839, evidence suggests that the Elysian Fields in Hoboken was the actual site of the first game of baseball as we know it now, held on June 19, 1846. New Yorker Alexander Joy Cartwright organized the Knickerbocker Baseball Club largely as a men's social club. He brought the team on leisurely ferry trips to practice in Hoboken in 1845 because open playing fields were already becoming scarce in lower Manhattan. Around this time, Cartwright revised some of the rules governing the game. Some of these changes included tagging runners out instead of pegging them with a thrown ball, establishing three strikes for an out, and limiting an inning to three outs instead of batting the entire order around. Cartwright found another team willing to play a game using his new rules. This club, known as the New York Nine, and the Knickerbockers ferried to Hoboken together for the June 1846 contest. The Nine defeated the Knicks that day, 23-1, in front of a small crowd on what is now Washington Street. The Elysian Fields became a center of early baseball activity during the Civil War era, and a crowd of 20,000 once gathered on the site to watch an important game between the New York Mutuals and the Brooklyn Atlantics—acknowledged to be the two best teams in baseball—in 1865. The new game was off and running, with men being paid to play baseball professionally by 1869.

In 1871, the National Association of Professional Baseball Players, the first professional baseball league, was formed. Composed mostly of teams in the big northeastern cities, the loosely organized league played until 1875, when the new National League replaced it one year later. New Jersey became represented in the National Association when the Resolute Club of Elizabeth formed in 1873. The Resolutes played their home games at the Waverly Fairgrounds, on a horse-racing track in what is now Weequahic Park. Even though they disbanded after achieving a dismal 2–21 record, the Resolutes nevertheless were a pioneering team in professional baseball and were New Jersey's first entry into the professional game. There were plenty more to follow.

By the mid-1880s, the best professional baseball players played for National League and American Association clubs. Access to these games was limited to those who lived within commuting distance to the ballparks. Nevertheless, baseball fans who could not travel long distances still had a desire to see live, competitive baseball. To satisfy this demand, regional professional leagues, which became known as "minor leagues," took root both in rural areas of America and in its smaller cities. Between 1880 and 1950, no fewer than fifteen New Jersey towns and cities played host to minor-league baseball teams, the most enduring being those located in Newark, Jersey City, and Trenton.[1]

NEWARK

The Newark Domestics were the city's first team to play minor-league baseball, beginning in 1884, finishing third in the newly formed Eastern League. Between 1884 and 1900, the club—also known at various times as the Little Giants, the Trunkmakers, and the Colts—played in five different minor leagues. The 1886 Little Giants finished in first place in the Eastern League and moved to the International League in 1887. A black catcher, Moses "Fleetwood" Walker joined the club in 1887, along with a black pitcher from Canada, the very talented George Stovey. They were immediately subjected to racial taunting throughout the league, setting the stage for Newark to be caught in the middle of one of the most infamous incidents in baseball history. The July 11, 1887, issue of the *Sporting News* editorialized against "certain baseball associations [which have] done more damage to the International League than to any other we know of. We refer to the importation of colored players into the ranks of that body." It was doubtlessly a reference to the Little Giants. Three days after the editorial was published, the Chicago White Stockings of the National League, later to be known as the Cubs, visited Newark for an exhibition game against the Little Giants. The White Stockings' star player, shortstop Adrian "Cap" Anson, also served as the manager. Anson, an Iowa native and future Baseball Hall of Fame member, held extreme personal racist attitudes that spilled over to his activities on the baseball field. He refused to let his White Stockings take the field against the Little Giants if Walker and Stovey played. Unfortunately, the Little Giants would not cross this "line in the sand" drawn by Anson, forcing Walker and Stovey to stay on the bench. Newly enabled, the mostly white minor leagues, one by one, voted against signing black players to their clubs, setting up the infamous color line that would not be broken until Jackie Robinson played at Roosevelt Stadium in 1946.[2]

The Newark club moved to the Central League in 1888, winning the league championship that season and moved again to both the Atlantic League and the Atlantic Association through 1900. In 1902, then known as the Sailors, Newark joined the newly formed National Association's Eastern League, one of the highest levels of minor-league baseball. The club performed poorly during the next decade, and even a name change to the Indians did not help. The Brooklyn Dodgers' owner, Charles Ebbets, was looking to diversify his baseball holdings and bought the Newark Indians in 1912, and whether coincidentally or not, the club responded with ninety-five wins and a first-place finish in 1913. Ebbets did not have a chance to enjoy the success of his investment, however, as an interloper joined the Newark baseball scene and quickly drove the Indians out of town.

Major-league baseball enjoyed a spectacular rise in popularity during the early twentieth century, resulting in the construction of new, larger ballparks made of concrete and steel in major-league cities.[3] These parks became necessary in order to hold the larger crowds that attended the games. More wealthy "sportsmen" wanted in on the ownership action, and there were not enough major-league teams to satisfy their desires to own baseball clubs. Few were ever for sale. In 1913, a group of mostly midwestern businessmen started the Federal League and were content to operate it as a minor league, even though it had already placed clubs in the major-leagues cities of Chicago, Cleveland, Pittsburgh, and St. Louis. Encouraged by a successful 1913 season, the Federal League owners decided to challenge the existing two-team major-league structure by declaring their league "the third major league" while expanding it into eastern cities. Two new, deep-pocketed investors who made this possible were Robert B. Ward, a Brooklyn bread-baking magnate famous for the Tip-Top label, and most important for Newark, an oilman from Oklahoma named Harry F. Sinclair. With its war chests filled with new money, the Feds took on the American and National Leagues. They built new stadiums, raided major-league rosters, and succeeded in enticing name ballplayers like Joe Tinker, Mordecai Brown, Eddie Plank, and Chief Bender to jump to their league, as well as many other major leaguers looking for a better paycheck.

Sinclair bided his time, determined to put a club of his own in the New York metropolitan area. With Brooklyn already claimed by Ward for his Tip-Tops, and with the Giants and the Yankees already crowding Manhattan, Sinclair decided to place his team across the Hudson River in New Jersey. Tunnels under the Hudson River made it a safe and easy trip by rail to Newark; in some cases, the trip was even shorter than that to the Polo Grounds in upper Manhattan, the home of the Giants and the Yankees. Seeing an opportunity, Sinclair purchased the Indianapolis Hoosiers, the 1914 Federal League champions, and brought them to Newark for the 1915 season. Sinclair, who also needed to spend considerable time tending to his oil wells in the Southwest, partnered with a New Jersey native and former National Association president, Patrick T. Powers, to buy the club. Powers provided the presence needed to make the Newark club operational in time for the 1915 season, giving New Jersey its very first major-league baseball team.

Sinclair and Powers considered locations on the outskirts of Newark for what they promised would be a spectacular new ballpark for the club. Curiously, they settled on a location across the Passaic River, in neighboring Harrison, bordered by Middlesex, Burlington, South Third, and South Second Streets. The new Hudson-Manhattan Transit lines (the Hudson Tubes, now know as the PATH system) ran one block from the stadium location, with the Pennsylvania Railroad lines also located nearby. The owners felt that mass transportation provided their biggest opportunity and would enable them to attract New Yorkers by the trainload to their new ballpark. The park was also a quick walk from the four corners of Broad and Market Streets in downtown Newark, while electric trolleys ran between Newark and Harrison. Harrison itself was a heavily industrial town inhabited by numerous blue-collar immigrants, described as a "beehive of industry" by president William Howard Taft during a campaign visit to Harrison in 1912. Harrison was growing by leaps and bounds, and the town officials welcomed the new stadium with open arms.

Ground was not broken for the stadium until approximately six weeks before opening day, and in an incredible construction feat, an all-wooden stadium with a listed seating capacity of 21,000 was ready, if not fully completed, for opening day on April 16, 1915. A giant celebration and parade marked opening day, with schools and businesses shutting down for a half day in order to participate in the festivities. Marching bands played, youth organizations marched, and politicians and fraternal organizations all turned out in their best attire to welcome the Peppers to Harrison Field. Pat Powers so named the club because, according to him, it would take "pepper" for a ballplayer to merit playing on the club, "pepper" to get the ballpark built in time, and "pepper" to play winning baseball. The press picked it up immediately, and fortunately the name was shortened to "Peps" before many games had passed. However, on this opening day, it was not unusual to see celebrants wearing green, red, or yellow peppers, bought from local markets, pinned to their lapels to show their allegiance to the new club.[4]

A crowd estimated at 32,000 jammed into the still-unfinished park to watch the Peps lose the Harrison opener to the Baltimore Terrapins, 6-3. The club—managed by Bill "Whoa" Phillips and, later in the season, by future Hall of Fame player and manager Bill McKechnie—played decently in 1915. It finished fifth in the eight-team league with a record of eighty wins and seventy-two losses. Its young outfielder Edd Roush, who later played for the Cincinnati Reds and the New York Giants, batted .298 for the Peps; and Ed Reulbach, previously a star pitcher for the Chicago Cubs, led the pitching staff with twenty-one wins. The Peppers became a big hit in Newark, garnering much more attention than the minor-league Indians across town.

In 1914, the defending International League champion Newark Indians slumped to fifth place with a 73-77 record. With all of the excitement created by the Peps, the Indians began 1915 in relative obscurity, playing at Wiedenmayers' Park in the Ironbound section of Newark. Charles Ebbets, looking to sell the club and unaware that his chief competitors in

Harrison would be out of the picture by the following year, had little patience for what he viewed as a hopeless situation. After only fifty-two games, he transferred the Indians to Harrisburg, Pennsylvania, where it finished the season. They would be back in Newark in 1916, and have the city all to themselves once again.

Unexpectedly, attendance in the Federal League overall fell far below projections, and between expensive players' contracts and continuous litigation with the American and National Leagues, the Feds were hemorrhaging money. Late in their only season, rumors circulated that the Peppers would be abandoning Newark in 1916 for a new superstadium to built by Sinclair on the east side of Manhattan. That, too, was not to be. Instead, all of the warring factions in major-league baseball entered into peace discussions, and the Federal League disbanded in December 1915.

The Indians, renamed the Newark Bears in 1917, took over Harrison Field and played there until it burned to the ground in a spectacular fire after a game in August 1923. The club again struggled on the field, and the fire forced it to play their home games at the Meadowbrook Oval on South Orange Avenue. Homeless once again, the Bears played most of the 1925 season in Providence, Rhode Island. Better days for the franchise were nearing, however.

A baseball enthusiast and semipro-club owner from Long Island, Charley Davids, bought the Bears and moved the club back to Newark for the 1926 season. He also started construction on what became the most famous baseball stadium in New Jersey's early minor-league history. His stadium was built on the far end of town, on Wilson Avenue, at the tip of the Ironbound section near what is today the New Jersey Turnpike. Known as Davids Stadium, it was built out of concrete and steel, and its 15,000 seats were ready for occupancy by May 1926. After two seasons, Davids's finances were drained, and he sold the club to newspaper publisher Paul Block. Block brought in future Baseball Hall of Fame members Walter Johnson and Tris Speaker to manage the club in the late 1920s, and even though their presence gave the team some box-office appeal, the Bears were perennial also-rans. The fortunes of Newark's International League club then took a most dramatic turn upward.

Prior to the 1932 season, New York Yankees owner Jacob Ruppert, who by this time had crafted the beginnings of the Yankee dynasty in the Bronx, bought the Bears from Block with the intention of making them the Yankees' top farm club. Newarkers hoped Ruppert's ownership might improve the fortunes of the often-struggling Bears, but they had no idea how incredibly fast it would happen. Between 1932 and 1942, the Bears finished in first place seven times, in second place once, and never finished in the bottom half of the league standings. Three times they won the Junior World Series, an annual championship series between the winners of the International League and American Association playoffs. Five times during this eleven-year period, the mighty Bears won more than one hundred games. From 1943 until the club's demise after the 1949 season, the team finished in a respectable second place four times.

The 1932 Newark Bears, managed by a Newark favorite, Bears pitcher Al Mamaux, boasted past and future major leaguers Johnny Neun, Red Rolfe, Marv Owen, George Selkirk, and Johnny Murphy on their roster. They won 109 games and finished 15½ games ahead of the second-place Baltimore Orioles. Newark fans responded by setting a new International League record attendance of 345,000. The Bears then defeated the American Association champion Minneapolis Millers in the Junior World Series in six games to win the championship.

Newark fans grew accustomed to winning, with the Bears finishing in first place again in 1933 and 1934. The club was competitive, if not spectacular in 1935 and 1936. Ruppert, Yankees general manager Ed Barrow, and Yankees farm-system director George Weiss found it convenient to keep a ready supply of almost-ready major leaguers within a short train ride of the Bronx should someone on the parent Yankees falter. Yet, nobody predicted the juggernaut that they would create in Newark in 1937.

The 1937 Newark Bears have gone down in history as one of the greatest minor-league baseball clubs of all time. By that season, Oscar Vitt had taken over as manager of the club. Buddy Rosar and Willie Hershberger shared the catching duties behind the plate. The infield included future major-leaguers George McQuinn at first base and Joe Gordon at second base. The capable Babe Dahlgren played third base. Dahlgren became better known as the man who replaced Lou Gehrig at first base for the New York Yankees in 1939. The outfield included the budding star Charlie "King Kong" Keller, along with Bob Seeds and Jimmy Gleeson. Atley Donald, Marius Russo, and Vito Tamulis led a very strong pitching staff.

How great were these 1937 Bears? They finished the regular season with 109 wins against only 43 losses, a winning percentage of .717, and a 25½-game margin over the second-place Montreal Royals. Yet, they fell behind in the Junior World Series against the American Association champion Columbus Redbirds, the top farm club of the St. Louis Cardinals. Remarkably, the Bears lost the first three games of the series at home at Ruppert Stadium. The final four games, if necessary, would all be played in Columbus. The Redbirds, needing only one more win, perhaps allowed themselves to become a bit overconfident. The struggling Bears postponed elimination by defeating the Birds in game four, 8-1. Game five became the ultimate momentum changer in the series when Donald three-hit the Redbirds, defeating them 1-0. The last two games were no contest, with the Bears soundly defeating the Redbirds 10-1 in game six, then 10-4 in the deciding game, completing the unlikely comeback. Newarkers went crazy for their Bears.

The Bears provided a futuristic glimpse of the partnership between a minor-league club and its community with the establishment of the Knot Hole Gang in the 1930s, which provided free bleacher-seat tickets to Newark kids. Originally a joint project between the Bears and the Newark Public Schools, the program became so popular that it expanded to private schools, parochial schools, YMCAs, and YMHAs. The Grizzly Club, an adult booster club, also raised money to sponsor a Knot Hole Band, a group of young musicians who marched on opening days and entertained during the designated Knot Hole games throughout the season.

The banner 1937 season earned Oscar Vitt a major-league managing job with the Cleveland Indians in 1938. Johnny Neun replaced Vitt from 1938 through 1941, and Billy Meyer managed the club through the World War II years. The Bears finished below second place only once during that time period—a fourth-place spot in 1939. Players came and players went, especially with onset of the war, but the Bears maintained their position as a force in the International League, setting the stage for the first postwar season of 1946.

The ex-Yankees and Bears outfielder George Selkirk took over the club as player-manager in 1946, and the Bears featured future Yankee stars Yogi Berra, Gene Woodling, and Bobby Brown. However, injuries and multiple roster changes limited the club to eighty wins and a fourth-place finish. Large crowds of 13,000 or more filled Ruppert Stadium during the Governor's Cup playoffs against Jackie Robinson's Montreal Royals, a series that the Bears lost in six games. Little was it realized that this was basically the last hurrah: the beginning of the end of the glory days of the Newark Bears. Events off the field began to conspire against baseball in Newark.

A competitive advantage that the Bears held for many years, even over the parent Yankees, was night baseball. Lights were installed at Ruppert Stadium in 1930, five years before the first major-league night game in Cincinnati in 1935. Night baseball was not played by the big-league teams in New York until 1939, when the Brooklyn Dodgers added lights to Ebbets Field. The Giants quickly followed suit in 1940, but then wartime restrictions intervened, cutting the number of night games that could be played between 1942 and 1945 due to blackout regulations. The Yankees used this restriction to hold fast against the installation of lights at Yankee Stadium. The general manager, Ed Barrow, while acknowledging the economic positives, did not think it was good for the players' health to upset their normal routines by playing night baseball. By 1946, the war was over and Yankee ownership passed from the Ruppert estate to a group that included Larry McPhail, the man who had introduced night baseball to both Cincinnati in 1935 and Brooklyn in 1939. Lights immediately were installed in Yankee Stadium.[5] The Bears fans who also considered themselves Yankee loyalists because of the affiliation of the two teams suddenly had a choice for their evening entertainment dollar. Ticket prices in the Bronx were relatively inexpensive in the 1940s, and the ride across the Hudson River, either by rail or by automobile, had not yet become an overcrowded hassle. Night-game attendance at Ruppert Stadium began to suffer. Night games being played by the New York major-league clubs posed one problem for the Bears, but the combination of night games and television proved to be too much to overcome.

Postwar prosperity and a maturing of the technology of television resulted in a boom in the number of home TV sets in the late 1940s. By 1948, the three New York major-league clubs televised all of their home games for free over the airwaves. Faced with a choice between driving to Ruppert Stadium and remaining in the comfort of their living room after work, people started to choose watching major-league baseball on the fuzzy black-and-white screen. In May 1948, the American Association president Frank C. Lane was quoted in the *New York Times* as stating that "when a night game is televised from one of the New York parks, attendance at two International League cities, Newark and Jersey City, falls off 20 to 25 percent."[6] Even if Lane was padding those numbers, it was clear that local television was badly hurting clubs like the Newark Bears. When the parent Yankees then deprived the Bears of their best prospects and players, Newark fans became angry and stopped showing up at Ruppert Stadium.

After an uncharacteristically poor 1947 season, when the Bears won only sixty-five games and finished in sixth place, the team rebounded strongly in 1948, led by future Yankees Joe Collins and Jerry Coleman. Pitcher Bob Porterfield was having a sensational season, with fifteen wins against only six losses, when he was called up to the Yankees in the beginning of August. Bears fans, angry at what they felt was a betrayal of the club by the Yankees front office, stayed away from Ruppert Stadium for the remainder of the year. Even though the Bears finished in second place with eighty wins in 1948, they ranked seventh out of eight clubs in attendance in the International League. Rumors circulated that the club would be sold and moved to Pennsylvania.

Newark officials, alarmed over possibly losing their club, agreed to increase the number of bus lines to Ruppert Stadium as well as to eliminate the smoky trash fires being created by private garbage-dump operators outside of the outfield fence. The smoke from those fires was a constant source of irritation to both fans and players alike. Unfortunately, the Yankees didn't hold up their end of the bargain to improve the club. They shipped an extremely poor team of players to Newark in 1949, and it became obvious that they reserved their best minor-league players for their Kansas City and Portland, Oregon, affiliates. If the Yankees had set out to devalue their Newark franchise and eventually rid themselves of it, they certainly succeeded. Fewer than 90,000 fans came to Ruppert Stadium in 1949 to watch a club so uninspiring that the *Newark Star-Ledger* actually refused to publish their standings out of protest. The once-proud Bears finished the season with a meager 55–98 record. After the season, the Chicago Cubs purchased the Bears for a fire-sale price of only $50,000 and moved them to Springfield, Massachusetts.[7] Newark was now without a professional baseball team for the first time since 1901, worsening the void left when the Newark Eagles of the Negro National League departed the year before.

Black baseball first gained prominence in New Jersey in Atlantic City in the 1920s. The Bacharach Giants, named after Atlantic City's mayor Harry Bacharach, played in the resort town for fourteen seasons and were a charter member of the Eastern Colored League in 1923. In 1926, the Giants played the Chicago American Giants in the third Negro World Series, losing five games to three. The shortstop and first baseman John Henry "Pop" Lloyd endures as one of the most famous of all the Bacharachs, and to this day, a baseball field near the marina district in

Atlantic City bears his name. The Bacharachs fell victim to the Depression and disbanded in the 1930s, at about the same time that black baseball took hold in Newark.

Up until this time, Newark had hosted some black baseball teams, but no franchise succeeded in the long term. In 1934 and 1935, a club called the Newark Dodgers played in the Negro National League. Across the Hudson River, in 1935, Abe and Effa Manley bought the Brooklyn Eagles, who played their games at the Brooklyn Dodger's Ebbets Field. Since World War I, Newark's black population had grown at a very fast rate as blacks moved from the South to take advantage of the industrial job opportunities created by the war. The Manleys decided that Newark was a much better place for their baseball team. They purchased the Newark Dodgers, merged them with the Eagles, and located their new club, calling them the Newark Eagles, at Ruppert Stadium, sharing the park with the Bears when the Bears were on the road. Abe Manley enjoyed traveling with the club and being a man in a man's world. Effa actually ran the franchise, and she became noted as a formidable baseball executive who combined the operation of the baseball team with a passion for activism in the black community. She became the treasurer of the Newark chapter of the NAACP and used the Eagles' visibility within the black community of Newark to help promote black causes. Effa was a players' owner, who sought to improve travel conditions for her club by purchasing an air-conditioned bus to take them on their long road trips. Most important, in a league where finances were often questionable, she provided her players with dependable and steady paychecks that they could count on. This helped her acquire and maintain star players.[8]

The Eagles peaked in 1946, winning the Negro National League's regular-season first- and second-half titles. Statistics keeping was not an exact science in the Negro Leagues, and the games were rarely publicized in the daily newspapers. Despite this, it was impossible to ignore the Eagles' 47–16 won-lost record and the exploits of their two young stars from New Jersey: sluggers Monte Irvin from East Orange and Paterson's Larry Doby. Leon Day led a strong pitching staff into the Negro World Series against the Kansas City Monarchs, and the Eagles won the championship in a hard-fought, seven-game series. However, much like their white stadium-mates, their days in Newark were numbered.

The reasons for the demise of the Eagles were not the same as those that led to the end of the Bears, but they were legitimate reasons nonetheless. The Negro Leagues in general and the Eagles in particular were victims of their own greatest accomplishment: the advancement of their players to white baseball. While black attendance at Brooklyn Dodgers games increased by an estimated 400 percent from 1946 to 1947 (coinciding with the arrival of Jackie Robinson to the Dodgers), the Eagles' attendance declined from 120,000 in 1946 to only 57,000 in 1947. The player exodus to the major leagues could not be stopped. Pitcher Don Newcombe left the Eagles for the Dodgers organization before the beginning of the 1946 season. Doby became the first black player in the American League, signing with the Cleveland Indians in 1947. Irvin followed Doby out of Newark after the 1948 season, signing with the New York Giants organization. By then, it was too late to save the Eagles. After losing a reported $50,000 during the 1947 and 1948 seasons, the Manleys sold the club, which then moved to Houston for the 1949 season as part of a consolidation of the American and National Negro Leagues. Ironically, established Negro Leaguers like Irvin and Hank Thompson of the Kansas City Monarchs moved across Newark Bay to begin their careers in integrated baseball with the Jersey City Giants. The Giants' own history also traces back to the beginnings of baseball in New Jersey.

Jersey City

The Jersey City Skeeters began play in 1885 and existed through the 1933 season as a member of both the Eastern and International Leagues. Their first home field was West Side Park, near the current site of New Jersey City University. West Side Park was known primarily for its abundant mosquitoes, hence the nickname Skeeters. The 1903 Skeeters won ninety-two games against only thirty-three losses, winning the Eastern League pennant. It was the only time that the Skeeters won a league championship. For most of their history, the Skeeters were a poor ball club, finishing in last place ten times. The Depression made it difficult for many minor-league clubs to survive, and this included the Skeeters. Plagued by low attendance and an abundance of red ink, the Skeeters relocated to Syracuse for the 1934 season. Jersey City did not have a minor-league club for the next three seasons.

President Franklin D. Roosevelt created the federal Works Progress Administration in order to create work for those left jobless by the Great Depression. The WPA specialized in the building of large public structures like post offices and stadiums. The largest WPA project in Hudson

County became a federally built stadium in Jersey City. Mayor Frank Hague was so grateful to acquire this project that he named it Roosevelt Stadium, after the president that he so admired. The New York Giants seized the opportunity to place their Triple-A club across the Hudson River from their home stadium, the Polo Grounds, and moved their Albany team to Jersey City for the 1937 season. The Jersey City Giants were known more for their record-breaking opening-day attendance numbers than for their success on the field. More than 50,000 people jammed the stadium for the opener in 1940, to be followed by an astounding 61,000 in prewar 1941, thanks to the ticket-selling efforts of Mayor Hague. The 1939 and 1947 Giants finished first in the International League, but neither club advanced beyond the first round of the postseason playoffs. These were the great days of the Newark Bay rivalry. The Bears and Giants staged their own baseball wars, befitting the great rivalries that played out on the other side of the Hudson between the Dodgers, Giants, and the Yankees. The Giants' future major-league stars Bobby Thomson, Don Mueller, Wes Westrum, and Whitey Lockman all played at Roosevelt Stadium, as well as the aforementioned black stars, Hank Thompson and Monte Irvin. Postwar attendance at Roosevelt Stadium peaked at a season total of 337,531 in 1947. Yet, the same factors that doomed the Bears started to work against the Giants, namely the televised games of the New York major-league teams. Mayor Hague left office in 1949, symbolizing the end of the great era of Jersey City minor-league baseball. Only 63,191 paid their way into Roosevelt Stadium for the entire 1950 season. With the Bears already gone, the Giants no longer had their traditional New Jersey rival to help create fan interest, and acknowledging that the age of television was here to stay, the club moved to Ottawa, Canada, for the 1951 season. New Jersey minor-league baseball, already on life support by this time, also fought a losing battle to survive in its capital city of Trenton.

TRENTON

The city of Trenton sits approximately sixty miles southwest of New York City. Because of its location on the Delaware River, Trenton grew into a major manufacturing area during the nineteenth century. Amateur industrial baseball teams flourished in Trenton after the Civil War. By the time minor-league baseball established itself in the 1880s, Trenton was considered a good location for a team because of the popularity of the industrial games.

After an initial season as part of the Interstate League in 1883, Trenton moved into the Eastern League for the 1884 and 1885 seasons, with the 1884 club winning the league championship. The Trentonians were managed by Patrick T. Powers, who later became the co-owner with Harry Sinclair of the Newark Peppers of the Federal League in 1915. Despite the success of the 1884 club, minor-league baseball in Trenton was not a big hit with fans, and the club moved out after 1885, leaving Trenton without professional baseball for the next twenty-two years. In 1907, the class B Tri-State League was formed, and the Trenton Tigers were charter members. Their high-water mark was a second-place finish in 1911, followed by a victory in the league playoffs. Unfortunately for Trenton, baseball economics took a serious downturn as World War I approached, with financial losses being felt all the way to the major-league level. The club in Trenton could not survive this and disbanded after the 1914 season. Again, minor-league baseball would not return to Trenton for another twenty-two years.

The mid-1930s marked the arrival of affiliated minor-league baseball teams, the first being the Trenton Senators. They began play in 1936 at Dunn Field, located on Route 1 at the Brunswick Circle. Dunn Field had a small wooden grandstand, which only sat 3,500 people, and a very inadequate lighting system that drew criticism throughout its existence. Yet, the minor leagues played there for the next fifteen seasons. The 1936 and 1937 Senators were led by outfielder George Case, who went on to a notable major-league career, mostly with the Washington Senators. In 1939, the Trenton Senators moved from the Eastern League to the class B Interstate League. Goose Goslin, a player-manager from Salem, New Jersey, who was finishing up his baseball career after eighteen years in the major leagues, led the team. The club shifted affiliations to the Philadelphia Phillies organization for 1942 and 1943, then became a Brooklyn Dodgers farm club in 1944 and 1945. In 1944, the club, renamed the Packers, was managed by career minor-league player Walter Alston. Alston later went on to manage the Dodgers in both Brooklyn and Los Angeles in a Hall of Fame managerial career that lasted into the 1970s.

The New York Giants purchased the Trenton club in 1946, operating it as their class B club in the Interstate League. It was under the Giants' ownership that early Trenton baseball would hit its highest level. After a seventh-place finish in 1946, the T-Giants took off, finishing first in both 1947 and 1948. Under manager Tommy Heath, the 1947 club put together an amazing finish to the season, winning fifty-two out of their final sixty-two games. Standing-room-only crowds of 5,000 and more pushed the season's attendance to more than 77,000 at the tiny Dunn Field, an Interstate League record. T-Giants players Bobby Hofman, Hal Bamberger, Andy Tomasic, Roger Bowman, and Paul LaPalme all eventually made it to the big-league Giants, most stopping along the way to also play in Jersey City at the Triple-A level. The 1948 club also won the league championship. Attendance increased to 97,389 that season, and the citizens of Trenton passed a referendum to build a new, larger ballpark for the club. A site was selected, designs were drawn up, but the new park never saw the light of day. Even though the 1949 club won the Interstate League playoffs, their fourth-place regular-season finish caused attendance to drop to 67,500.[9]

Without a new stadium, the Trenton Giants could not survive, and it became apparent that 1950 would be their final year in Trenton. Trenton was treated to one more great baseball moment when the parent Giants signed a nineteen-year-old outfielder from the Birmingham Black Barons of the Negro League and placed him at Trenton. He was none other than the future Hall of Fame outfielder Willie Mays. Mays made his Trenton debut in June 1950 and batted .353 in eighty-one games for the T-Giants. He also gave the local Trentonians a glimpse of the acrobatic fielding ability that would become his standard during his baseball career. Mays himself could not save the T-Giants, however, as only 48,300 fans turned out at the dilapidated Dunn Field for the final season. The club moved to Salisbury, Maryland, and minor-league baseball did not return to Trenton until the arrival of the Trenton Thunder in 1994.

The minor leagues effectively passed from the New Jersey scene for the greater part of the next forty-four years. There were some occasional attempts to revive it. Baseball at Roosevelt Stadium in Jersey City had some brief moments during the next thirty years, none of them lasting very long. Brooklyn Dodgers owner Walter O'Malley took the very unusual step of moving seven Dodgers home games from Ebbets Field to Roosevelt Stadium in both 1956 and 1957, seeking to use Jersey City as leverage in his battle with New York City officials for a new stadium in Brooklyn. Some people thought that the Dodgers might actually make Jersey City their eventual permanent home, but when the Dodgers finally did get a commitment for a new stadium, it was about three thousand miles west of Roosevelt Stadium, in Los Angeles.

In 1960, the island of Cuba was newly taken over by the forces of Fidel Castro. The games of the Havana Sugar Kings of the International League were interrupted by revolutionary activities and demonstrations, and gunshots were actually heard at the Havana ballpark during a game. League president Frank Shaugnessy, fearing for the safety of American ballplayers in Cuba, pulled the club from Havana in mid-July and placed it at Roosevelt Stadium, renaming it the Jersey City Jerseys. The Triple-A affiliate of the Cincinnati Reds had many Latin Americans on its roster, including such notable future stars as Leo Cardenas, Luis Arroyo, Orlando Pena, and Jose Azcue. The Jerseys' July opener attracted 7,155 curious fans, and it was thought that with the Yankees being the only club left in New York after the Dodgers' and Giants' 1958 move to California, the Jerseys would not have to contend with as much televised competition. Even though this was the case, most people still chose to stay home and watch the Yankees on TV. In 1961, the Jerseys averaged only 1,357 fans per game at Roosevelt Stadium, and many blamed the poor attendance on the predominance of Latin American players on the roster, as well as the lack of a local baseball hero to associate with the club. Faced with increased competition from the new New York Mets in 1962, the Reds moved the Jerseys club to Jacksonville, Florida, for the 1962 season.[10]

Roosevelt Stadium did not host minor-league baseball again until 1977, when the Cleveland Indians moved their Eastern League Double-A affiliate from Williamsport, Pennsylvania, to Jersey City. The Indians, managed by New Jersey native and former major-league catcher Johnny Orsino, posted only forty wins against ninety-seven losses, a record not designed to stimulate much fan support. The club changed affiliation to the Oakland A's organization for the 1978 season, and despite the presence of a fleet-footed nineteen-year-old outfield prospect named Rickey Henderson, the A's won only fifty-four games, finished last, and drew sparse crowds. Two light towers at Roosevelt Stadium fell from atop the stands during a severe winter storm that off-season, and repairs could not be made in time for the 1979 season. The club moved out, and minor-league baseball left both Roosevelt Stadium and the state of New Jersey.

The euphoria of that opening day in 1946 became just a distant memory. Minor-league baseball in general experienced a contraction of teams and leagues from the 1950s to the 1970s. This, combined with the failures of the franchises in Newark, Jersey City, and Trenton, convinced the so-called experts that the minor leagues would never again succeed in New

Jersey. Player-development contracts with major-league organizations kept the minor leagues in business during this period, but the country began to change. People became used to more mobility, they were moving in large numbers from the cities to the suburbs, and they enjoyed increased entertainment options. The minor leagues had to reevaluate their approach to the fan market before they could start the long climb back to sustained growth.

2

The Decline and Reinvention of the Minor Leagues, Post-1950

Unlike the declining state of professional baseball in New Jersey by 1949, it took a year or two before other ball clubs throughout the United States felt the same financial strains. In 1949, more than 39.8 million fans attended games fifty-nine minor leagues operating 448 teams, an attendance record not broken until 2003. It was easy to see how television had hurt the New Jersey clubs, especially Newark and Jersey City. First, there were an unusually high number of major-league teams in the region, with three in New York City alone. These clubs televised their games into northern New Jersey. In addition, the New York metropolitan area had a higher percentage of households with television sets than did most of the nation. But in the rest of the country, especially

Dunn Tire Field in Buffalo, New York, originally Pilot Field. Photograph courtesy of the Buffalo Bisons baseball club, 2007.

the rural areas that were supporting minor-league baseball, most homes were not within the airwave range of a major-league club. By 1950, only 23 percent of the homes in America had television sets at all. Clearly television was a factor in the decline of minor-league baseball after 1950—a decline that would level off but not reverse until the late 1980s—but it was not the only factor. In 1950, attendance at minor-league games fell by five million fans, followed in 1951 by another drop of eight million fans. The national minor-league scene was not immune to the same pressures first faced by the Garden State teams. In fact, the New Jersey situation foreshadowed the decline of minor-league baseball everywhere during the 1950s.[1]

A major factor in the rapid decline of the minor leagues immediately after 1950 was the overexpansion of the minor leagues after the Second World War. Players who served in the armed forces returned to baseball in 1946 in large numbers, and the nation was not in the mood to tell its war heroes that there was no place for them in the national game. New leagues and teams were created to handle the surplus of players. The country still hadn't quite taken to the road in their automobiles as of yet, which created a situation that made for some prosperous years for minor-league teams in towns big and small. Local entertainment options still dominated a population that had not realized the potential of its mobility. This tremendous postwar expansion in minor-league baseball had inherent dangers, however; as business executives acknowledge that a boom in an industry that is caused by overly exuberant expansion will most certainly be followed by a painful bust. In minor-league baseball, that bust took place quickly after the peak season of 1949. For better or for worse, America began to change and the minor leagues would have difficulty adapting to those changes.

Increased mobility was the basis of the new American society. The postwar period saw the building of better highways, culminated by President Eisenhower's Interstate Highway System of the early 1960s. The automobile became king. A Sunday drive began taking the place of a day at the ballpark. Families were on the move, not only on weekends but also on a permanent basis. Members of the new middle class, spurred on by a prosperous postwar economy and the shifting of the industrial base, moved out of the cities and into the suburbs. They also moved into areas previously thought to be unreachable—the West Coast and the Sun Belt. The population of America underwent a dramatic migration, away from the traditional northern and eastern manufacturing centers and into more temperate areas that promised a more comfortable lifestyle.

Previously successful minor-league cities like Atlanta, Denver, Houston, Los Angeles, Minneapolis, and San Francisco grew in population. The minor-league clubs in those cities were quickly replaced by major-league expansion teams or by relocated major-league franchises. In their haste to bring their product to as many growing markets as possible, major-league owners destroyed the minor leagues by moving into these successful minor-league cities without an adequate plan to keep the rest of the minor leagues viable. But it would be inaccurate to lay the blame for the decline of the minor leagues in the 1950s and 1960s solely on the expansion of the major leagues. The minor-league owners themselves were slow to adjust to the shifting population patterns and new consumer needs. They stubbornly kept clubs in areas that could no longer support them, often in outdated stadiums, while ignoring the ongoing shift to the suburbs that was taking place. These owners were also old-school baseball people who thought that opening the gates on a game night was enough to attract fans into the stands. They saw no need to try to compete with other entertainment venues by improving their facilities and making them more fan-friendly and comfortable. Marketing was a concept taught at the local universities, but it was not practiced in the local minor-league front offices. Baseball was supposed to be a serious business, according to baseball owners. Publicity stunts and contests between innings were thought to be hokey and beneath the game. Or this is what the owners believed while completely ignoring their declining attendance.

Tastes were also changing in the 1950s. Professional football was gaining in popularity, taking some of the fan attention away from baseball, particularly among the young followers. Professional basketball was also beginning to gain some attention. The spirited spectacle of professional football and the nonstop action of basketball mirrored the new aggressiveness of the postwar society. Baseball, to some, seemed slow and boring in comparison. In addition to increased competition from other spectator sports, people were also spending time at newly constructed alternative recreation and entertainment venues. Bowling became a popular family participation sport in the 1950s, and bowling alley construction boomed. An air-conditioned, inexpensive family evening at a modern bowling facility became a more appealing alternative on a hot sticky night than going to an older, poorly maintained minor-league ballpark. Drive-in theaters flourished in the 1950s to accommodate the new automobile age. And, for those who did not want to suffer through the summer heat at an outdoor movie, the indoor movie theaters all rapidly became air-conditioned. None of these factors alone could have killed minor-league baseball, but combined they posed a serious problem for the sport. If not for the major league's player-development needs, the minor leagues might have died altogether after 1950. Fortunately, the minors were still the main outlet for young players to develop their skills and prove themselves under the watchful eye of experienced baseball men from major-league organizations. To this day, college baseball has failed to capture the sort of national attention enjoyed by college football and basketball. Professional football and basketball teams recruit their new players mostly through NCAA Division I collegiate competition. Although college baseball has become a more important professional player source in recent years, from the 1950s to the 1970s it was most common for younger players to go directly from high school baseball into a club's minor-league network. College attendance was not yet considered to be mandatory for employment survival in later life. Few players passed up an opportunity for a baseball paycheck, regardless of how small it might be, to play the game they loved and to have a chance to eventually make the majors.

By 1962, major-league baseball executives recognized that minor-league baseball might be heading for extinction, so they decided to try to help it survive by changing the way the leagues were governed and financed. Baseball established the 1962 Player Development Plan, which realigned the minor leagues into Triple-A, Double-A, Single-A, and rookie levels. The plan guaranteed that enough clubs would remain in business to stock a team at each minor-league level for all twenty existing major-league clubs. Major-league owners signed player development contracts (PDCs) with the minor-league clubs at all levels, spelling out the operating relationship between them. In most cases, the parent team paid all of the salaries of the players, managers, coaches, and medical staff. Other operating expenses, like player equipment, were also provided for by the major-league organizations. This left the minor-league owners having to concern themselves only with providing for the front-office staffing, local broadcast rights, sponsorship incomes, stadium maintenance, ticket selling, and (heaven forbid) marketing. Talent scouting, procurement, and player supply became the sole responsibility of the major-league parent organization.[2]

This improved relationship with the major leagues did not reverse the decline of the minor-league industry in any meaningful way during the 1960s. In 1967, minor-league fan attendance reached rock bottom when 6.9 million people attended the games of 112 minor-league teams, compared with the 39.8 million fans who attended the games of the 448 teams in business in 1949. The country was going through the political and social upheaval of the Vietnam war period. The relevancy of old, established institutions like baseball was being questioned, especially by young people. By 1967, the National Football League was booming in popularity. In the National Basketball Association, the emergence of great players like Bill Russell and Wilt Chamberlain elevated the sport from a game that was played in front of small crowds in dingy arenas to national popularity. More and more people paid to see the faster action of the NFL and the NBA. The country no longer seemed to have the time or the temperament for something as traditional and as passive as minor-league baseball. Wholesomeness was out of favor. Families and communities had a lot on their minds and were not focused on their local minor-league baseball clubs. The malaise for minor-league baseball continued into the mid-1970s as clubs lost money and were sold for next to nothing. Then, the national bicentennial celebration in 1976 regenerated Americans' feelings for their older traditions and, in turn, their national game. Minor-league baseball, even though still seriously depressed, took a small step upward. Attendance improved to more than nine million fans in 1977. The old guard of minor-league owners was starting to give way to a new breed of younger ownership, and these new owners were busy trying to find the right formula to transform their clubs into more of a business and less of a hobby.

The 1980s saw the minor leagues sitting in idle gear, much like a race car in the pace lap awaiting the starting flag. The industry then experienced two critical events that helped launch a new era. Both of these events occurred in 1988. One event was fact; the other one was fiction; and both had a major impact on the development of the modern era of minor-league baseball in the United States.

THE FACTUAL—BUFFALO, USA

Chapter 1 described the failure of the Jersey City Indians to rekindle the minor-league flame in New Jersey in 1977 and 1978. However, it was the demise of the Jersey City franchise that gave rise to the situation that helped revolutionize the way owners looked at their minor-league ball clubs.

Buffalo, New York, had been without minor-league baseball since 1970, the result of the poor economy that beset many of the smokestack cities of the Northeast over that time period. During the winter after the 1978 baseball season, the Eastern League umpire and Buffalo native Pete Calieri called the league president, Pat McKernan, in search of his end-of-year W-2 wage and tax statement. During the conversation, McKernan told Calieri that Jersey City had just withdrawn from the Eastern League and that the search was on for a replacement city. Calieri suggested his hometown of Buffalo. McKernan liked the idea and, after some political maneuvers, came up with funding to bring an Eastern League team back to the old War Memorial Stadium, which up to that point was best known as the original home of the Buffalo Bills football team. Affectionately known as "the Rockpile," War Memorial Stadium was ill suited for base-ball. Its only baseball claim to fame was when it was turned into the fictional home of the New York Knights for the filming of *The Natural*, with Robert Redford playing Roy Hobbs. The new Eastern League Buffalo Bisons performed as the pre-Hobbs Knights did—losing more often than winning and alienating their new fan base. The parent Pittsburgh Pirates did not provide the caliber of players to make the Bisons a competitive team, and after only 77,077 fans paid their way into the Rockpile in 1982, it looked as if the three-year experiment of returning minor-league baseball to Buffalo was about to end.[3]

Enter the frozen-food magnate Robert Rich Jr., family heir to the Rich Products Corporation. Rich had a vision of turning the Bisons into a financial success through aggressive marketing and promotions. Along with his wife Belinda, who was the Bisons' executive vice president, and Mike Billoni, the club's general manager, Rich focused on corporate sponsorships, group ticket sales, special events, and game-day music concerts to attract larger crowds. Regardless of the quality of the baseball, Rich resolved to make the game experience fun for fans and even to make baseball relevant to their lives. He went as far as to hold a special "Unemployment Day" in 1983 in acknowledgment of the recession in the Buffalo area. His efforts resonated with the city; attendance immediately jumped to more than 200,000, tripling the number of fans attending Bisons games from the year before.

Rich did not rest on his laurels. He bought the rights to a Triple-A minor-league club in 1985 and placed his Buffalo Bisons in the American Association as an affiliate of the Chicago White Sox. Once again, attendance rose to 362,762. Around this time, rumors circulated that the National League would be expanding by two clubs in the not-too-distant future. Rich thought, "why not Buffalo as a major-league city?" Along with Buffalo mayor James D. Griffin, Rich proceeded to sell New York governor Mario Cuomo on his plan to bring a major-league franchise to Erie County. Faced with formidable competition from cities like Denver, Washington DC, Tampa–St. Petersburg, and Miami, Rich and Griffin persuaded Cuomo to provide a $22.5 million interest-free loan for construction of a new, expandable stadium to replace the Rockpile. With assurances of extra funding via Erie County and the city of Buffalo, Rich was in a position to be able to offer a 20,000-seat stadium for the Bisons, expandable to 42,000, as an enticement to lure a National League club to Buffalo.[4]

Unfortunately, Rich's best efforts did not result in a major-league expansion franchise for Buffalo, something that he greatly wanted. What he accomplished with the new Pilot Field, however, set the standard for future minor-league baseball stadium construction. It was the first of the retro-style stadiums, designed to evoke memories of the old ballparks like Brooklyn's Ebbets Field. Buffalo fans responded overwhelmingly to the new park. An astounding 1,186,651 spectators paid their way into Pilot Field to see the Bisons in 1988, followed by another 1,132,183 in 1989. Between Rich's marketing and promotional flair and the new Pilot Field, organized baseball was forced to sit up and take notice. Baseball executives began to contemplate changes in the Professional Baseball Agreement with the minor leagues when it came up for revision again in 1990. While the factual saga of the Buffalo Bisons and Pilot Field was occurring in 1988, another event, this time fictitious, was helping to convince America that minor-league baseball was indeed really "cool."

THE FICTIONAL—*BULL DURHAM*

The writer-director Ron Shelton set out to produce an American romantic comedy with the filming of *Bull Durham*, starring Kevin Costner, Susan Sarandon, and Tim Robbins. The film depicts the activities of the minor-league Durham Bulls. The young, untested pitcher "Nuke" Laloosh (played by Robbins) was sent to be tutored by the hardened, veteran catcher "Crash" Davis (played by Costner). Of course, the two attract the attention of minor-league groupie Annie Savoy (played by Sarandon), and the rest is history. Released in 1988, *Bull Durham* skillfully blended its characters with glimpses of life in the minors from both the players' and fans' perspectives. The movie became a box-office success. It also developed into probably the single most important advertisement that minor-league baseball could have ever asked for. But for the real Durham Bulls and their owner Miles Wolff, it was a mixed blessing.

In 1979, Wolff invested a paltry $2,417 for the right to bring Single-A baseball back to Durham, North Carolina, which had been without a club since 1972. Wolff worked tirelessly to make the Bulls a success, using a hands-on approach, working sixteen-hour days, and marketing the club's effort to provide family entertainment at the old Durham Athletic Park, known as the DAP. At the time of the filming of *Bull Durham* in 1987, the real Durham Bulls were a moderately successful Single-A franchise in the Carolina League. After the movie's success, the DAP would never be the same for Wolff and the residents of Durham. Tourists and other curiosity seekers found the park, and by 1989, Wolff pushed for a new park to be built in Durham to attract a Triple-A club. A referendum for a new park that Wolff wanted was initially defeated by Durham voters, but the park eventually was built. When Wolff sold the Bulls in 1990, his $2,417 investment returned a cool $4 million. Minor-league baseball was taking off in an upward direction. More important, Wolff would go on to play the leading role in the rise of independent professional baseball in the United States in the 1990s, a movement that would spur the growth of independent leagues like the Atlantic League and the Northeast–Can-Am League, leagues that New Jersey baseball fans have come to know very well.[5]

Between the bonanza in Buffalo and the success of *Bull Durham*, organized baseball awakened to the culture and financial opportunity of minor-league ball. Not everyone was immediately convinced. In fact, in 1990, the noted baseball historian and author Neil J. Sullivan, in his book *The Minors*, gave his assessment of the future of the minor-league game this way: "The present condition of the minors is about as good as it will ever be. For the moment, leagues are growing, and franchises are stable. Some clubs are making a little money." It was an extremely cautious view of the future of the minors. Neither Sullivan nor many other experts were prepared for the explosive growth that was about to engulf the minor-league game in the 1990s. And, quite ironically, one of the biggest pieces of the puzzle that would help catapult the minor leagues into their new era was the result of good, old-fashioned major-league greed.

Major-league owners started to notice the resurgence of the minor-league game during the latter portion of the 1980s. Just as attendance neared the 20-million-per-year mark, the majors decided that they, with a new professional baseball agreement due in 1990, would seek a bigger slice of the revenue pie for themselves. At first, the minors felt that the new 1990 agreement was oppressive and economically stacked against them. In fact, it turned out that the terms imposed on them by their major-league partners helped spur their tremendous growth in the 1990s.

First, major-league baseball executives demanded that the minor-league clubs hand over 5 percent of their total ticket revenues to them. This ensured that efforts like those of Buffalo, which drew more than a million fans for five consecutive years starting in 1988, would benefit the bank account of the major leagues. Up until this agreement, most minor-league clubs had shoddy accounting practices by today's standards. This new agreement forced the minor-league owners to keep better financial records, helping them transform from the mom-and-pop outfits that they had been into modern business operations. As they became more aware of the bottom line (and were also forced to cede some of their profit to the majors), minor-league owners began to take their marketing and promotional efforts more seriously. Major League Baseball also revised the PBA rules to give Major League Baseball Properties, a subsidiary of Major League Baseball, control over the sale of all minor-league apparel, enabling it to profit from the licensing and sale of all items containing a minor-league team logo. Although this seemed like a suffocating business relationship at first, it actually helped the minor leagues by providing increased marketing opportunities, which resulted in greater revenues from the sale of items with the minor-league logos.

The third condition imposed by the new PBA seemed to be the most unreasonable of them all, but it ultimately provided the minor leagues with the biggest benefit. Major-league baseball set new minimum stadium standards for their minor-league affiliates. Single-A clubs were now required to provide at least 4,000 seats for fans, and Triple-A parks needed to have at least 10,000 seats. Locker-room facilities had to be expanded and playing-field conditions improved. This caused a wave of new stadium construction, with fan-friendly amenities also taking priority in the stadium designs. Suddenly, the new ballparks became popular places to bring whole families, not only because of their increased comforts but also because of what they represented in terms of being the anti–major leagues. The resurgence of minor-league baseball in the 1990s was no accident. The off-the-field conduct of major-league baseball players actually helped drive fans back toward the minor-league environment.[6]

While the minor leagues were struggling to survive in the 1960s, 1970s, and 1980s, major-league baseball practices began to try fan patience and loyalty. The first unpleasant situation created for the fans, well intentioned as it seemed, proved to be disastrous in the long run. By the 1960s, the old ballparks constructed during the first part of the twentieth century were deteriorating, and most of them needed to be replaced. The clubs and their home cities, looking to create efficiencies and economies of scale, decided to pursue the concept of multipurpose and multiuse stadiums to suit both the baseball clubs and the pro football teams in a city. Shea Stadium in New York, Busch Memorial Stadium in St. Louis, Veterans Stadium in Philadelphia, and Three Rivers Stadium in Pittsburgh were just some examples of the characterless architecture that replaced the venerable old parks. Large, circular concrete bowls with seats far away from the baseball diamond replaced the traditional smaller parks. Bigger was better when it came to the new stadiums, as crowds exceeding 60,000 were commonplace for pro football games. Unfortunately, this created poor sight lines for baseball viewing. Instead of sitting close to the field of play, fans were now forced to sit a good distance from the action in these coliseum-type buildings. As the years wore on, fans began yearning for a more intimate ballpark setting that would allow them to be closer to the field.

The other changes that affected major-league baseball fans' attitudes were not so well intentioned. Players' salaries were skyrocketing, making it harder for average fans to identify with their ballpark heroes. As recently as the 1960s, players could be seen in the off-season working regular jobs to augment their baseball income. Fans' perception of baseball players began to change. The new salary structure itself would not have been so bad if fans knew that the players they rooted for would be playing their entire careers for the home team. Free agency, which granted the players the right to change teams upon the completion of a contract, changed all of that. Correctly, any proponent of the free-market system will tell you that employees should have the freedom to move to any job that they please at the best salary they can make. This is the American way, so why should baseball players have it any differently? However, in the baseball fans' minds, it became extremely difficult to identify with the millionaire ballplayers who showed no loyalty to the people who were paying the increasingly higher ticket prices to help support their salaries. This situation made the next issue of fan alienation even more difficult to take, the issue of baseball's never-ending labor troubles.

From 1972 to 1994, baseball and its fans suffered through eight work stoppages due to either player strikes or owner lockouts. In the United States, we have labor laws that give unionized employees the right to strike if they cannot negotiate an acceptable contract with management. This is the American way, and why should a baseball player, who is the employee of a baseball team, not have that right? But the perception of baseball is different. Even to the most hardened union person, baseball is a game. Many see it as a public trust, where the owners and players share the obligation to keep the gates open regardless of the labor situation. In the early days of the players' union, the players had a good level of sympathy from fans. The owners were looked at, quite deservedly, as robber barons taking advantage of the poor players who were bound for life to their teams. The players had no freedom of movement, and they had to sell cars or men's suits during the off-season to boot! Free agency and multimillion-dollar contracts changed this view. By the time of the devastating 1994 baseball strike that led to the cancellation of the end of the regular season and the World Series, fans started looking at the players as being greedy millionaires who were willingly depriving them of their summer escape and enjoyment. People lost patience with both the players and owners.

In *Minor League Baseball: Community Building through Hometown Sport,* sports sociologist Rebecca S. Kraus defines a community in terms of a sense of belonging and a quality of life. Major-league baseball fans had always felt a sense of community with their hometown clubs, and the success or failure of the clubs was a very personal thing. Big business changed that intimate feeling. The major-league ballpark experience in the 1990s was now dominated by a constant bombardment of marketing and boisterous advertisements. Postseason games now began at 8:30 PM on the East Coast in order to ensure a prime-time television audience on the West Coast. Those unfortunate enough to live east of the Mississippi River had to go sleepless in October if they wanted to watch the playoffs and the World Series. Ticket and concession prices were making a night at the ballpark for a family of four a $200 outing at the minimum. In short, there was a sharp loss of community among major-league fans, who began to feel a sense of abandonment by the players, owners, and executives.

While the fans' feelings of discontent toward the major leagues grew, minor-league owners discovered the recipe for capitalizing on the legions of baseball fans looking to recapture the game of their past, as well as on young families with disposable incomes who were looking for a fun, inexpensive night out. By 1990, the affiliated minor leagues stressed a relaxed atmosphere fed by zany between-innings promotions and plain old fun to attract audiences. No longer was loyalty to a player enough to sustain the minor-league fans' allegiance, as players came and went from minor-league rosters quite quickly. Owners realized that the people who attended their games needed to be treated more as customers rather than as fans.

There is no better example of this change of attitude toward the entertainment factor by minor-league ownership than the constant stream of sometimes irreverent and always funny themes and skits that now dominate minor-league games. The greatest practitioner of this type of entertainment, who brought it to the minor leagues into the 1990s and beyond, is Mike Veeck, son of the legendary baseball owner Bill Veeck. The elder Veeck owned the Cleveland Indians in the 1940s, the St. Louis Browns in the early 1950s, and the Chicago White Sox twice—in the late 1950s and again the 1970s. Bill Veeck was known as a baseball maverick during his day, pulling stunts at the ballpark that were unheard of in the staid old major leagues of that time. He was responsible for signing a midget to a one-day contract and sending him up to pinch-hit for the Browns. He held a formal funeral procession and burial for the 1948 Indians' World Championship flag when it became obvious that they would not repeat their championship in 1949. Bill Veeck gave baseball the exploding scoreboard at Comiskey Park in Chicago in the 1960s, and who could forget his White Sox in their disco-era shorts and knee-high socks in 1976? Mike Veeck took over his father's zany legacy. In describing him, baseball writer Alan Schwarz wrote in *Inc.* magazine in April 2005, "This nut didn't fall far from the tree."

Mike Veeck's contribution to his father's White Sox in 1979 was his ill-fated Disco Demolition Night promotion idea, when Chicago fans stormed the field between the games of a twi-night doubleheader to profess their hatred of disco music by setting fire to and otherwise destroying disco music records. Needless to say, the event turned into a full-scale, on-field riot, resulting in the field being rendered so unplayable that the White Sox were forced to forfeit the second game of the doubleheader. Mike Veeck took the blame for this fiasco, and as a result, could not get another job in baseball for ten years afterward. In 1989, Marvin Goldklang, owner of the Miami Miracle, an independent team operating in the Florida State League, decided he needed someone to perk up his franchise and decided to take a chance on Veeck. The rest is minor-league history.[7]

Veeck is mainly responsible for what you see in minor-league parks today. He introduced pranks like having a pig deliver baseballs to the home-plate umpire, a Blow-up Bat Day sponsored by Viagra, and nuns giving massages to fans in the stands. He is responsible for 5:30 AM games on Mother's Day (so fans can go to the Mother's Day game and make it to Mom's house in time), free vasectomy giveaways on Father's Day, and, of course, free admission for all pregnant women on Labor Day. Thanks to the inspiration of people like Mike Veeck, a minor-league baseball game became more of an entertainment event than a ballgame, and fans began showing up at parks as much to see the between-innings "dizzy bat race" as a sparkling play by a shortstop. Suddenly, there were more communities and regions willing to host minor-league baseball and build stadiums than there were minor-league clubs to inhabit them. This, too, changed quickly.

In 1993, the aforementioned Miles Wolff led a movement that would further revolutionize lower-level professional baseball by forming the Northern League, an all-independent league completely unaffiliated with the major leagues. Wolff, like Veeck, was another baseball maverick who favored being able to "go it alone" as opposed to being tied to the whims of the major-league franchise. Many potential owners felt the same way as Wolff, and they invested heavily in the Northern League and other independent leagues like the Atlantic League and, in later years, Wolff's Can-Am League. Independent baseball ownership is risky, and many teams and leagues have failed. But enough have survived to make them a very important part of the landscape of community-based baseball. The key to success was researching and finding areas where the concept of a town-based team and community pride meant more than a major-league affiliation.

The alienation of the fans from the high prices and relentless marketing of big-time sports and entertainment was causing many people to turn inward and look for ways to reconnect with their communities by participating themselves in local entertainment and recreation. Independent baseball fit this new attitude perfectly. Going to the ballpark with friends and neighbors helped contribute to a sense of belonging, an amount of civic pride in the home team, and a feeling of a better quality of life, which could not be generated by a long, expensive trip to a major-league city. The average fans in an independent-league park are not concerned with whether the players they are watching are future budding major-league stars. They are in the park to be entertained and to relax.

There is certainly no lack of good players for these independent leagues. Up until the independents came into being, if a player was cut by a major-league organization because he wasn't progressing in their system fast enough, his career was basically over. There was no other place to go practice his craft as a ballplayer, unless another major-league organization was willing to take a chance on him. If he was a talented college player who, for whatever reason, went unselected in the major-league amateur player draft, again, his career was pretty much ended. Independent professional baseball gives forgotten players a second chance. Many players have used independent baseball to sharpen their skills and return to major-league organizations. It is enough of an incentive to keep the players hungry for that second chance, which makes the product on the independent playing fields a very entertaining one for the fans who go to the games. The proliferation of independent professional baseball helped populate New Jersey with six of its eight baseball clubs by 2006.

The stage was now set for the explosion of minor-league and independent professional baseball in the 1990s and into the new century. Minor-league attendance in 1993 totaled more than 30 million fans, not counting the independents. New minor-league stadiums dotted the country, and in areas where there was no minor-league baseball, savvy public officials and potential franchise owners were plotting to cash in on the new minor-league popularity.

But, if you lived in New Jersey then, you still needed to venture into either New York City or Philadelphia to see live baseball, and if you preferred something less expensive, the closest minor-league clubs were in distant Pennsylvania, Delaware, or upper New York State. Even though historically loyal to either the Yankees, Mets, or Phillies, the New Jersey fans were no different than their counterparts in the rest of the country in their growing disenchantment with the big business and high cost of major-league baseball. It was time for New Jersey to get back into the ballgame. A whole generation of New Jersey baseball fans had never experienced having local minor-league baseball teams to root for. Their wait would end in 1994 with the creation of the Trenton Thunder and the New Jersey Cardinals.

3

Baseball Returns to
New Jersey in 1994

The two men who brought professional baseball back to New Jersey were as different as night and day. One lived in the city, the other in the country. One was a slick, hard-driving Trenton politician who could work a room with the best of them. The other was a low-keyed businessman who commuted to New York City every day from his home in rural Sussex County. Bob Prunetti of Trenton and Rob Hilliard of Vernon shared the dream of bringing minor-league baseball to their respective areas of New Jersey. Their methods differed but their goals and results were the same, resulting in brand new ballparks and minor-league baseball in Trenton and Frankford Township for the 1994 baseball season.

The entrance to Skylands Park, Augusta, Sussex County, which was built to resemble a barn. Photograph by Bob Golon, 2005.

In 2007, fourteen years after professional baseball returned to the state, it is hard to believe that as recently as 1993, New Jersey baseball fans experienced nothing but rumors, broken promises, and failed attempts to bring the game back. New Jersey professional sports experienced a rebirth in the 1970s and 1980s, and the efforts were strictly major league. It started in the 1970s, when the New Jersey Sports and Exposition Authority convinced the New York Giants of the National Football League to play in the new Meadowlands Sports Complex in East Rutherford. The 76,500-seat Giants Stadium opened in 1976, and it became an immediate hit among football fans. Eight years later, oilman Leon Hess, owner of the NFL's New York Jets, abandoned Shea Stadium in Flushing Meadows, Queens, and joined the Giants as tenants in Giants Stadium, making New Jersey the professional football capital of the Northeast. In the late 1970s, Giants Stadium became the focal point of the short-lived North American Soccer League, as well. The league's flagship team, the New York Cosmos, filled the stadium to capacity a number of times, a rarity for soccer in the United States. Heartened by their success, the Sports and Exposition Authority sought approval for and built a 20,000-seat indoor arena at the Meadowlands, immediately attracting both the National Basketball Association's New Jersey Nets and the National Hockey League's Colorado Rockies (later renamed the New Jersey Devils) to play in it.

New Jersey became a hot sporting commodity, but there was still no professional baseball being played in the Garden State. Governor Thomas Kean and the Sports and Exposition Authority looked across the Hudson River and spotted what they thought might be a willing partner to fill the baseball void. The New York Yankees continually grumbled about needing a new home, and the Meadowlands looked enticing. Moving a storied franchise like the Yankees to New Jersey could be discussed only then because at that time, they were not the most popular team in New York City.

In the mid-1980s, the New York Mets of Dwight Gooden, Darryl Strawberry, and their other colorful teammates dominated the New York baseball headlines. The Mets won the World Series in 1986 and drew big, enthusiastic crowds to Shea Stadium. Meanwhile, the once-mighty Yankees fell upon some hard times at Yankee Stadium in the Bronx. Questionable player deals and numerous managerial changes taxed the patience of even the most dedicated Yankees fans, and empty seats became a common sight at Yankee Stadium. The front office attributed the lack of attendance to the Bronx neighborhood itself. People didn't feel safe coming to the

Bronx, claimed Yankees executives, and even those who did were being turned off by the constant traffic delays due to the outdated highways leading to and from Yankee Stadium. The Yankees told anyone who would listen that they were in need of a new ballpark and would consider alternative locations in the New York City area if a deal could be struck.

New Jersey governor Kean, with the backing of the Sports and Exposition Authority and state business and labor leaders, placed a $185 million stadium bond issue on the ballot in 1987. If the bond issue passed, the state would have the funding to build a 45,000-seat baseball stadium in Lyndhurst, adjacent to the Meadowlands complex. A commitment for a team to relocate to the new stadium had to be in place prior to construction, and many thought that the Yankees would be that team. The bond issue's supporters claimed that major-league baseball would create thousands of jobs in Bergen County and be a positive stimulus to the New Jersey economy. The opponents of the bond issue thought it was a risky proposition. Attendance at games could not be guaranteed, and a realistic cost assessment of a new ballpark was in the neighborhood of $400 million. A "north-south" theme also developed within New Jersey, with many residents in the southern part of the state complaining that all of the major Sports and Exposition Authority projects benefited only northern New Jersey. Opposition to the plan increased, and despite the political backing, the voters defeated the bond issue by a two-to-one margin. The Yankees never officially committed to New Jersey, and whether they would have moved or not is simply conjecture. One New Jersey official very close to the negotiations with the Yankees was Robert Mulcahy, currently the athletic director of Rutgers University who was the longtime president and CEO of the New Jersey Sports and Exposition Authority. Mulcahy recalled that Yankees owner George Steinbrenner had genuine interest in the Meadowlands site. "We had very serious conversations that included layouts of what the stadium might be. George made some helicopter flights over the sites that we had either adjacent to or on the Meadowlands, and frankly his attraction was to the Meadowlands because he felt it was the symbol of success. So, how close it ever got? You know, it's hard to know when people would pull a trigger on something like that, but I can say that we had some very serious discussions about it." Unfortunately, Mulcahy and New Jersey never got the opportunity to present a firm plan of financing to the Yankees once the bond issue was defeated. The idea of building a major-league baseball stadium in New Jersey died along with the referendum.[1]

Despite this failure, the talk of bringing baseball to New Jersey created considerable interest from local businessmen. With the defeat of the bond issue, discussions began to bring minor-league baseball back to the state. A Chester, New Jersey, investment banking and brokerage firm, Cathedra Investment Corporation, announced their intention to buy a minor-league club, move it to New Jersey, and finance the building of a new minor-league ballpark somewhere in the central portion of the state. In June 1989, the firm announced that it would build a 5,500-seat ballpark on the grounds of the Six Flags Great Adventure Amusement Park in Jackson. Cathedra targeted the 1990 season for opening, provided that it could arrange the $6 million financing privately, negotiate a lease with Six Flags and Jackson, arrange for all of the construction permits necessary, and most important, purchase a team. Cathedra seemed serious and it had some momentum, and New Jersey baseball fans were cautiously optimistic. However, 1990 came and went without a shovel ever being turned in the soil of Jackson, and by 1992 it became apparent that the Cathedra initiative had died a very quiet death. If Cathedra had waited two or three years to initiate the project, it might have been successful. The minor leagues did not expand until 1994.

Cathedra had talked of bringing an existing minor-league club to New Jersey while minor-league baseball was undergoing a period of stabilization. Many clubs were making money in their existing locations, and there were no available clubs to purchase at either the Triple-A or Double-A levels. Without an immediate minor-league expansion, the possibility of purchasing a baseball team to bring to New Jersey did not exist. Cathedra lost the momentum and faded from the picture.

In Atlantic County, freeholder Kirk Conover championed the idea of bringing a Double-A club to Atlantic City to complement the casino tourism industry by bringing a family entertainment option there. Conover had neither a baseball club nor the financing for a stadium project. He hoped that the Sports and Exposition Authority would purchase the Atlantic City Race Course in nearby May's Landing, making it possible for him to propose a bond issue to finance a minor-league stadium at that location. Conover's plan stalled when the Sports Authority declined to purchase the racetrack. The option of asking Atlantic City voters to publicly finance a ballpark looked like a risky proposition, one that they would never approve. As late as 1992, a group calling itself New Jersey Professional Baseball Incorporated attempted to convince the Atlantic City Council to pursue an $8 million loan from the Casino Reinvestment Development Authority for construction of a ballpark on the grounds of the Bader Field airport. The council declined to pursue the idea by a four-to-three vote. New ideas were needed for baseball to come back to New Jersey.[2]

Meanwhile, in Trenton, Robert Prunetti had just taken office as the new Mercer County Executive. He had a plan for the economic development of the city of Trenton, and it included baseball. Prunetti, determined to succeed where others had failed, intended for his plan to work.

BOB PRUNETTI'S THUNDEROUS PLANS

Minor-league baseball wasn't the only entertainment option experiencing a growth boom in the 1980s. All across the nation, cities with abandoned waterfronts reclaimed them for tourism and recreation. Projects at the Inner Harbor of Baltimore and Penn's Landing in Philadelphia showed that with vision and creativity, waterfront areas could once again prosper and attract visitors. These city waterfronts had been centers of industry and commerce up until the mid-twentieth century. Large commercial port operations made it possible to transport manufactured goods to destinations via ship. Advances in transportation technology caused massive changes that affected these ports. Jet air transport and containerized trucking made the local port system obsolete. City waterfront areas began a long period of decay and neglect, and the once bustling port of Trenton was no exception. Route 29, a state highway constructed in the 1950s, physically cut off the downtown Trenton area from the Delaware River. The road acted as a barrier between the waterfront and potential visitors, further eroding economy of the Trenton waterfront, and the area decayed.

The slogan "Trenton Makes, the World Takes" is displayed on a bridge that crosses the Delaware River between Trenton and Pennsylvania. The slogan reflects the major manufacturing center that Trenton once was. When industry moved out, the city suffered economically. A 1989 survey of Mercer County area incomes showed that Trentonians earned an average of only $11,018 per capita per year and that 17.3 percent of Trenton's residents lived below the national poverty line. The same survey showed that the per capita incomes in the towns surrounding Trenton were much higher, West Windsor ($30,761) and Lawrence ($23,605) in particular. Urban flight to the suburbs affected Trenton like any other city in America. Bringing people back into the city and to the waterfront, even if only for a few hours of recreation, required new ideas and bold initiatives.[3]

County Executive Prunetti knew the Trenton territory. A native of the Chambersburg section of Trenton, Prunetti graduated from both Trenton High School and Trenton State University. Despite being a Republican politician in a predominantly Democratic Party area, Prunetti had the drive and initiative to take on big projects and succeed. The revitalization of the Trenton waterfront became Prunetti's priority, and he insisted that Mercer County and the State of New Jersey take an active part in making the waterfront into a regional attraction that residents, state workers, and tourists could enjoy. The thirty-four-acre American Bridge Company site along Route 29 attracted Prunetti's interest. Plans were already in place to build a new, $150 million Riverview Executive Plaza and a restaurant at the site of the old Cooper Iron Works next door to the Bridge Company site. The accessibility of the property to Route 29 and the commercial development happening on the waterfront made this an ideal location for a baseball stadium, according to Prunetti.

Critics questioned why Prunetti was so vehement about baseball in Trenton. Prunetti explained that before Trenton could accomplish great things as a city, it first had to begin to believe in itself. Christopher Edwards, the author of *Filling in the Seams: The Story of Trenton Thunder Baseball,* quotes Prunetti as saying, " First of all, we wanted to show that a professional sports franchise could work in this area [Trenton]. . . . We wanted to show that we could change the image of the city of Trenton, both from within, the spirit from within, and the perception of the city of Trenton from outside. We wanted to demonstrate that if we brought class acts to this town, people would frequent them." Craig H. Skiem of Coopers & Lybrand's professional sports industry services, agreed. "The presence of a sports stadium can build name recognition for and can attract people to an area and in the process help diversify its economic base," Skiem told the *New York Times* in October 1993. "The potential is there for the people who come [to a ballpark] to channel money into local businesses, and the investment in the stadium itself shows investment within the area." Prunetti spent 1992 and 1993 convincing state and local agencies to support his project. By the middle of 1993, he successfully obtained a $4 million state loan for the Mercer County Improvement Authority and convinced the authority to sell an additional $9 million in bonds for the ballpark project. Prunetti's style of pushing his proposals through local government without ever letting the voters of the county decide if they wanted to spend the money through a ballot referendum drew criticism. His judgment, plus the experience of the Sports and Exposition Authority in 1987 in failing to convince voters to approve a baseball stadium in the Meadowlands, convinced him that public funding referendums for baseball stadiums could not succeed. His ego and drive took over. Mayor Doug Palmer of Trenton explained in the *Trentonian,* "If you mix ego with Bob's intelligence and charisma, that's what fueled him to be able to do what he did in bringing baseball in [to Trenton]." The Republican consensus-builder Prunetti and the Democratic governor of New Jersey, James Florio, took turns turning shovels at the groundbreaking ceremonies for Waterfront Park on September 29, 1993. Bob Prunetti's tireless work had pushed the stadium through governmental red tape. While this took place, another group, led by Sam Plumeri, worked with Prunetti to secure a minor-league baseball franchise for Trenton.

Samuel Plumeri Sr., a successful real estate developer, also had his own vision for baseball in Trenton, albeit a more personal one. Plumeri's father, Joseph, owned part of the Trenton minor-league club in the 1920s. As a child, Sam attended many games and developed a lifelong affinity for baseball. In the early 1990s, Plumeri and the Cherry Hill real estate developer Joseph Caruso purchased the Eastern League's London, Ontario, franchise with the intention of moving the club to Trenton. The London franchise had difficulties meeting the minor league's new requirements for minimum stadium-facility conditions, and its stadium lease with London was expiring. Plumeri and Caruso met with Prunetti and offered to lease the new Trenton stadium if they were successful in convincing minor-league baseball executives to approve moving the team to Trenton. Not only did Prunetti have his plan for a Trenton baseball stadium, he now had a potential team to play there. Plumeri and Caruso added law firm partners Joe Finley and James Maloney to their group of investors. Maloney, the former chairman of the New Jersey Democratic Party, was politically well positioned. Finley turned his attention from the legal practice to baseball, eventually becoming a successful owner of multiple minor-league teams. This diverse group would not be denied in their quest to bring their baseball team to Trenton. "We had no real business plan and we were trying to put a team in Trenton when businesses and people were running away from the city," Finley told the *Asbury Park Press* in May 2006. "Sam Plumeri would not have it any other way. He was a Trenton guy and thought the team could make it there." Extensive behind-the-scenes negotiations with minor-league baseball executives during the 1993 season resulted in the announcement in October that the London Tigers were moving to Trenton to become the Trenton Thunder in 1994.

The owners realized that for all of their financial ability, they did not know the finer points of operating a minor-league club on a day-to-day basis. The leadership team they assembled to run the baseball operation of the Trenton Thunder would determine the degree of success of the franchise for many years to come. The new Thunder needed experienced, young, energetic minor-league executives for the formidable task of introducing the ball club to the public.

Wayne Hodes, a twenty-nine-year-old native of Watchung Hills, New Jersey, was hired to be the first general manager and chief operating officer of the Trenton Thunder. Hodes received a master's degree in sports administration from Montclair State University, worked as an intern with the Tidewater (Norfolk) Tides of the International League, then headed west to become the assistant general manager of the Rancho Cucamonga Quakes of the California League for their inaugural season in 1993. With the Quakes, Hodes acquired the skills needed to run a new stadium operation, a job very similar to the one awaiting him in Trenton. Brian Mahoney, the Quakes' director of ticket sales in 1993, joined Hodes in Trenton as the assistant general manager. Tom McCarthy, a twenty-five-year-old sportswriter for the *Trenton Times* and graduate of Trenton State University, left the print journalism field and joined the Thunder front office as director of public and media relations and, more critically, the Thunder's first radio play-by-play voice. McCarthy believed in the future of baseball in Trenton, and his enthusiasm for it both on the air and behind the scenes was infectious. McCarthy became the "voice of the Thunder" to area fans as well as the team's best salesman in their early days.[4]

McCarthy, currently a member of the Philadelphia Phillies radio broadcasting team, has fond memories of Sam Plumeri and his passion for getting the Thunder started. "Sam was such a sweet guy and a great guy. I still live for fact that I have memories of him walking into my office and just chatting. He was just a special, special guy. He had such an impact on all of us in the front office, because of his personality and the way he treated us," explained McCarthy. He added, "I think the Thunder was very important to Sam. This was his town. He made his mark in this city.

He loved this city. He was raised in this city. His kids were raised in this city. Everything about Trenton was important to Sam, and I think that he wanted to see something special be left for the city before he would go eventually. This gave him passion. I mean, he acted so young for his advanced age but had such an impact on the younger folks that he came in contact with. I always say to my wife that there are a handful of people that we were fortunate that we got a chance to meet because they made our lives better. He's one of them."[5]

As December 1993 approached, the team unveiled its new logo, enabling Trenton Thunder shirts and hats to be sold just in time for the holiday gift season. As construction crews worked to complete Waterfront Park in time for opening day in April, Mother Nature intervened. New Jersey suffered through one of its harshest winter seasons ever, with snow and ice storms a weekly occurrence. Construction slowed to a crawl. A heavy layer of ice on the grounds delayed the installation of the playing field, and by March 1, team officials conceded that the park would not be ready in time for the April 16 opener. The Thunder arranged to play its first scheduled home games in Veterans Stadium in Philadelphia as well as in the minor-league park at Wilmington, Delaware. The Waterfront Park inaugural was rescheduled for April 27 against the Albany-Colonie Yankees. Trenton and Eastern League officials determined the playing field to be ready, even though wide ruts were visible between the layers of sod. Yankees manager Billy Evers inspected the field personally, decided that it was unsafe for his players, and refused to let his club take the field. Privately, the Thunder players agreed with Evers's assessment of the playing conditions. Tom McCarthy remembered the night like it was yesterday. "I remember there being such a buildup," explained McCarthy. "There are certain events that you look at in your life, whether it is your marriage, the birth of your first child, your graduation from college, where you build and you build and all of the sudden it's there and it whisks by so quickly. We had a packed house and people wanted to see baseball for the first time in their ballpark. Billy Evers just didn't feel that the playing conditions were up to par and he didn't want to send his players out to the playing field, and in hindsight, he was probably right. The ground was very soft and the sod had not planted itself yet. When you walked on it, you did sink a little bit. It was a frenetic night. It did put a negative spin on what was supposed to be a great night, but you can look at public relations in two different ways. Positive public relations are great, but negative public relations, no matter what form, gets your name out there. I think people got intrigued because they saw the pictures of the ballpark in all the papers and they said, wow, this is a pretty special looking place. I remember Bob [Prunetti] telling everybody over the public address system that the Yankees did not want to play. I forget the way he phrased it, but I was standing right next to him when he announced it and I looked at the person standing next to me and said, 'oh, that's not good.' But as it turned out, it was just one of those pages in the long chapter of that first Thunder year. I look back and I chuckle at it now, but it was still a great night because out of it, the players, led by [future major-league slugger] Tony Clark, walked into the stands and signed autographs and really made people feel like that team was part of their community." Regardless of what took place on opening night, the experience did not sour the fans. They returned to Waterfront Park in great numbers after the club played some additional "home" games in Reading, Pennsylvania, while allowing the new sod to settle and grow. The history of Waterfront Park as home to the Trenton Thunder officially began on May 9, 1994, when Bill Pulsipher, who later played for the New York Mets, pitched the Binghamton Mets to a 5-3 win over the Thunder before 6,941 fans.

The Thunder averaged 6,263 fans per game in 1994, far exceeding the expectations of even its most optimistic backers. They became the first Eastern League franchise to draw more than 435,000 fans for two consecutive seasons (1995 and 1996). By the end of 1996, the Trenton Convention and Visitor's Bureau called the Thunder the single biggest entertainment attraction in the city. Prunetti did not stop with Waterfront Park in his quest to rebuild Trenton's tourism and entertainment base. He helped create the Sovereign Bank Arena, adding to Trenton's entertainment and sports venues, as well as other new waterfront destinations. The general improvement of the Waterfront Park area, including the Route 29 tunnel, can be traced to Prunetti's initiatives. His successful 1995 and 1999 election campaigns demonstrated the faith that Trentonians put in him. Bob Prunetti left the office of Mercer County Executive at the end of 2003, with Waterfront Park and the Trenton Thunder a major part of his legacy. "You ought to use politics to make positive change," Prunetti told the *Trenton Times* on December 28, 2003. "We got things done." Indeed they did.

"If you build it, they will come" became a popular phrase after the 1989 movie *Field of Dreams* caused Americans to romanticize about small ballparks in rural farm settings. That mysterious voice from above that drove Kevin Costner's character, Ray Kinsella, to build a ballpark in a cornfield in Iowa seemed to influence others nationwide to emulate the film's protagonist. Bob Prunetti's field of dreams lacked a cornfield, but he did build it and they certainly did come to the Trenton Thunder games. In Vernon, New Jersey, a rural community in the northwestern-most part of the state, Rob Hilliard, a public relations executive in his mid-thirties, also caught Ray Kinsella's fever. There were plenty of corn-fields in Sussex County, and Hilliard decided to pursue his dream of a ballpark in that area at the same time Prunetti was building his ballpark in Trenton. The result was a second minor-league ballpark in New Jersey built for the 1994 season.

ROB HILLIARD'S BALLPARK—PUBLIC SUCCESS, PRIVATE NIGHTMARE

Rob Hilliard loved minor-league baseball since his days as a young-ster growing up in Jersey City. He attended Jersey City Eastern League games in old Roosevelt Stadium in the late 1970s, watching future major leaguers like Rickey Henderson develop their skills. The club left Jersey City in 1979, and shortly thereafter Hilliard left too, eventually settling in Sussex County with his young family. Minor-league baseball came relatively close to northwest New Jersey in 1989 when the Philadel-phia Phillies established a Triple-A franchise, the Red Barons, at the new Lackawanna County Stadium in Scranton, Pennsylvania. Hilliard packed his wife and kids into the car for the short ride to Scranton to see a Red Barons game. The intimacy of minor-league baseball once again impressed Hilliard, and afterward, every time he drove through the corn-fields of Sussex County, visions of Ray Kinsella's field of dreams danced in his head.[6]

America suffered through a white-collar recession in the late 1980s, and Hilliard became a victim of corporate downsizing. He was without work, but he had a dream, and suddenly he also had the time to devote to that dream. Hilliard attended a minor-league executive meeting in Texas during the 1989 off-season, where he heard that the Hamilton (Ontario) Redbirds were for sale. Determined to purchase the Single-A club but short on cash, Hilliard sought investor partners. A mutual friend intro-duced him to Barry Gordon, a money fund manager from Long Island City, New York. Gordon had a baseball background, being a broker of baseball memorabilia as well as a part owner of the Albany-Colonie Yankees of the Eastern League. Using all of his public relations skills, Hilliard convinced Gordon and Gordon's partner, Marc Klee, that Sussex County was the perfect place for a "field of dreams" type of park. On the fringes of the New York and Philadelphia major-league markets, Sussex County had approximately 135,000 residents with an annual mean income of $48,000. Another 3.5 million potential fans lived within a thirty-five mile radius of the planned ballpark.[7] Hilliard felt that many of the suburban residents would make the drive to see minor-league baseball, much as Hilliard and his family drove to see the Red Barons only a couple of years before. The tourism industry already attracted hundreds of thousands of visitors to Sussex County each summer. Surely, a baseball game in a rural setting would be the ideal complement to a day of camping, fishing, and hiking.

Convinced by Hilliard's enthusiasm, Gordon and Klee's company, called Minor League Heroes Inc., joined Hilliard in purchasing the Redbirds for approximately $1.4 million in 1990. Hilliard's new company, the Skylands Park Management Corporation, accounted for 25 percent of the purchase price, with Gordon and Klee supplying the other 75 percent. Shortly thereafter, the New York–Penn League, in which the Redbirds played, granted permission to move the club to New Jersey if the group could get a stadium financed and built. All it needed was a cornfield and about $10 million. Hilliard realized that a public bond issue referendum for a ballpark would never pass in conservative Sussex County. He took the unusual approach of raising funds for the project privately, offering two million shares of common stock in Skylands Park Management to small investors via the NASDAQ stock exchange. Ballpark builders typically depended on state and local governments to provide financing for their projects. Privately financing Skylands Park, as risky as it seemed, attracted the interest of a different type of small investor. Many nonsavvy investors were willing to pay the $7 initial cost per share to invest in minor-league baseball, feeling that they were contributing to a noble cause of bringing family entertainment to northwestern New Jersey while actually owning "a piece of the action." The stock offering raised approximately $6.5 to $7 million dollars, while Hilliard successfully raised another $2 million in private capital.

Skylands Park Management used some of the proceeds from the stock sale to purchase the land for the ballpark, spending $1.1 million for a 28.5-acre parcel at the intersection of Routes 15 and 206 in Frankford

Township, known as Ross Corner. The plans for the complex called for a 4,200-seat baseball park, a 17,000-square-foot recreation center for parties, batting cages, miniature golf, a sporting goods store, and a museum devoted to the history of minor-league baseball as well as a Sussex County Sports Hall of Fame. Construction began in June of 1993.

The same rough winter that delayed the progress of Waterfront Park in Trenton also delayed the Skylands Park project. The colder temperatures of the northwest corner of New Jersey led to greater amounts of snow and ice accumulating on the construction site and posed an even bigger problem than in Trenton. The New York–Penn League season did not begin until the middle of June, which gave contractors more time to complete the park than their Trenton counterparts had. Unfortunately, the weather delays and overtime needed to rush the stadium to a condition where it could be opened inflated the original cost estimate by $1.2 million. Rob Hilliard, sensing trouble, resigned his position as president of the baseball team in February 1994 to devote his full energies to finishing the park. Management of the team now settled into the hands of Barry Gordon, Marc Klee, and the new Cardinals general manager, Tony Torre. Torre, a native Canadian, had worked for the club while it was located in Ontario. He moved with it when it temporarily located to Glens Falls, New York, for the 1993 season. Minor League Heroes offered Torre the general manager's position with the Cardinals, and he embarked on a bizarre journey to bring the Cardinals to life.

With the financial problems mounting, Hilliard arranged for a $3.5 million loan from a group of local banks to finish construction of the stadium, but the banks pulled out of the deal when rumors of the cost overruns surfaced. Skylands Park Management filed for Chapter 11 bankruptcy protection on June 2, 1994, citing a total of $5 million in debts to 150 different creditors. Hilliard turned to a Hackensack lending company, Kennedy Funding, for a $2 million loan to satisfy the contractors, who were refusing to finish their work on the stadium. Kennedy Funding pulled out of the deal when the creditors objected to the high interest costs of the loan agreement, coupled with the fact that one of Kennedy's officers was once involved with a securities fraud judgment.[8] Rob Hilliard's field of dreams was turning into a financial nightmare. The public cared little about Hilliard's money problems as advance tickets for the Cardinals games sold in large numbers. With Skylands Park not nearly ready for occupancy, Torre realized that he needed to take the lead to get the stadium opened in time.

The day before opening day on June 16, the ballpark had no sewer or water hookups. The concession stands were not ready, the skyboxes weren't built, and the manager's office and clubhouses were empty rooms. Torre reached into team funds to convince contractors to complete enough of the work so that Frankford Township would grant the park a temporary certificate of occupancy for opening day. Portable toilets were brought in. Young Cardinals players, just out of college, were introduced to professional baseball by having to build their own lockers. Temporary coolers and concession facilities were put up. Torre and his staff worked around the clock.[9] When the gates opened on opening night, a sellout crowd of 4,200 cheered the Cardinals as they defeated the Hudson Valley Renegades, 6-3. The fans kept coming back despite long lines at the temporary concession stands and portable toilets. The Cardinals set a New York–Penn League record for attendance in 1994, drawing 156,447 fans. They averaged 4,050 fans per game in a stadium that seated 4,200. Sellouts were common. Skylands Park was a hit with New Jersey Cardinals fans, even in its unfinished state.

Success on the field matched the success at the box office. The 1994 New Jersey Cardinals, under manager Roy Silver, celebrated their first season at Skylands with a 43-32 record, good enough to finish in first place in the New York–Penn League's McNamara Division. Then, in what turned out to be their only appearance ever in the playoffs, the Cards defeated both the Jamestown Jammers and the Auburn Astros to win the league championship. Catcher Brian Silvia and first baseman Mike Taylor represented the Cardinals on the New York–Penn League 1994 all-star team, and pitcher Scott Cunningham led the Cards with nine victories.

Sussex fans got a brief chance to see a local Seton Hall University favorite and future major leaguer Matt Morris pitch for the Cardinals in 1995. Even though the team slipped to third place in the standings, a franchise-record 176,788 fans paid their way into Skylands Park, which now boasted finished restrooms and concession stands. Cardinals attendance did not fall below the 170,000 mark through the 1997 season.

This success can be attributed to the dedication and hustle of Tony Torre and assistant general manager Herm Sorcher. The pair integrated the Cardinals into the Sussex County community, actively participating in youth events, charitable organizations, and local business opportunities. The club formed numerous advertising and promotional program relationships with local companies and organizations. The triple-tiered advertisement boards along the outfield fence perimeter were fully sub-scribed, and a host of sponsors appeared regularly in the Cardinals pro-gram. The Cards became a consistently visible part of the Sussex County summertime experience, and fan support could always be counted on. One can only imagine the local fans' disappointment when rumors began late in the 2005 season that the Cardinals owners were selling the club to a group that would move it to a new ballpark at State College, Pennsylvania.

In retrospect, Rob Hilliard's private corporation that was respon-sible for Skylands Park's being built also led to the Cardinals' demise. As sincere as Hilliard was about building his field of dreams in the cornfield, he did not possess the navigational skills to pull Skylands out of the finan-cial tailspin that began with the howling winter of 1994. Bad decisions and fractured relationships characterized the next ten years of business.

From the very beginning, Hilliard felt that nonbaseball events such as concerts, flea markets, and wrestling programs would be critical to the financial success of Skylands Park. The original agreement with Frank-ford Township that enabled Skylands Management to build the ballpark called for the township to have control of the park for nonbaseball events. The relationship between the township and the club soon became acri-monious. Each time Skylands Management wanted to book an event at the park, it had to pay a $200 application fee to the township, and long de-lays ensued while the requests were evaluated. The township acquiesced to concerts at the park in 1997, but only after Skylands Management threatened a lawsuit. Part of the agreement stated that concert seating was not allowed on the grass playing field, limiting attendance at the con-certs. This hurt ticket sales, and after one concert was only marginally successful, the concert promoters canceled the rest of the programs. In addition, the township's zoning laws prohibited the installation of an electric marquis sign outside the ballpark entrance to advertise the day's events. Such a sign would have been very helpful to inform traffic of up-coming events at an intersection as busy as Ross Corner. Yet, despite all of the conflicts, Frankford Township could not be held solely responsible for the difficulties of Skylands Park.

Management turmoil and missteps became the hallmark of Sky-lands Management Corporation. Exhausted and exasperated by his in-ability to turn the situation around, Rob Hilliard had resigned his posi-tion as president of Skylands in October 1996 and left the board of directors six months later. Hilliard explained to writer Fred J. Aun in the July 7, 1997, edition of the *Newark Star-Ledger* that he resigned in order to spend more time with his young family. In the same article, Barry Levine, hired by Barry Gordon and Marc Klee to replace Hilliard as head of Skylands Management Corporation, said that it was "a mutual decision" between Hilliard and the Skylands shareholders. Gordon and Klee became directors of Skylands Management and changed the name of the company to Millennium Sports Management Inc. Telling Aun that his job was like that of "rearranging the deck chairs on the Titanic," Levine set out to fix things, but some of his logic and methodologies were questionable. More problems followed.

Millennium lost nearly $1 million per year in both 1996 and 1997, but in spite of this, it awarded stock compensation of $750,000 to its executives and directors, above and beyond their salaries. It invested another $175,000 in a partnership led by two of its major shareholders to build a golf stadium in Florida, which failed miserably. To make matters worse, the investment company Millennium was using to help raise capital for the golf stadium ran afoul of securities regulators for misrepresenting the profitability potential of the project as well as the overall financial stability of Millennium stock. An ugly property tax fight developed with Frankford Township over the township's restrictions on the park's nonbaseball uses, and more rumors of bankruptcy surfaced. Despite the steady stream of negative news surrounding the management of Skylands Park and its financial condition, the fans of the New Jersey Cardinals never stopped coming to their games, and they were rewarded with a replacement club, the Sussex Skyhawks of the Can-Am League, after the Cardinals moved out.[10]

The New Jersey Cardinals and the Trenton Thunder set the stage for a broader growth of both minor-league and professional baseball in New Jersey. Neighboring communities and regions looked at the success of both franchises and decided to pursue baseball teams themselves, eventually resulting in stadiums being built in Camden, Atlantic City, Bridgewater Township, Lakewood, Newark, and Little Falls. The off-the-field problems of the Cardinals did not temper the enthusiasm of those who sought baseball for their communities, and the astounding success of the Trenton Thunder served as the model to emulate. The Thunder showed the rest of the state how it could be done and established Trenton as the "Capital of New Jersey Baseball."

The Trenton Thunder

The Capital of New Jersey Baseball

T he meeting room in the executive offices of the Trenton Thunder, below the stands at Waterfront Park, is relatively small. Early on this Labor Day morning, twenty-five Thunder staff members—both male and female, full-time and intern, some standing, some leaning against the wall—pack every corner of the room, awaiting the day's marching orders. The banter is friendly and casual. These people,

Mercer County Waterfront Park, Trenton, New Jersey, home of the Trenton Thunder. Photograph by Bob Golon, 2007.

after an entire season, seem to still genuinely like each other, no small accomplishment in such a high-pressured environment. As I kneel in the corner to take notes of the proceedings, general manager Brad Taylor opens the meeting by announcing, "We have finally reached the end of the regular season after starting out 0-10. Today should be, relatively speaking, a piece of cake. Wednesday, however, will be quite different." Taylor is referring to the fact that the Trenton Thunder began the season by losing their first ten games but recovered to win the 2006 Eastern League Northern Division. The veiled reference to Wednesday is in anticipation of game one of the best-three-out-of-five Eastern League semifinal playoffs, and the appearance of New York Yankees star Hideki Matsui in a Trenton Thunder uniform for an injury rehabilitation assignment. Labor Day afternoon games are normally fairly laid-back events, but that will all change by Wednesday night, when the playoffs begin. The staff needs to be ready for the media circus and large crowds that will accompany the appearance of yet another Yankees star in the Trenton Thunder pinstripes. A high-profile rehabilitation assignment is a mixed blessing for the Thunder, as are many issues that arise out of being the Double-A affiliate of the most visible team in major-league baseball. The constant balance between the business needs of the Trenton Thunder and the baseball needs of the New York Yankees is something that the management and employees of the Thunder deal with on a daily basis. But for now, there's the matter of the final regular-season game of the season, a Labor Day afternoon game against the Reading Phillies.[1]

Labor Day signifies the unofficial ending of the summer season. It is also the day designated to honor the working people of America. It's a holiday of parades, barbecues, political speeches, and of course that American staple, baseball. Labor Day marks the beginning of the stretch drive for the postseason playoffs in the major leagues, and it also signals the imminent ending of the regular season in the minors and the independent leagues. For many years, Labor Day for New Jersey baseball fans meant watching the Yankees, Mets, or Phillies play holiday doubleheaders either in person or on television. The days of single-admission Labor Day doubleheaders are long gone, and New Jersey fans now have the option of attending minor-league and independent professional Labor Day baseball games at their local parks, in an atmosphere that's as American as apple pie. Labor Day might have been intended as a day of rest for the working class of America, but it is just another long day at the office for Brad Taylor and his young staff.

After a tumultuous weekend of rain and wind leftover from Tropical Storm Ernesto, this Labor Day Monday at Waterfront Park in Trenton dawns sunny with temperatures in the sixties. There's a hint of autumn in the air. Pulling into the parking area at 9:30 AM, I notice numerous Thunder front-office staffers carrying large containers of coffee and other beverages from their cars to the Thunder office. There's a spring in their step, and they don't look tired. Not only is it the end of a long season, it also has already been a very long weekend that, for the staff, began at the same time as the aforementioned Ernesto.

Friday night's game against Reading was postponed due to the rain. A twi-night doubleheader was scheduled for the following evening at 5:05, with a promise from the local weatherman that Ernesto would leave the area by early evening. The weatherman had it wrong by about an hour or so. After a lengthy delay, the doubleheader began at 6:30, and the first game proceeded to take eleven innings. The second game did not end until long after midnight. The Thunder and Phillies played again the following day, Sunday evening at 6:00, and the exhausted Thunder staff had no time to rest as 7,698 fans jammed Waterfront Park on that night. When it was over, Taylor and his management team credited the staff with a near-flawless performance, not only in the handling of the big crowd, but also in performing the evening's duties of promotions and fan activities with virtually no errors. No small accomplishment, considering the multiple hats worn by minor-league and independent professional baseball staff members, as compared with their major-league counterparts. The major-league teams employ staffers that have clearly delineated, narrower responsibilities. In an office such as Trenton's, the same person booking corporate sponsorships and selling group ticket packages is also in charge of helping the grounds crew cover the field with the tarpaulin in case of rain. Keeping a harried staff happy, especially on a long, rainy weekend such as this one, is one of the many challenging aspects of the general manager's job.

A minor-league general manager should hold the title "head of household," because that is what he really is. He's in charge of balancing all of the competing allegiances associated with an affiliated minor-league club, from the welfare and motivation of the staff to the appearance of the ballpark and from the satisfaction of the parent club to the satisfaction of the fans. The days are long, followed by longer nights. In an August 18, 2005, article in the *Star-Ledger*, writer Erin Farrell described the minor-league and independent professional baseball general manager the following way: "Strong legs. The ability to handle a walkie-talkie . . . and flip a burger . . . and handle a rake. . . . Oh, and that's just during the game, after you've already put in eight to ten hours behind the desk in your office." Brad Taylor joined this exclusive group of workaholics when he was named the successor to Rick Brenner in Trenton in September 2005. A native of Virginia, the thirty-seven-year-old Taylor served his apprenticeship working in minor-league towns like Fayetteville, North Carolina, and Huntington, West Virginia, before arriving in Trenton as director of business operations in 2000. A self-described "stadium rat," Taylor was promoted to assistant general manager one year later, where he not only helped run the sales and promotional tasks of the club but also managed the day-to-day baseball operations by being the primary interface with the parent club, first the Boston Red Sox and later the New York Yankees. These duties typically involved arranging housing and transportation for players being shuffled to and from the Thunder from other levels within the parent organization. Now, the Thunder was his club to run in its entirety, and on this Labor Day, he and his staff gathered at 10:10 AM for their daily meeting to discuss the previous day's performance and today's plan of action.

The Trenton Thunder offices are on the ground floor of Waterfront Park. It's a simple office area with all of the trappings of a midsize business, from copier machines, personal computers, and printers humming away in the office cubicles to refrigerators and bottled-water coolers in the hallways for the staff. The cubicles are small and some of the desks are cluttered, reflecting the nonstop activity of the operation. There are many reminders on the walls of the Trenton Thunder's history, from pictures of old Thunder players to mementos of the time that Yankees star Derek Jeter played there in a rehabilitation assignment. The official office greeter is none other than Chase the Golden Thunder. Chase is a six-year-old golden retriever who carries player's bats back to the dugout like a batboy during early innings of a game, brings drinks to umpires, and catches Frisbees between innings. Chase, who stays at the house of Eric Lipsman, the vice president of marketing, when he's not at Waterfront Park, makes numerous appearances at schools and other youth events with Thunder representatives in the off-season as well. This morning, Chase has the run of the office. As I sat down on a chair after arriving in the office, Chase approached and presented me with a dog toy that he had been carrying around the office. I guess that was his way of welcoming me to the family and making sure that I was okay to be involved with the Thunder staff meeting.

After Taylor opens the staff meeting, Lipsman speaks next, running down the promotional activities scheduled for the day. Lipsman is the senior member of the Trenton front office, having arrived in Trenton in late 1993 to help launch the new club to the public. He had prior experience working for the Single-A Wilmington (Delaware) Blue Rocks. "That guy can flat-out sell," said Tom McCarthy, an original Thunder front-office member and current Philadelphia Phillies broadcaster, "and that's important when it comes to minor-league baseball, to nurture relationships and to get [the club] out in the public."[2] Even though a bit older than most of his fellow staff members, the environment seems to energize Lipsman. "Today is Aim Toothpaste Fleece Blanket Day, with the first 1,000 fans receiving the blankets. There will be eight ceremonial first-pitch throwers from our group outings, as well as one celebrity first-ball thrower, Mr. Peanut from Planters," explains Lipsman. "There will also be a softball home-run-hitting exhibition prior to the first pitch today by Mike Hamilton of the Mastery Prison Ministry softball team, otherwise known as the Hammer." Hamilton does the gentle work of tending to the spiritual needs of prisoners via the ministry, but today, he'll be providing thrills with a display of brute strength: hitting a softball. Lipsman adds, "2007 schedules are to be given to all fans leaving the stadium, and we will be putting playoff ticket flyers on parked cars during the game." The director of merchandising, Joe Pappalardo, chimes in, asking the staff's assistance in moving all of the blankets from the hallways out to the entrance-gate areas and to "get rid of them all," meaning he didn't want any leftover blankets at the end of the game. The food services manager, Kevin O'Byrne, talks about his staff's readiness for Dollar Hot Dog Day, a Labor Day special, and how "this will not be an easy day for the concession guys" because of it.

After going around the room, asking everyone whether they had any reports or input, and getting none, Taylor uses the rest of the meeting as an opportunity to prep the staff for the upcoming Eastern League playoffs as well as for Hideki Matsui's arrival in Trenton on Wednesday afternoon. The Trenton Thunder have the advantage of being the highest affiliated level of minor-league baseball played in New Jersey. Double-A baseball has long been the level known for housing genuine prospects for the major leagues. Triple A also has prospects, but their rosters are also dotted with players "on their way down," who simply remain with their organizations as insurance policies for the major-league club should somebody get injured. The Thunder's affiliation with the New York Yankees appeals to the baseball purists in the state who are willing to drive extra miles, past unaffiliated clubs that might be closer, to see tomorrow's up and coming Yankees stars. Rehabilitation assignments by current Yankees only add icing on top of the cake for the Trenton Thunder fans.

The Thunder organization is used to having high-profile Yankees spend a few days with the club in order to rehabilitate injuries prior to returning to action in the majors. In the previous three years, Yankees Steve Karsay, Kevin Brown, Carl Pavano, Bernie Williams, Robinson Cano, Kenny Lofton, and Derek Jeter all wore the blue Thunder pinstripes. A rehab appearance poses a unique challenge for the Thunder front office, from accommodating the increased press coverage to arranging for additional security. "When we had Derek Jeter here," explained Taylor, "it was close to being a stampede to get to him for autographs. And, fortunately, people behaved themselves, but we had to set up about eight to ten additional security people, professionals from an outside company that we normally don't have here." Taylor also coordinates the security details with the head of New York Yankees security. Yankees representatives attend and assist the Thunder when a high-profile Yankee rehabilitates in Trenton. Such scrutiny from the parent club only adds to the pressure felt by Taylor and his staff to provide not only for the needs of the local fans but for those of the Yankees as well.

The crowd of writers and photographers attracted by a Yankee rehabilitation case presents an additional challenge for the Thunder's director of media relations, Dan Loney. In discussing the Jeter visit, Loney explains, "We went from having normally five to six media members here to having seventy-five, and that included pretty much all of the television stations from New York and Philadelphia, the writers from New York, some of their radio stations, so, suffice [it] to say, it was probably the busiest time that I've had in terms of setting up media relations in my ten years working pro ball."[3] Matsui's visit provides an added challenge for Loney, as the Thunder anticipated at least seventy-five Japanese media members in addition to the New York and Philadelphia media. Taylor explains at the staff meeting that additional tables to handle the crush will be set up along the railings of the concourse, and that the photography contingent might have to be seated in the picnic area down the left-field line if there's no room for them elsewhere. The small press-box facilities notwithstanding, the Thunder provide an ideal situation for the Yankees to rehabilitate players. Besides the excellent playing facilities at Waterfront Park, the proximity of Trenton to New York makes it an easy trip for the Yankee players and officials. The rehabbing player's stay in Trenton is usually a brief one, no more than a game or two. It is a way for the Yankees to gauge how well a player has recovered from an injury and whether he is ready to rejoin and contribute to the big-league club. They do force regular Thunder players to the bench to create a space in the lineup to accommodate the big leaguer, making the task a bit tougher for manager Bill Masse. However, the Yankees call the shots, and they are much more concerned about their multimillion-dollar stars' ability to rejoin the big club than they are about a minor-league kid who may or may not be a genuine prospect. In this case, Masse will not have to worry about replacing a player in the field, as Masse has strict instructions to use Matsui only as a designated hitter and not to risk further injury by having him play in his customary position of left field.

Otherwise, rehabilitation assignments are a win–win situation for both the Yankees and the Thunder. On the aforementioned Jeter rehabilitation assignment, the gates at Waterfront Park opened one hour earlier than normal for the Saturday evening game, and even though Jeter did not appear on the field until right before game time, the fans arrived early, hoping to get a glimpse of their hero. Most of the early arrivals visited the concession areas multiple times, providing more revenue for the Thunder than on any other, ordinary evening. The team received an extra boost with Matsui being scheduled to appear in an Eastern League playoff game. Although making the playoffs is a big accomplishment for any minor-league organization, it doesn't necessarily always translate into a bonanza at the box office. Playoff games do not appear on anyone's advance schedule, making it impossible for fans to plan on attending them ahead of time. Except for the die-hard fan base, good walk-up sales are vital to attain a large crowd. Playoff games are typically played after the school year begins, making for smaller crowds as school nights do not draw as well as the midsummer evenings. Taylor and the rest of the staff feel that the Matsui appearance will translate into a larger gate by attracting the curious Yankees fans. The *Trentonian*, one of two Trenton newspapers that cover the club, helped the cause by screaming in tabloid fashion across its back page, "ADDED THUNDER" superimposed on a full-page picture of Matsui. "We didn't have to pay for any of this," laughs Taylor.

After reviewing playoff travel arrangements for both the Thunder and potential playoff opponents, Taylor ends the staff meeting with instructions to the stadium operations staff to get the patriotic playoff bunting in place and to replace the American flag on top of the stands behind home plate that was torn by the wind from Tropical Storm Ernesto. This all had to be done before Wednesday night. He reminds everyone that there will be additional staff meetings at 1:00 PM on both Tuesday and Wednesday, and that the office will open at 9:30 AM on Tuesday, even though it is an off day. The meeting adjourns at 10:35 AM and the staff scatters throughout Waterfront Park to begin performing their game-day tasks. Taylor retreats to his office to take care of some leftover business from the night before.

Brad Taylor's office looks lived in, because it certainly *is* lived in during the baseball season. His desk decorations show that he's a Washington Redskins football fan, and his walls are lined with overhead shots of Waterfront Park and photos of Trenton Thunder players. There is a clothes locker, much like the lockers that the players use, to the left of his desk. In it are numerous changes of clothing and shoes. The clothing choices are designed to fit any situation that might present itself during his long work day, including "mudders" that are used for helping to pull the tarpaulin onto and off the playing field during rain. To Taylor's right are a small refrigerator and water dispenser. His meeting table is fairly cluttered with trade literature and bobble-head dolls left over from various promotional nights. Even Chase the Golden Thunder and the head-groundskeeper, Nicole Sherry, have gotten their likenesses on bobble-head dolls. Nobody's effort, neither dog or person, goes unnoticed by the Trenton Thunder! Two long leather couches line the back of Taylor's office, which I can only imagine have been used for an overnight or two. "This is not like your Monday through Friday 9 AM to 4 PM job," says Taylor. "We spend more time together here than we do with our families."

Upon returning to his office, Brad makes a telephone call to a fan who qualified for the finals in the "Win a Chevy Tahoe" contest the night before but could not make it to the game to participate. Taylor is concerned that the fan misunderstood the contest and the tremendous odds that he would have been up against to win the Tahoe, even if he had been able to attend. In order to win, the fans chosen for the finals had to throw a number of baseballs from the pitcher's mound through a twelve-inch circle cut out of an advertising board at home plate. Nobody won. After explaining the difficulty to the missing contestant, Brad asks "Everything OK?" and the fan assures him that it is. Satisfied, Taylor ends the phone call. It is hard to imagine a major-league general manager like Brian Cashman of the Yankees feeling compelled to make such a telephone call. Bill Cook, the director of public relations, then enters Taylor's office to get his approval on the press release that Cook had written regarding Hideki Matsui's arrival. Taylor reads it over carefully and approves the release for publication. After a quick telephone call to the Yankees security office in New York, Brad sets out at 10:40 AM on his daily walk through the locker room and playing field to see if any of the baseball-related staff needs assistance from the front office regarding game-day matters.

The atmosphere leading to the locker rooms, trainer's room, and coaches' areas mimic the Yankees spring-training and minor-league complexes in Tampa, Florida, as much as possible. In the style of Yankees owner George Steinbrenner, and according to his personal wishes, the walls of the hallways are painted with inspirational statements by people like Joe DiMaggio ("I'd like to thank the good Lord for making me a Yankee"), former New York mayor Rudy Giuliani, and football coaching legend Vince Lombardi. You can't help but notice the subtle message above the whirlpool tub in the trainer's room: "You can't make the club sitting in the tub." The tub is empty on this particular morning.

Taylor checks with Thunder manager Bill Masse to see if there is anything he needs before the game. Masse is in a jovial mood, having clinched the division crown some days ago. A former Minor League Player of the Year in 1993 while playing for the Yankees Triple-A farm club in Columbus, Ohio, Masse had the misfortune of being an outfield prospect with the Yankees at the same time the Yankees were developing outfielders like Bernie and Gerald Williams. His batting statistics started to decline in 1994, so Masse decided to pursue a coaching career. After spending some time in the Montreal Expos organization, Masse rejoined the Yankees as manager of the Tampa Single-A club in 2003 and was promoted to the Thunder in 2005. After the Thunder earned two consecutive playoff births, the Manchester, Connecticut, native had the right to feel good about his job status. That changed at the end of September 2006 when Yankees general manager Brian Cashman abruptly fired him, citing some differences in philosophy. The conflict that arises between a minor-league club's need to focus on player development for the parent club versus providing a winning team for the fans cost Masse his job. "According to Cash [Cashman], I put winning ahead of development," Masse told *New York Post* sportswriter George King after being fired. Masse categorically denied disobeying the Yankees orders to limit innings pitched by prized prospects or to give players predetermined spots in the batting order that might not match the needs of the rest of the Thunder lineup. "I hate to be let go for a reason that never happened," Masse explained to King. "That is unacceptable. If it was a personality conflict, I can accept that." Luckily for Masse, Rick Brenner, the former Thunder general manager who successfully teamed with Masse in Trenton in 2005, became the general manager of the New Hampshire Fisher Cats. Brenner immediately hired Masse to manage the Cats, the Eastern League affiliate of the Toronto Blue Jays, for the 2007 season.

On this Labor Day, Masse's Thunder players were now arriving at the park and were lounging in front of their lockers, enjoying a large breakfast spread carefully assembled by the home clubhouse manager, Tom Kackley. The pitching coach, Dave Eiland, greets Taylor as he makes his way into the coaches' room. Eiland, who pitched for three major-league clubs in his ten-year major-league career, carefully charts every pitch thrown by the Thunder pitching staff and is constantly reviewing and teaching the young prospects coming through Trenton. Before joining Bill Masse's staff in 2005, Eiland coached the pitchers at the short-season Single-A Staten Island Yankees, and he is considered one of the hardest-working young pitching coaches in the organization and in all of minor-league baseball. The batting coach, Ty Hawkins, worked this morning with some players in the batting cages under the stands. Hawkins uses video technology to analyze player's swings to find possible flaws, then takes them to the batting cages underneath the stands to work with them to correct those flaws.

Next, Taylor inspects the strength-and-conditioning room, which on this morning is empty. He points out that most players use this room after the game, which might seem unusual to outsiders but is very common among ballplayers. The players don't want to risk injury or fatigue prior to performing their jobs for the day but, rather, use the weight room as a place to relax and work off their remaining energy afterward. The room is filled with $20,000 worth of exercise equipment paid for by the Trenton Thunder as part of their affiliation agreement with the Yankees. While fulfilling their responsibility to provide quality major-league prospects to their minor-league affiliates like the Thunder, the major-league clubs hold those affiliates to strict stadium-equipment and facilities standards, and it is no different in Trenton. If these standards are not lived up to, the affiliation can be taken elsewhere. Farther down the hall, the visiting team clubhouse manager, Daniel Rose, readies the locker room for the Reading

Phillies, who have yet to arrive. Rose has the newly washed Reading uniforms neatly hung up in the players' lockers and is in the process of laying out his own large breakfast spread for the Reading players. Because today's game follows a night game, and also because this is the Reading Phillies' final game of the season, it is not unusual that they will be arriving at Waterfront Park a little later this morning.

The last stop of Taylor's locker-room-area check is the auxiliary room, which is the farthest down the hall. The club maintains this area as a storeroom and dressing room for Boomer the mascot and the batboys. At the far end of the room is the press conference area, a very modest backdrop filled with Trenton Thunder logos with a lectern placed in front of it. This is where all of the important press conferences take place, and it is hard to imagine how crowded this small area will be when Hideki Matsui holds his press briefing on Wednesday afternoon.

Satisfied that the Thunder coaches and staff don't need his assistance today, Taylor now heads to the playing field area to check on conditions. As he steps into the tunnel leading to the Thunder dugout, the Trenton first baseman Shelley Duncan takes hold of the wireless microphone used for on-field promotions. Using his best NBA arena public-address announcer's voice, Duncan belts out an introduction for "the Big Man . . . Braaaad Taaaaaylorrrrrrr." Duncan's voice reverberates around the still-empty ballpark.

The head groundskeeper, Nicole Sherry, kneels behind the pitchers mound, busily making some adjustments to the turf area. The playing field is like a tightly woven carpet; not a bare spot anywhere. Sherry gained notoriety three seasons ago when she came from the grounds crew staff at Camden Yards in Baltimore to become the first woman head groundskeeper in the Eastern League. Tending to the grounds of a ballpark has become a science. In fact, Sherry earned an undergraduate degree in agricultural science from the University of Delaware in preparation for this sort of a job, even though being a baseball groundskeeper was not in Sherry's long-term plans. "When I graduated with my associate's degree, I wasn't really sure if I wanted to go on and get my bachelor's degree right away," explained Sherry. She took a job at a golf course as a greenskeeper. "I did that for a summer, and I said, oh my goodness, this is a really fun job," she continued. "You're out by yourself cutting grass and it's neat, learning all about different sorts of things to keep a golf course beautiful." The golf course experience helped Sherry when she remembered a contact she made at Camden Yards in Baltimore when touring there as a student. After a telephone call, the Orioles offered Sherry an internship as a groundskeeper. "So, I packed up, quit my job at the golf course, and it turned the Orioles opportunity into a seven-month internship. I went back to school at the University of Delaware, then after two months was offered a full-time position with the Orioles. I moved back to Baltimore and commuted an hour each way to school every day, and worked at the ballpark every day. So, I finished up school, I was working at Camden Yards, got my bachelor's degree, and now, here I am at Trenton." explained Sherry. At the completion of this 2006 season, she became only the second woman head groundskeeper in the history of major-league baseball when the Orioles hired her to return to Camden Yards in that capacity.[4] On this Labor Day, her job is made somewhat easier because the players don't have on-field batting practice, in order to get more rest after last night's game. The field won't take any pregame damage that she would have to fix with a rake or a shovel.

Taylor retreats back to his office for another check of his computer. He shows his obsession with weather by checking the Doppler radar repeatedly to make sure that no showers are heading toward Trenton. Rain delays make a general manager paranoid, and today is no different. Never mind that it is a cloudless day with no prediction of rain whatsoever. Not only does a rain delay cause the entire staff to drop what they are doing at that moment to help put the tarpaulin on the field, it also causes some fans to leave the park, lessening the revenue potential of the day or evening. Should rainouts occur, scheduling becomes difficult, necessitating single-admission doubleheaders that cause even more revenue loss. Taylor then checks attendance figures from the night before not only for his Eastern League counterparts but also for the other clubs in New Jersey, including the independent professional clubs, as well as the Staten Island Yankees and the Brooklyn Cyclones. He next allows himself a quick look at CNN's Web site. The long hours at the park put him out of contact with the rest of the world, and the news-oriented Web sites are his quick window back in. He also takes this opportunity to update the owners of the Trenton Thunder—Joe Finley and Joe Caruso—via e-mail. Taylor does so daily, even though the owners are very hands-off and not prone to micromanage. He expresses some concern that he has not heard from Finley in more than thirty-six hours, unusual but not unexpected, as the Finleys were expecting twins "any moment," according to Taylor.

While Taylor is occupying himself in cyberspace, the assistant general manager, Greg Coleman, interrupts him by carrying into the office a large bundle wrapped in foil. "It is a day game tradition," claims Coleman. One of the Waterfront Park ushers, a fellow named Walter, always stops by his favorite delicatessen on the morning of a day game and brings to the senior staff some breakfast sandwiches that are strictly Trenton delights. "Pork roll, potatoes, cheese, and eggs on a roll," says Taylor between bites. "Probably not too good for me, but pretty hard to turn down." Later on, some season-ticket holders bring trays of Italian pastries into the Thunder ticket office for the staff. The regulars treat the staff, from Taylor on down, like their own children, making sure they are well fed and taken care of. "It's like one big family here," explains Taylor.

At 11:15 AM, Bill Cook comes running into Taylor's office, exclaiming excitedly, "Brad, Matsui is out!" Taylor's jaw drops and a look of horror crosses his face as visions of the rehabilitation appearance of Hideki Matsui and the big crowd to go along with it vanishes in Taylor's mind with the news. Seeing his expression, Cook backtracks. "No, no, I mean, the Matsui press release is out!" Taylor exhales in a big sigh of relief, again able to enjoy the pork roll, egg, and cheese.

Two hours before game time, at 11:25 AM, Coleman and Lipsman appear in the hallway outside of Brad's office, like clockwork, without being asked. It is time for their daily walkthrough inspection of the stands and concession areas of Waterfront Park. It resembles a white-glove inspection, with the cleanliness of Waterfront Park the major concern. Starting in the left-field corner by the picnic area, Coleman finds a stray drinking straw on the ground from the night before and immediately picks it up. Taylor notices some promotional signs from last night's Chevy giveaway still hanging up in the concourse area, and calls the stadium operations staff on the walkie-talkie to ask them to send someone up to the concourse to remove all of the signs. Suddenly, from high atop the left-field fence, from the vicinity of Sovereign Bank advertisement sign, a loud noise is heard.

Bang! A softball hits off the wall. "The Hammer," Mike Hamilton, has arrived, and needs to test out some new underhand pitchers for his exhibition. *Bang, bang!* One ball after another hits off the fence. Everyone on the field witnessing this practice session oohs and ahhs. The Hammer then proceeds to hit a couple of low line drives, with backspin, off the left-field grass. The spinning balls create golf-like divots in the turf. "I hope Nicole is not watching this," Taylor laughs. *Bang!* This one caroms off the Amtrak sign, and then another bounces off the Aztec Graphics ad. Satisfied, Hamilton walks off the field, bats on his shoulder, to conserve his energy for the pregame exhibition.

On the way toward the home-plate area, Taylor explains that an outside firm is in charge of the postgame cleaning of the grandstand area, but it is his job to make sure that 100 percent cleanliness of the park is the order of the day. "Parents won't have a problem bringing their kids back to a clean stadium," Taylor reasons. The inspection winds its way around toward the right-field line, then up along the first-base concourse area, ending at the kids' video arcade. The upper-management triumvirate judges Waterfront Park to be in good condition, ready for the arrival of season-ticket holders, for whom the gates open one-half hour before all other fans.

As they proceed back downstairs to the office area, Coleman is still unsure what to expect with today's fan turnout. "Labor Day is typically one of the dog days of the minor-league season," he explains. As evidence, he points to a list of names of groups that are scheduled to attend today's game. The list only fills one-half of a page. Typically, the list fills two pages. Minor-league baseball depends on group attendance, and Coleman knows this, having had experience operating both minor-league teams and an independent professional league.

Greg Coleman came to Trenton with more baseball experience than your average thirty-one-year-old. The native of Hamilton, New Jersey, worked for the Modesto A's, the Single-A California League affiliate of the Oakland A's, from 1999 to 2003. During Coleman's time in Modesto, he served as assistant general manager, general manager, and vice president of the club. Coleman's work caught the eye of David Kaval, a former Silicon Valley executive who was determined to start a new independent professional league in California and Arizona. Kaval succeeded in launching the Golden Baseball League in 2005 and hired Coleman to serve as the chief operating officer and vice president of the new league. The Golden League's concept is a radical one. Golden League member clubs are centrally owned by the league and their general managers report to the league's front office. "I was in charge of the activities of all of the general managers of the league," explains Coleman. The open Trenton Thunder assistant general manager's position at the end of the 2005 season presented a difficult career choice for Coleman, but he chose to return home to the Trenton area. "The Golden League experience was a great one, but I chose to return to affiliated ball in Trenton with a great franchise."

At 11:45 AM, Taylor and Coleman meet with representatives of a design firm regarding some future club activities. Some of these discussions are confidential club matters, so I go off by myself to wander around the stadium. While surveying the scene in the still-empty park, I realize that even though the park has been open since 1994, it still looks virtually brand new in its thirteenth year of operation. In a previous interview, Taylor explained to me, "Every year, we try to pick a project, a capital project that we can improve something physical here, so that people notice there's perpetual updating and taking care of this facility going on. The one thing I always hear this year when people come in here is 'this place is thirteen years old?' It sure is. It doesn't look it, and that's the best compliment we can get."[5] I notice that the owners have maintained the unobstructed view of the Delaware River beyond the right-field fence by limiting the levels of advertising allowed between the right-field scoreboard and foul territory.

Preparations for today's game proceed smoothly. The sweet smell of fresh-cut onions wafts throughout the concession areas once the vegetables are placed into all of the condiment bins that line the railings of the concourse. The ushers, who are now on duty and waiting for the fans' arrival, go from seat to seat in their assigned sections, carefully wiping them off with rags. "The Hawk," a classic-rock FM radio station from the Trenton area, is playing over the stadium loudspeaker, but it is not overbearingly loud like in some parks. The low volume of the music in the park is indicative of the consideration the Thunder have for everyone who enters the park. They cater to all types and ages of fans, and they try to make sure that none feel left out or alienated. At noon, the season-ticket holders leisurely start filtering through the stands, some wrapping themselves in their new Aim Toothpaste fleece blankets, even though it is now a very sunny and warm early afternoon. These fans talk and laugh with the ushers and other stadium employees. I can tell that many of them are regular attendees who have established relationships with those working around them. At 12:20 PM, almost one hour before the scheduled first pitch, I go down the long stairwell toward one of the main fan entrance gates of Waterfront Park. A very long line of fans, waiting for the gates to open, stretches about one-quarter of a mile to the street area, down toward the Riverview Executive Plaza buildings. Eric Lipsman is monitoring this unexpected activity. Eric doesn't think that the people are waiting in line because of the blanket promotion, because "there wasn't much advance publicity given to this." Obviously, the bad weather forecasts kept some local residents at home on this Labor Day weekend, and today they are taking advantage of the nice day by attending a baseball game. It will be a larger walk-up crowd than anticipated.

Underneath the stands, at 12:30 PM, Brad Taylor's meeting breaks up, and he changes into his Trenton Thunder Staff shirt, looking much like any other game-day staff employee and enabling customers to recognize him as a staff person during the game should they need his assistance. He goes to the ticket office to survey the activity there and is surprised to see that the large walk-up business has necessitated the opening of four ticket windows for a game that was supposed to be "quiet." Taylor leaves the ticket office and goes outside to greet fans arriving at the park. Satisfied that preparations have gone as well as they could for today's game, he goes inside, takes the elevator up to the luxury-box level, to do a last-minute check on how the group using the Yankee Club and Conference Center is enjoying their outing. The Yankee Conference Center sits between the luxury boxes directly above the press area behind home plate. Seating approximately 120 people, it is a fully catered restaurant and bar, with a seating area outside on the ledge. The room is carefully decorated with Yankees and local Trenton baseball memorabilia, donated mostly by noted sports collector Barry Halper. A small group from a local brewery is using the club today, and it seems oblivious to Taylor's appearance. Outside, Hamilton has begun his exhibition of softball skill and strength. The crowd goes wild with every long ball, as play-by-play announcer Dan Loney gives a running account of the Hammer's exploits from the on-field microphone. As Hamilton finishes his Babe Ruthian demonstration, Taylor proceeds back to the grandstand level, where he assumes his position as "everyone's assistant." The carefully choreographed hours of pregame planning and execution now give way to observing and reacting as the staff spreads out through the stadium to take care of today's crowd's every need.

I make my way down to my seat behind home plate, settling in with two "dollar dogs" and a large Diet Coke as a local vocalist sings the national anthem. The sun is warm, the crowd is big, and it is time to play ball. The Thunder players end the weekend with a solid win. First baseman Randy Ruiz does his best "Hammer" imitation in the bottom of the first inning by hitting a long, two-run home run over the left-field wall.

The Thunder score the bulk of their runs in the first inning, and cruise to a 7-2 victory over the Reading Phillies for their eightieth victory of the Eastern League season. There are 6,794 fans watching the game in the park. A meaningless, final regular-season game tends to have the same intensity as a spring-training game under the Florida sun, and this one is no different. With the Thunder comfortably ahead for most of the game, the crowd seems to be focusing more on their conversations with each other than the action on the field. Many begin to leave the park after the seventh inning, content that the Thunder has the game won and wanting to beat the Labor Day traffic home.

As I walk through the concourse and toward the exit of Waterfront Park at the end of the game, I notice Taylor near the entrance portal at the aisle next to the press box. He introduces me to Thunder owner Joe Finley, who is holding his young daughter and looking out on his club. I guess the Finleys' expected twins must be waiting for another day. Not only have the Thunder made it to the postseason, but the other New Jersey club that Finley owns, the Lakewood BlueClaws, qualified for the playoffs for the first time in their history. "I'll be at Lakewood on Wednesday evening," I inform him. "Bring home another win," he replies.

The Trenton Thunder drew more than 413,000 fans in 2006, marking the twelfth consecutive season that the club exceeded 400,000, a first for a minor-league club at the Double-A level. Stadiums like Waterfront Park have enabled Double-A franchises to draw 400,000-plus since the stadium-building boom of the early 1990s. Yet, few franchises have been able to maintain that level of attendance as consistently as the Thunder. They averaged 5,986 fans per game and rewarded those fans with a good on-field performance, culminating in the Northern Division championship and a berth in the Eastern League playoffs against the Portland (Maine) Sea Dogs. Ironically, the Sea Dogs are the Double-A affiliate of the Boston Red Sox and the same franchise that switched its affiliation from Trenton after the 2002 season. The Yankees–Red Sox rivalry takes on additional meaning even at the minor-league level, and it promised to be a hard-fought, entertaining playoff series.

On September 6, two days after the Labor Day game against Reading, 5,114 fans came to Waterfront Park to see game one of the Trenton-Portland series as well as Hideki Matsui's return to competitive baseball. The crowd was smaller than a typical summer-evening regular-season crowd but considerably higher than the usual midweek minor-league playoff game in September. Matsui's appearance was worth at least an additional 1,000 fans at this game. The fans were not disappointed in either the Thunder or Matsui. Behind a thirteen-strikeout performance by top Yankees pitching prospect Philip Hughes, the Thunder defeated the Sea Dogs, 3-1, to take a one game lead in the series. Matsui singled home the Thunder's third run in the seventh inning, going one for three with one walk that night. Approximately seventy-five Japanese media members were on hand to witness Matsui's return. Matsui is considered a national treasure in Japan and his every move is scrutinized, so surely the Trenton Thunder received a good deal of international exposure during his stay with the club. In the end, however, Matsui couldn't provide enough hits to win the series for the Thunder, as the tables turned in the second game.

Game two, also played at Waterfront Park, drew a crowd of 4,765, considered a good Thursday night playoff turnout. The fans happily witnessed the Thunder pull out to a quick 2-0 lead in the bottom of the second, but as television sportscaster Warner Wolf said during his sportscasts many times, "You could have turned your sets off right there." The Sea Dogs scored two runs in the third inning, two more in the sixth inning, and six runs in the seventh inning on their way to a 10-3 rout of the Thunder to tie the series at one game apiece. The series moved to Portland and would not return.

The Sea Dogs prevailed in two hard-fought, close contests, defeating the Thunder 5-4 in game three and 4-3 in game four to win the best-of-five series and send the Thunder home to Trenton. Matsui only managed three hits in eleven at-bats with six walks in his four games with the Thunder, but the series must have prepared him well for what was ahead. On September 12, Matsui returned to the Yankees' lineup after four months on the disabled list and went four for four, eventually helping the Yankees win the American League Eastern Division championship.

Back in Trenton, the lights went dark on another Eastern League season. The summer interns are back in college, and Brad Taylor's front-office staff gets some much needed rest, but not too much, before starting to plan for the 2007 season. "The most challenging thing is being the GM of a successful team," explained Taylor. "That sets the bar higher every year. We never really stop to pat ourselves on the back, and even when we think we've had a good year, you know what? They're going to expect more next year, which is fair; and we want to give everybody more the next year because our goal is always to be the best, not only in the state of New Jersey, but also in the industry." Taylor loves the baseball landscape of New Jersey. "It is amazing to me that a state the size of this state, geographically and obviously demographically, has so many people that are so into one sport, and that sport is baseball. I think that is why there are currently eight teams in this state."

Any pessimism that existed when the Thunder began play in 1994 about whether they would be able to survive for the long term has long since ended. Their success helped spawn the creation of more professional baseball teams in New Jersey, mostly of the independent, nonaffiliated variety. The independent clubs have similar company philosophies when it comes to attracting fans for a night of relatively inexpensive family entertainment for all ages. Unlike the Trenton Thunder, they do not have a major-league parent club to answer to, which can be both a blessing and a curse. In 1998, the newly formed, independent Atlantic League of Professional Baseball Clubs placed teams in Atlantic City, Somerset, and Newark. Ironically, the Atlantic League was born out of a territorial conflict between major-league owners and an affiliated minor-league club owner who had a vision of a "boutique league" in the Northeast.

5

A League of His Own

Frank Boulton and the Atlantic League

Major League Baseball rule number 52 (a)(4) allows any major-league club to block any other major- or minor-league club from playing within its territorial area without permission. Territories are defined by geography, and they were expanded between 1990 and 1994 to include the surrounding areas of a major-league city in order to ward off rampant intrusions of major-league territories by minor-league clubs. Major League Baseball executives feared that the stadium-

Atlantic City, one of the original home cities of the Atlantic League. Photograph by Bob Golon, 2005.

building boom of the early 1990s and the tremendous growth of the minor leagues might lead to the encroachment of its traditional marketing areas, resulting in decreased revenues for major-league clubs. If baseball were a normal business, subject to the rules of free enterprise, it could not get away with territory blocking. However, since the 1920s, baseball has been protected by a congressional exemption from antitrust law, giving it the ability to act as a monopoly in many cases. In the greater New York area, the territory of the Yankees and Mets is jointly defined as any part of the five boroughs of New York City, plus Nassau, Suffolk, Westchester, and Rockland Counties in New York.[1] A Long Island native named Frank Boulton ran headfirst into this baseball rule in 1993, setting in motion a chain of events that eventually resulted in the creation of the independent Atlantic League of Professional Baseball Clubs. Frank Boulton's "league of his own" altered the landscape of professional baseball in New Jersey.

Boulton spent twenty-five years as a successful Wall Street financial executive, working for companies such as Smith Barney and the Union Bank of Switzerland. Like many who worked in the high-pressure environment of financial trading, Boulton sought enjoyment in other areas of endeavor; in his case, it was minor-league baseball. Boulton became involved in the minor leagues as a part owner of the Peninsula Pilots of Hampton, Virginia. In 1993, the Pilots moved to a newly built ballpark in Wilmington, Delaware. Playing in the class-A Carolina League as an affiliate of the Kansas City Royals, the newly renamed Blue Rocks were an instant success. Technically, they were encroaching on the territory of the Philadelphia Phillies, but nobody at the major-league level raised any objection to it. Boulton's success with the Blue Rocks gave him ideas about moving the other minor-league club that he owned part of, the Albany-Colonie Yankees of the Eastern League.

The Double-A affiliate of the New York Yankees, Boulton's Albany club played in the antiquated Heritage Park, a substandard facility according to the new ballpark requirements established by the Professional Baseball Agreement. It became clear that the Albany-Colonie Yankees would have to leave Albany soon unless a new facility was forthcoming. Frank Boulton had an ideal solution in mind.

In 1992, after consulting with the parent New York Yankees, Boulton embarked on an effort to move the club to the Central Islip area of Long Island in Suffolk County. Westernmost Suffolk County resided in the New York Mets' territory as defined by Major League Baseball. After conducting careful research of baseball's territorial mileage limits, Boulton determined that the Central Islip location was indeed east of the Mets' territory. He received the permission of the Eastern League to move the Albany club to Long Island, then he set out to arrange funding for a new, modern minor-league park. Boulton succeeded in raising the capital by working with the local government and business leaders. The future looked bright for an Eastern League club in Central Islip.

By this time, Boulton had risen to the rank of vice president of the Eastern League, as well as becoming a well-connected, successful minor-league baseball owner. The Yankees approved moving their Albany affiliate to Long Island. The New York Mets, however, did not allow it, citing the major-league territorial restrictions rule. Boulton took his case to the MLB executive committee. "I flew to Texas," recalled Boulton, referring to an executive committee meeting, "and walked in with an architect's ruler, a Hagstrom map, and a copy of the baseball rules. I handed the rules out, and said I needed ten minutes to make my case. I showed everyone on the committee that Hagstrom had been in the map business for over 100 years, and the ruler was an accurate architect's ruler. It [Central Islip] was clearly outside of the Mets' territory, and . . . in fact it was an open territory." When put to a vote, five members voted for Boulton, nine against. In some cases, owners voted against Boulton because they looked at a yes vote as a vote for George Steinbrenner. "[Hall of Famer] Hank Greenberg's grandson worked for Major League Baseball at the time," explained Boulton. "Jackie Autry [the wife of Los Angeles Angels founder Gene Autry] looked to him and said, 'What is this all about? Who are we voting for?' And Greenberg's grandson said, 'A yes vote is for George Steinbrenner, a no vote is for [New York Mets owner] Fred Wilpon.' They voted no."[2] Boulton did not hide his disappointment, on February 17, 1993, telling *Long Island Newsday:* "It was certainly a kangaroo court. . . . I'm shocked at the decision. The Mets have gone and put pressure on to turn this around. It's a very sad day for the two and one-half million people of Long Island and . . . I'm ashamed of the Mets and their entire organization."

Boulton faced a difficult decision. He could pursue the issue further. He had overtures from U.S. senators to take his case to the government in order to assist them in getting baseball's antitrust exemption removed. Boulton decided not to push the envelope, explaining, "I had enjoyed owning the Wilmington Blue Rocks, which was clearly inside the Philadelphia Phillies territory, and I had owned other minor-league teams, and

I decided that life was too short. I really didn't want to be the poster child for baseball losing the antitrust exemption because some people decided to make a decision and make two plus two equal eight on that particular day." The Long Island idea died, and the Albany-Colonie team eventually moved to a new ballpark in Norwich, Connecticut, in 1995. But the seeds of the Atlantic League were planted.

Jay Acton, a literary agent from New York, also became involved in minor-league baseball ownership during this time period. Acton had sold the Peninsula Pilots to Frank Boulton, and he admired Boulton's business acumen. In 1993, Acton and Nick Bakalar coauthored the book *Green Diamonds: The Pleasures and Profits of Investing in Minor League Baseball.* Boulton was interviewed for a chapter detailing the art of doing a successful baseball deal, and his expertise attracted the attention of officials in Atlantic City. The gambling town had unsuccessfully attempted to secure an Eastern League franchise in 1992, but the officials still aspired to bring professional baseball to the city in order to enhance its tourism and family entertainment options. They were also aware of the success of Boulton's new Wilmington Blue Rocks, not very far away from southern New Jersey in Delaware. The *Atlantic City Press* dispatched a photographer to a Wilmington game and ran a picture of Rocky Bluewinkle, the team's mascot, dancing and otherwise entertaining the fans from atop a dugout. The caption read, "Wilmington Living Atlantic City's Dream." Mayor James Whelan and New Jersey assemblyman William Gormley contacted Boulton, and expressed interested in joining a new league, even one that was not affiliated with minor-league baseball. Boulton then received a telephone call from mayor Joseph Ganim of Bridgeport, Connecticut, about the possibility of building a baseball park in the Bridgeport Harbor area and participating in a new independent league. Independent professional baseball attracted the attention of local officials in the mid-1990s because of the success of Miles Wolff and his Northern League in the Midwest.

Wolff relaunched independent professional baseball in the United States when he organized the Northern League in smaller midwestern cities in 1993, and the league's success made the baseball establishment as well as potential investors take notice. Communities like Atlantic City and Bridgeport, both looking for the opportunity to build ballparks and participate in the resurgence of minor-league baseball, now found themselves with the opportunity to do so without having to be concerned about the major-league territorial rules. Independent baseball in the Midwest was the starting point, and the time was right for it to expand and move to the East Coast.

Central Islip still had the desire to build a ballpark, so as Boulton explained, "now, I have three [cities], and all of the sudden, I'm starting to get some critical mass. I knew that Newark [New Jersey] had been interested. Rick Cerone, my former partner [with the Blue Rocks] grew up on the streets of Newark. He was the ex-Yankees catcher, and he'd be perfect to someday be involved with Newark. My mind started putting these pieces together, and that's when I decided that I was going to leave my job on Wall Street. I sold the Blue Rocks to my partners, and I started visiting other cities." In Wilmington, Boulton's partners also included ex-Mets shortstop and manager Buddy Harrelson. Cerone and Harrelson were both enthusiastic about joining Boulton's possible new venture, and they became visible advocates of the project who gave Boulton's idea "major-league credibility" with investors. Cerone introduced Boulton to Steve Kalafer, a successful automobile entrepreneur from Flemington, New Jersey. The Somerset County, New Jersey, government had expressed interest in building a baseball park on a former industrial site in Bridgewater. Kalafer joined the effort to create financing for a Bridgewater ballpark. Groups from Nashua (New Hampshire) and the Lehigh Valley (Pennsylvania) also expressed their commitment to Boulton. He now had six locales within a four-state area interested in a new independent league, which he christened the Atlantic League of Professional Baseball Clubs. More work was necessary to get the ballparks built, work that Boulton was very astute at accomplishing. "To date, we have raised $83.5 million in public funds to build stadiums," Boulton told the *Atlantic City Press* in August 1997. "Either I'm a really great salesman or I've got a terrific product. I'd like to think it's a little of both." [3] Minor-league executive Peter Kirk, a director of the Carolina League when Boulton owned Wilmington, became another enthusiastic adviser in the Boulton camp. Kirk's company, Maryland Baseball, owned successful minor-league clubs in Hagerstown and Frederick in said state, and his insights were valuable to Boulton's growing vision. Eventually, Kirk himself joined Boulton to become actively involved in the ownership of Atlantic League clubs. Boulton's concept of what his independent league should bring to both the baseball player and the fan enabled him to convince investors that his concept was a good one. Boulton's particular experience with a new, state-of-the-art minor-league ballpark in Wilmington influenced his thinking. "I wanted to play in new facilities," explained Boulton. "Our emphasis [in planning the Atlantic League] was on facility development. I could have gone up to tired, old, abandoned ballparks, the way most independent leagues went, but I chose not to because I thought that for our long-term growth, we wanted to be in new facilities." Boulton decided that the facilities in the Atlantic League had to be up to the standards of Triple-A or Double-A minor-league ballparks, because substandard facilities would not attract top-flight players. The Atlantic League ballpark guidelines, as set out by the league in its official literature, state that "new Atlantic League ballparks must fully comply with the 'Facilities Standards' as defined by the National Association. Players will be assured of field conditions that meet or exceed the standards for 'Triple A' classification National Association facilities. Communities must demonstrate market size sufficient to support a minimum ballpark size of 5,000 to 7,500 seats."[4] It is interesting to note that even though the Atlantic League has no affiliation with the National Association of Professional Baseball Clubs, the governing body of Minor League Baseball, it was using the association's guidelines for ballpark construction.

The player-procurement philosophy developed by Boulton also differed from that of most other leagues in independent baseball. The old Pacific Coast League model intrigued him. The original, pre-1958 Pacific Coast League (PCL) was designated as an open league that attracted ex-major-league players finishing out their careers as well as eager youngsters trying to get noticed by major-league organizations. The caliber of baseball in the old PCL was considered to be above that of the Triple-A minor leagues. The jet age put an end to the independent PCL as the major leagues, now able to travel easily to cities like Los Angeles and San Francisco, relocated clubs to cities on the West Coast after 1957. It spelled the end of high-level independent baseball. Boulton and Harrelson saw that there were plenty of baseball players fitting the old PCL category who needed places to continue playing.

The ballpark in Homestead, Florida, originally built to be the spring-training home of the Cleveland Indians, was virtually destroyed by Hurricane Andrew's 140-mile-per-hour winds in 1992. The park was eventually rebuilt but the Indians left it to sit empty, and instead it became home to a free-agents' baseball camp in 1995, a place for disenfranchised professional players to stay in shape while awaiting an opportunity to re-sign professional contracts. Harrelson and Boulton traveled to this camp to investigate what type of players they would have available to them once it became time to stock the new league. Boulton explained,

"We didn't want to get involved with players that weren't professional players. We wanted to do this at the top of the food chain, so my model was, after interviewing a lot of the players at the Homestead free-agent camp, that these were good players who just needed a place to play. For various reasons, for numbers reasons, for economic reasons, all of these guys were excessed out of playing the game of professional baseball, and there were many guys in that camp who went on to play many years after that." Boulton also wanted to become an independent, high-level partner of Major League Baseball, much like the old PCL. He wanted his league to be a place where the major leagues could go to add players to their organizations when the need arose without overextending their minor-league systems. "I thought that a boutique league that could play at a AAAA level [higher than the highest level of the minor leagues] and have a mix of major leaguers and minor leaguers would be the successful model," Boulton explained. It was a philosophy that caught on with both players and fans, because the players who came to the Atlantic League felt that they could still play baseball at the highest level, and they were motivated to play hard and win games.

Bob Wirz is the president and founder of Wirz and Associates, a public relations and marketing firm that focuses on baseball-related activities. Wirz spent considerable time in major-league baseball, working as a spokesman for baseball commissioners Bowie Kuhn and Peter Ueberroth, as well as spending six years as the publicity director for the Kansas City Royals. He is also an expert on the business of independent baseball, having been a part of it since his involvement in the management of the Thunder Bay Whiskey Jacks in the original Northern League in 1993. Wirz continues to be active in independent baseball today in Connecticut, as well as publishing the *Independent Baseball Insider* newsletter. He was quick to jump on the independent-baseball bandwagon, and he explained its popularity. "The affiliated minor leagues today," said Wirz, "they're doing very well, and I'm not here to condemn them in any way, but as far as the baseball purist [believes], affiliated minor-league baseball is not 'win at all costs,' it is 'develop at all costs.' Independent baseball is where winning matters. From a business standpoint, it is also creating many more fans, and it's giving so many more communities a team that they would otherwise not have."[5] The emphasis placed on playing to win in the independent leagues enables players to showcase their skills to major-league scouts who attend independent ball games. Some purists might disagree with Wirz because in their estimation, minor-league baseball is where the future major-league prospects are. For Boulton to make his independent Atlantic League successful in the Northeast, where baseball fans are some of the most passionate and knowledgeable, he had to find a way to bridge serious player development with affordable community entertainment. Fortunately for Boulton, ex-major-league general manager Joe Klein was available in the mid-1990s, and he became the Atlantic League's link to major-league organizations looking for quality players.

Klein had spent six seasons as a big-league general manager, first with the Texas Rangers and the Cleveland Indians in the 1980s, then with the Detroit Tigers in the 1990s. He possessed the kind of professional baseball experience necessary to develop the Atlantic League's baseball operations, and he had an insight that told him that the Atlantic League would work if structured properly. "The more I heard about this league from Frank [Boulton]," Klein explained while sitting behind his desk in the Camden, New Jersey, headquarters office of the Atlantic League in 2005, "the more I was convinced that it was the same thing that we had been talking about for twenty years in farm directors', scouting directors', and general managers' meetings [in the major leagues]. A place to park veteran players who would definitely be needed, not so much as one of the 500 or 600 players on opening day, but as one of the 1,200 to 1,300 that would be needed throughout the season. Farm directors were always looking for a way to streamline their operations, to make their farm systems work more economically by having a place outside the organization to purchase fill-in players that they would need, not only at the major-league level but at the minor-league level as well to get through the season." Boulton hired Klein to be the Atlantic League's executive director. Before the league ever played a game, Klein helped shape what it would become. "I helped with the bylaws, their rules and regulations, their contracts, setting up the structure of the league, and dealing with everything that had to do with the baseball operation," said Klein.[6]

Klein's expertise in player evaluation and development helped the Atlantic League find the experienced professional ballplayers it was seeking. He focused mainly on the veterans who played six years or more of professional baseball and were stuck in their current affiliated systems as well as on players who were just released by a minor-league club. These players had to possess the desire to make it back to affiliated baseball through improving their game. Klein focused his attention on player agents who could provide a steady pipeline of available players for the league.

The league originally scheduled to begin play in 1997, but the ballparks could not be constructed fast enough for that to be possible. Though they were eager to build, municipalities and county governments had to sort through considerable red tape to get their stadium financing approved and building permits in place. The Atlantic League's first season was postponed until 1998. The Bridgeport Bluefish and the Atlantic City Surf were the first two clubs to have their new ballparks completed. Bridgeport built the 5,500-seat Ballpark at Harbor Yard, nestled in the area between Interstate 95 and the Bridgeport Harbor. Ferry boats and Amtrak trains could be seen operating beyond the outfield fences during games, providing a picturesque environment for fans. Atlantic City had talked of building a baseball park since the early 1990s, and that became a reality with the new, 6,000-seat Sandcastle Stadium on the southern end of Atlantic City. Two ballparks did not a league make, however, and Boulton, along with the rest of the league owners, scrambled to assemble a complete, six-team league for 1998. Nashua (New Hampshire) and Newburgh (New York) were added to the original Atlantic League lineup. The Nashua Pride played in the historic Holman Stadium, a 4,500-seat, older facility that previously housed a lower-level farm team for the Brooklyn Dodgers in the 1940s. The league hoped to be able to field a team in Pennsylvania's Lehigh Valley, but funding for the ballpark could not be completed, and there was no timetable for its construction. They decided to place the club in Newburgh for one season while the situation in the Lehigh Valley was resolved. The Newburgh Black Diamonds opened in Delano-Hitch Stadium, which was built in 1926 and named after the aunt of former president Franklin Delano Roosevelt. Delano-Hitch seated only 3,100 fans, and was far below the ballpark standards set by the league. Newark had not yet broken ground for the Bears' new park as multiple delays, resulting from litigation regarding Cerone's plans to build at Riverbank Park, near Newark's Ironbound section, put the project on hold. Plans were made for the Bears to play all of their home games at Harbor Yard in Bridgeport in 1998. Construction was under way in Bridgewater for the Patriots' new park, but it had no chance of being ready for 1998. The Patriots played all of their games as a road team their first season. Despite this patchwork arrangement, it was time for the Atlantic League to play ball.

The 1998 Atlantic League managerial list was impressive, with ex–major leaguers Sparky Lyle (Somerset), Tom O'Malley (Newark), Doc Edwards (Atlantic City), Willie Upshaw (Bridgeport), Wayne Krenchicki (Newburgh), and Mike Easler (Bridgeport) patrolling the dugouts. The six clubs played a 100-game schedule. The Atlantic City Surf, behind the slugging of Will Pennyfeather and Juan "the Large Human" Thomas, defeated the Bridgeport Bluefish in the playoffs in the very first Atlantic League championship.

The Newark and Somerset ballparks opened in 1999, and name players like Ruben Sierra, Hensley "Bam Bam" Meulens, and Darrin Winston joined Atlantic League rosters. Other ex–major leaguers quickly followed in subsequent years. Jose and Ozzie Canseco, Jose Lima, future Hall of Famer Rickey Henderson, Carlos Baerga, and Pete Rose Jr., to name just a few, all performed with distinction in Atlantic League uniforms, as did hundreds of younger ballplayers looking for that second chance to get back into affiliated baseball. As of spring 2007, the contracts of more than 200 Atlantic League players have been sold to minor-league clubs affiliated with the major leagues in the ten years of the league's operation.[7]

Atlantic League players do not make the millions of dollars that their major-league counterparts do, which is why they are so eager to get back into the big leagues. There is no formal, hard salary cap in the Atlantic League, but there is a salary "understanding" among the member clubs, according to Boulton. The top salary of any player is in the neighborhood of $3,500 per month. This even applies to the Cansecos and Hendersons of the world. "They fall right into the salary structure of the league in every case," states Klein. "We have not had a player making Triple-A baseball money playing in the Atlantic League. Most of the time, when you get a high-profile guy like a Sierra or a Lima or any of the other significant major-league service-time players who play here, they're looking for the opportunity, not the money. They understand it's a short-term thing, and we're happy to have them. In most cases, it's worked out." The evidence supports Klein's assertion. Sierra played seven more years in the big leagues since reestablishing his career in the Atlantic League. Lima won thirteen games for the 2004 Los Angeles Dodgers after making a stop with the Newark Bears a couple of seasons before. But even without the big stars, the caliber of play in the Atlantic League has been high throughout its existence. The typical player sought by the league, according to Klein, "knows how to play and knows how to help a team win. That's what an Atlantic League player learns to be. We found players starting to improve once they were in this league, and we know we're on the right track from a development standpoint. Every year, we feel comfortable that we have increased the quality of play in this league."

It is noteworthy that, as of 2006, only one club in Atlantic League history, the Somerset Patriots, has repeated as champions. This plays into what Boulton wants: not to have any one team dominating or any one owner "buying" the championship. The gentlemen's agreement to hold the line on salaries has not been violated. "We're memberships, not franchises," stated Boulton. " I think it's understood throughout the league. Let's try to stay to the [salary] guideline, because we all want to be successful, and that way we keep everything competitive, and we keep the league healthy and alive and moving forward."

Not everything has come up aces for Boulton and the Atlantic League. An unstable ownership situation prevented the Lehigh Valley Black Diamonds from ever completing their new stadium. After the stadium site was abandoned due to lack of funding, it sat unfinished for many years. The Black Diamonds became the Road Warriors, reflecting a unique independent-baseball concept in which a team plays its entire schedule as a road team to maintain an equal schedule for the league. Another club in Aberdeen, Maryland, failed. Nashua and Atlantic City were plagued throughout their Atlantic League existence by low attendance. Both clubs eventually transferred to the short-season Can-Am League: the Pride in 2006 and the Surf in 2007. The Bears are still struggling for an identity in Newark and seeking to increase their attendance. In future chapters, I will discuss how location and demographics are major factors in defining the level of financial success of minor-league or independent professional baseball franchises. Clubs in locations surrounded by populations with higher disposable incomes tend to do better than those depending primarily on inner-city fan support. The Atlantic League is a combination of all of these situations. At times, the owners of its ball clubs have had to intervene in the affairs of clubs other than their own to ensure the stability of the league. This was the case with the Camden Riversharks.

In 2001, Camden real estate developer Steve Shilling entered into a unique partnership with the city of Camden and Rutgers University–Camden to build a baseball park on the banks of the Delaware River. The Campbell Soup Company, founded in Camden in 1869 and a major employer in the area ever since, bought the naming rights to the new ballpark, which sits on the site of its former manufacturing plant. The park, built at the foot of the Benjamin Franklin Bridge that connects Camden and Philadelphia, offers a breathtaking view of the bridge and the Philadelphia skyline. The club enjoyed immediate success, drawing more than 4,000 fans per game on average. Yet, in 2003, the league almost lost the club. The Riversharks' owner, Shilling, passed away unexpectedly after a short battle with brain cancer. The club was left in the hands of its trustees, and a chaotic financial situation ensued. In the spirit of the member-owners of the league, Steve Kalafer, Frank Boulton, and Peter Kirk, all owners of their own Atlantic League teams, jumped in to take over the ownership of the club, saving it from bankruptcy for the community and for the league. The Atlantic League would have sustained a major public relations hit if the Riversharks failed after having been perceived a successful operation. The league owners felt that Camden gave them a regional presence in the entire Camden–Cherry Hill–Philadelphia area and ought not be abandoned. Also, the owners viewed the league more as a sum of its parts and were willing to do whatever was necessary to ensure its continued prosperity. Multiple-club ownership and cooperation between owners are common in both minor-league and independent professional baseball. Such cooperation among owners is virtually nonexistent in major-league baseball. Major-league franchises in financial crisis, if not relocated to another city, are typically sold to other entities with deep pockets that are willing to sustain the losses while attempting to right the ship, with little collective concern for their industry as a whole.

Frank Boulton wants the Atlantic League to eventually contain twelve member clubs. In 2005, Lancaster (Pennsylvania) completed the construction of its Clipper Magazine Stadium, and the Lancaster Barnstormers, under owner Peter Kirk, joined the league. In 2007, a club in York (Pennsylvania) began play as the York Revolution. Because of its proximity to Maryland, the York club features four former Baltimore Orioles in the dugout leading the club: Chris Hoiles manages the team and is joined by coaches Ryan Minor, Tippy Martinez, and Al Bumbry.

The Southern Maryland Blue Crabs have been announced to begin play in 2008, if their new stadium in Waldorf, Maryland, can be built in time. There has been discussion of additional Atlantic League teams in Yonkers (New York) and northern Virginia in coming years. The future of the Atlantic League might also include another club based in New Jersey, the long-rumored Bergen Cliff Hawks. The Somerset Patriots' owner, Steve Kalafer, has been involved in serious and, at times, acrimonious negotiations with the developers of the Xanadu retail and entertainment complex for the construction of a ballpark at the East Rutherford site. As of January 2007, ground had yet to be broken for the park, and it remained to be seen if Kalafer could clear the legal and financial barriers that delayed his quest to bring an Atlantic League club to the Meadowlands Sports Complex. "It [Xanadu] is something like a $2 billion project, a huge project," explained Boulton. "What happens is that when you have these huge projects, unless you do a carve-out, you get caught up in the planning, and the inertia sets in, and sometimes it's tough to put your fingers back into the project. Now, if anyone can, Steve Kalafer can, and I know it's something he wants to do. He has 100 percent of our support and we'll do whatever we need to do to add Bergen County to the Atlantic League."

Would nine clubs be too much baseball for New Jersey, considering that Bergen County would give the Atlantic League four New Jersey clubs once again, along with the three in the Can-Am League and the two affiliated clubs in Trenton and Lakewood? "New Jersey is a big, big state," said a confident Boulton. "The ballparks are spread out. Where they're closer together they're in denser demographics, and where the ballparks are a little more spread out, the demographics are less dense. So, I think they are all well positioned."

The lingering doubt about the proliferation of the independent teams in New Jersey is how will they fare attendance-wise, considering that there are major-league teams in New York and Philadelphia and affiliated minor-league teams, not only in Trenton and Lakewood, but also a short drive away in Staten Island and Brooklyn. The results have so far been staggering, as baseball attendance is up at all levels. In 2006, the Mets and Yankees attracted a combined attendance of more than 7 million fans. The Philadelphia Phillies drew 2.7 million fans. The New Jersey minor-league and independent clubs drew another 2 million. Add in the Brooklyn Cyclones' and Staten Island Yankees' numbers, and the combined baseball attendance in the tri-state area approached 12 million paying fans.

On a given Saturday night, the Mets or the Yankees will have 50,000 spectators in their ballparks, and another 25,000 to 30,000 will be enjoying minor-league and independent professional baseball across the Hudson River in New Jersey. On top of all of this, Boulton's Long Island Ducks, in his original targeted location of Central Islip, have led the Atlantic League in attendance since their formation in 2000 and topped all other independent professional baseball teams in America in attendance in 2006. Boulton proved to be correct in his original assessment that the major-league territorial restrictions needed to be challenged and that there was certainly enough room for everyone.

The dynamic between minor-league and independent professional baseball is an interesting one. There are more similarities than differences in the business models. The major difference is from a baseball purist's perspective. "Minor League Baseball" is a brand name, and executives of affiliated clubs are very quick to point that out, maintaining that independent clubs are misleading the public if they position themselves as "minor-league baseball." For the most part, the independent clubs are extremely careful not to refer to themselves as minor-league baseball. The Atlantic League specifically instructs their clubs not to do so. The died-in-the-wool baseball purists probably drive the extra miles to see and track a player's progress as he make his way up or down a parent club's organization, and they have difficulty accepting independent baseball. I can cite my own skepticism about what I was watching the first time that I went to Commerce Bank Ballpark to see the Somerset Patriots play in 1999. To my knowledge, there has never been a formal survey taken of the percentage of fans that attend minor-league games who would not be seen in an independent team's park. I have to believe that percentage, however, is very small.

Again, I have to cite my own epiphany. I have grown to love and appreciate independent professional baseball as much as I do the pure minor leagues. This is where the business models come together, and where the similarities between the two far outnumber the differences. As I have sat in Somerset, Newark, and other independent clubs' parks over the years, as well as affiliated clubs' parks in Trenton and Lakewood, I've seen the same efforts being made by the local staffs. They all strive to provide affordable family entertainment in a clean and safe environment. The target audiences are basically the same: people looking for a fun night or afternoon out. The staffs are all young, eager, and energetic. The Atlantic League at its best is usually on display at the Commerce Bank Ballpark in Bridgewater, where Sparky Lyle and his Somerset Patriots have endeared themselves to the local community. That is where we are heading next.

6

The Somerset Patriots
Location, Location, Location!

For the Somerset Patriots of Bridgewater Township, New Jersey, the investment in home is so strong that the ball club's players and management believe in bringing a bit of their ballpark with them wherever they go. On one particular early autumn evening in 2005, the scene was Holman Stadium in Nashua, New Hampshire, some forty miles north of Boston. Nashua has long identified itself with the trials and tribulations of the Boston Red Sox. It also has an eventful baseball past of its own. Built in 1937, Holman Stadium witnessed a dramatic moment in both American social and baseball history when the Nashua Dodgers, a farm club of the Brooklyn Dodgers, played there. In 1946, Dodgers owner Branch Rickey intended to integrate the major leagues

Commerce Bank Ballpark, Bridgewater, New Jersey, home of the Somerset Patriots. Photograph by Bob Golon, 2007.

with black players. Seeking the tolerance of a liberal northeastern town, Rickey sent young black players Roy Campanella and Don Newcombe to play in Nashua, and the city welcomed them with open arms. Under the guidance of future Dodgers' Hall of Fame manager Walter Alston, Campanella and Newcombe led Nashua to the New England League championship.

Almost sixty years later, on October 2, 2005, a small crowd of 1,148 Nashua Pride loyalists gathered at Holman Stadium to witness game three of the 2005 Atlantic League Championship Series between the Pride and the visiting Somerset Patriots. Postseason baseball was in the air. The batting-practice screens were being dismantled, and the players slowly returned to their clubhouses to complete their pregame preparations. Meanwhile, around the infield, important business was taking place.

As the early-arriving fans watched, a group clad in Patriots jackets roamed the bases, sprinkling dirt from a jar first behind home plate, then carefully around first base, then second base, then third. When Pride manager Butch Hobson witnessed the ritual in progress, he sauntered out to the group and nicely but firmly asked that the activity be stopped. Hobson and the Somerset group amicably shook hands, but as Hobson returned to the outfield area to resume his pregame activities, the Patriots backers continued their mission of soil spreading, completing it before being further detected. This was important. Even though they were ahead 2-0 in the best-of-five series, the Patriots entourage sought to influence the baseball gods by bringing a little bit of New Jersey ground to New Hampshire.[1]

The dirt sprinkled across the playing field in Nashua was sacred, lucky soil from the infield of Commerce Bank Ballpark in Bridgewater. The man who led the effort was none other than Steve Kalafer, patriarch of the most successful of the independent professional baseball clubs in New Jersey. The Patriots defeated the Pride that evening, 6-1, winning their third Atlantic League championship in five years. They probably didn't need the ceremonial act, but Kalafer left nothing to chance.

In a state with major cities like Trenton, Newark, Camden, and Atlantic City, it seemed unlikely that a baseball empire could rise in a nondescript area like Bridgewater Township. But a closer look reveals the ingredients of success that Kalafer saw as he embarked on his effort to bring the Atlantic League club to Somerset County in the mid-1990s. In fact, Bridgewater, with its suburban middle-class demographics, willing politicians, and open space in need of redevelopment, had just the combination of ingredients that make for a successful minor-league or independent baseball franchise. Those who seek this formula are best served by getting in their cars and driving out to Commerce Bank Ballpark.

To get to the park, you can begin the journey at the Outerbridge Crossing from Staten Island to New Jersey, where it empties onto Route 440 in Perth Amboy. Make your way west through the northern portion of Middlesex County, where Route 440 becomes Interstate 287. Interstate 287 is often congested at rush hour. It is a much-cursed, concrete testament to Eisenhower's Interstate Highway System in central New Jersey, designed to form a loop around the New York City metropolitan area. The highway intersects with the Garden State Parkway at exit 129, then with the New Jersey Turnpike at exit 10. Throughout the ride, the landscape is marked by a never-ending succession of industrial parks, commercial areas, strip malls, and hotels catering to the businessperson, shopper, and traveler. The area does not possess a whole lot of redeeming character. Or so it seems.

The signs along I-287 make reference to the towns of Edison, Metuchen, South Plainfield, and Highland Park. "That's good," you're thinking. "People do live around here; it's not just businesses." As you make your way through Piscataway and into Somerset County, you arrive at Bound Brook Borough and the Township of Bridgewater. Bridgewater's municipal Web site describes the town this way: "Our 32 square mile community in central Somerset County borders 11 other municipalities. We are home to 3600 acres of public and private parks and recreation opportunities. Bridgewater boasts Blue Ribbon schools, job opportunities in national and international pharmaceutical and biotechnology firms, and is home to the championship winning Somerset Patriots and Bridgewater Commons Mall, as well as numerous other shopping opportunities and hotels." Well, okay, I guess we have arrived at the home of the Somerset Patriots![2]

Somerset County does not appear to be an area meant for anything but clean, suburban living which is perhaps why it is an ideal spot for a baseball team looking to attract a fan base of young families with few other sources of local entertainment to distract them. With a population of approximately 315,000 residents in twenty-one municipalities, Somerset County placed second in the nation in 2004 with a median household income of $84,892, according to the U.S. Census Bureau. It is bordered to the west and north by Hunterdon County, whose approximate population of 250,000 earned a median income of $79,888. Middlesex County, to the east and south, had an estimated 2003 population of 781,000, with a median household income of $61,446. That makes a combined population in the three-county area of approximately 1,350,000, with a median income of at least $60,000 a year.

Many of these households are made up of young families, possibly looking for a source of affordable entertainment besides the movies, school plays, ice skating, bowling, and shopping. When baseball successfully returned to New Jersey in the mid-1990s, its success in Trenton and Sussex County caught the attention of the forward-thinking Somerset County Board of Chosen Freeholders, the elected group of public officials who manage the county's affairs. They were seeking ways to turn otherwise unproductive properties into revenue generators that would benefit the residents and bring in new business.

The American Cyanamid Company owned and operated a chemical manufacturing facility in Bridgewater along I-287 until the mid-1990s. During that time, 800,000 tons of chemical waste were dumped into various lagoons and containment pools on the approximately 575 acres the firm occupied. Considerable groundwater and soil contamination resulted. In 1982, the Environmental Protection Agency added the Cyanamid property to the list of hazardous-waste sites needing cleanup. It was the second-largest cleanup site in New Jersey.[3]

The EPA defines "brownfields" as "real property, the expansion, redevelopment, or reuse of which may be complicated by the presence . . . of a hazardous substance, pollutant, or contaminant." According to county freeholder Denise Coyle, the Somerset County Board was looking for ways to transform the brownfield Cyanamid site from "a dying, decrepit dump that was just a drain on a community" into land that can be of a "mix-used retail, office, and condominium living space."[4] Fortunately, the front portion of the Cyanamid property, approximately one hundred acres that had been primarily used for parking and factory office space, was already decontaminated and considered to be safe. Those one hundred acres were destined to become the Commerce Bank Ballpark site.

Enter Steven B. Kalafer, a New Jersey native and resident of Annandale. He is also an automobile-dealership tycoon, award-winning documentary filmmaker, and baseball enthusiast. Owner of the highly successful Flemington Car and Truck Country, a large and multifaceted automobile sales and service business, Kalafer read correctly the demographics of central New Jersey that screamed for a baseball club. He petitioned Minor League Baseball, the governing body of the minor leagues, for an affiliated franchise for Bridgewater. He was rejected because Bridgewater was considered to be the exclusive territory of the Trenton Thunder by Minor League Baseball rules. Kalafer then got in touch with Frank Boulton, the architect of the coming new independent professional baseball league, the Atlantic League. Boulton had tried to place his own affiliated club in Long Island and was refused for the same reason as Kalafer. Boulton's vision for the Atlantic League provided Kalafer with a platform for his future Bridgewater Township team.

His next, more difficult step would be convincing the freeholders and taxpayers of Somerset County that a ballpark built in Bridgewater could and would be economically successful. "Location, location, location. Demographics, demographics, demographics," Kalafer stated as the reason behind his sales pitch to the county. "All of our surveys said we'd be successful. We've exceeded those surveys. It's not 'build it and they will come.' Build it in the right market, satisfy the public, provide value, and they will come."[5] The partnership between Kalafer and Somerset County was immediate but not without reservations. "Quite frankly, I was not on board with the stadium, because it's $17.5 million of the taxpayers' money," explained Coyle. "What I loved about the idea was reclamation of a brownfield site. In fact, that was what finally won me over, after we got the financials down on the stadium. The ball field had to make social sense, economic sense, and it had to make community sense."

The stadium plan created by Kalafer, Coyle, and her county associates became one of the most innovative financial deals in the country, according to Coyle. The debt on the stadium would be paid off without the use of taxpayer dollars if the Patriots managed to average 3,100 fans per game on a regular basis. Given that the Patriots averaged greater than 5,100 fans in a ballpark that seats 6,100 in each of their first seven seasons, Coyle's goal of 50 percent attendance has been easily attained. "I felt very strongly that we had to break even at 50 percent attendance," explained Coyle. "We are doing incredibly well. But this is our seventh season. Our first season was in 1999. And how is it going to be in our twentieth season? I don't know, but I felt really comfortable with the social-economic class in Somerset County and with what people like to do here that the ballpark would succeed as long as we could make 50 percent attendance. I wasn't going to count on 75 percent attendance to not have the support to be taxpayer neutral." Most stadium projects, particularly those in major-league cities, turn out to be a drain on the taxpayers' money while providing little tangible payback in return. Not so for the deal in Somerset County. For every season thus far, the Patriots presented a check to the county large enough not only to satisfy the yearly $1.3 million debt payment but also to place a profit of approximately a quarter of a million dollars into a special county fund designed for stadium repairs and improvements. So far, so good for Coyle and the county freeholders.

Even the stadium naming-rights deal, reached with Commerce Bankcorp of Cherry Hill, New Jersey, is unique by being more favorable to the county than the usual naming-rights deals. Under the arrangement reached with the bank in 2000, Commerce agreed to pay the county and the ball club $3.5 million over fifteen years for the park to be called the Commerce Bank Ballpark. The county gets 30 percent, or $70,000 a year, for each of the fifteen years. The Patriots receive the rest of the money, approximately $160,000. However, the money is prioritized for the county, with the county receiving its payment every year before the Patriots do. Jim Grinstead, the editor of the *Revenues from Sports Venues* newsletter, was quoted in the *Bridgewater Courier News* at the time of the deal, "The fact that the county got anything out of the deal speaks well for them. . . . Usually, the team gets all the revenue." In return, Commerce Bank has a link on the Patriots' Web site and visible advertising rights in the ballpark, but most of all, it can use this opportunity to increase its image in a very competitive banking region as a good corporate citizen and supporter of recreational activities in the area. How does it help the bank? Dr. Larry McCarthy, professor of economics at Seton Hall University's Stillman School of Business and a published expert in sports economics, says it is not all about finances and the bottom line. "What they may be doing is setting themselves up in terms of corporate philanthropy and contributing to the community, contributing to the area where they're located, and being a significant corporate citizen," said McCarthy. "Three to five million dollars is a significant amount, but it recognizes . . . the contribution of baseball perhaps to the communities, and their [Commerce Bank's] need or their understanding to be associated with that."[6]

As Coyle pointed out, sports economists have long argued the value of a sports franchise to a city or a region concerning the benefits of ballpark building. Most politicians seeking stadium deals claim that such projects will create jobs, drive new business, and promote area economic growth. McCarthy took a more guarded view. "It is questionable at best," he suggested, "because many of the jobs that are associated with the actual park itself are going to be part-time jobs. . . . [T]here's more benefit to putting up a Macy's instead of putting up a ballpark, because the jobs in Macy's are full-time. . . . [T]hey are open for longer periods of time than the stadium, so the types of jobs you get [with the stadium] don't justify the argument for it." There are exceptions, and McCarthy felt Somerset might be one of them. "If you put it in the heart of a commercial center, as it appears to be happening in Somerset, it will have long-term benefits, all right." Commerce Bank Ballpark sits on the edge of a major shopping district that includes such big-box retailers as Home Depot, Costco Warehouse, and Target and such chain stores as Old Navy, Bed Bath and Beyond, and Marshall's. Hilton has built a Garden Inn at the complex, and Applebee's opened a restaurant nearby. The area attracts a constant stream of heavy commercial traffic all year round. Even the most pro-ballpark politician and sports economist would have to admit that the commercial and retail complex in Bridgewater described above would probably be successful, ballpark or not, because of its proximity to I-287 and the heavily populated areas. There is no evidence available that the ballpark has helped spur the business development there, but there is no evidence against it, either. Taking it one step further, an argument can be made for the businesses helping to spur the growth of the attendance at Commerce Bank Park. The brick facade and tall light towers of the ballpark became a familiar sight to everyone who has visited the stores and dined near the complex since its completion in early 1999.

Even though the new Patriots were scheduled to begin play in the Atlantic League's initial season in 1998, groundbreaking for the Bridgewater ballpark did not take place until April of that year. This meant the Patriots would have to play their first season, an abbreviated 100-game schedule, as a road club, without a home field to call its own. They won only forty games that first season. As the club prepared to begin the 1999 season, the Somerset ballpark neared completion. Designed by Clarke Caton Hintz and the SSP Architectural Group, the 6,100-seat ballpark closely resembled Mercer County Waterfront Park in Trenton. All of the box and reserved seating is located in front of and below a wide main concourse, with the concession stands, rest rooms, and gift shops all accessible from the concourse. Quickly dubbed "the Jewel of the Atlantic League," the park opened on June 7, 1999, with a standing-room crowd of 6,500 fans witnessing a Patriots loss to the Lehigh Valley Black Diamonds. The Patriots finished last in the Atlantic League's first half, but they rebounded nicely by winning the second-half title and qualifying for the league playoffs for the first time. The roster included local Rutgers University favorite Darren Winston and Bobby Bonds Jr. (yes, Barry's brother). But no player was more closely identified with the Patriots by their fans in 1999 than first baseman Brian Traxler.

Brian Lee Traxler was listed in the scorecard as being five feet, ten inches tall and weighing two hundred pounds. The scorecard flattered him. In reality, Traxler's weight was somewhere above two hundred fifty, with all of it seemingly settled into his very large stomach and ample, round face and chin. In fact, Brian more closely resembled a refugee from a Sunday morning men's beer softball league than an ex-major-league prospect and player. But a player he was, drafted by the Los Angeles Dodgers in the sixteenth round of the 1988 amateur draft, and briefly making it to the major leagues with the Dodgers for eleven at-bats in 1990. In affiliated baseball, his short stature and big stomach worked against him. Those same qualities, however, endeared him to the Somerset Patriot fans, along with his ready smile and easygoing nature. Brian let the world know that he liked to have a couple of beers every so often, and that he ate whatever and whenever he felt like it. He was a poor man's David Wells (the ex-Yankee pitcher with similar appetites and physique), someone with whom the common fan could identify. Known for his ability to hit stinging line drives, Brian contributed twelve home runs and sixty-one runs batted in for the 1999 Patriots. Afterward, with his playing career nearing an end, Brian played briefly in the independent Northern League. He then returned to the Dodgers minor-league organization as a hitting coach. Sadly, Brian Traxler never made it back to the major-league level as a coach. After a short illness, Brian died in November 2004.[7]

Steve Kalafer scored his biggest victory for his new club by securing the services of the well-known ex-Yankees relief pitcher Sparky Lyle as the Somerset Patriots' first manager. Lyle took to his role as the face of the Patriots franchise so well that he has been the club's only manager through the 2007 season. The American League Cy Young Award winner in 1977, Lyle spent sixteen seasons in the major leagues, seven of those as a central character of the "Bronx Zoo" Yankees of Billy Martin, Reggie Jackson, and George Steinbrenner. Known for his quick wit and handlebar mustache, Lyle was shopping for a car when he met Kalafer at one of his auto dealerships in 1997. He came out with both the vehicle and the job. Unproven as a manager, Lyle quickly earned praise as a no-

nonsense type who treats players fairly, playing to win every game. He is also a shrewd judge of player talent who is involved in many of the club's roster decisions. Recently retired Patriots infielder and captain Emiliano Escandon said of his experiences with Lyle, "I've loved him from day one. He says, 'You play hard, you play the game the right way, and you produce, you're going to play for me,' and that's all I ever asked for. He is very big on being professional, on and off the field. He wants you to present yourself the way the New York Yankees did, and it [has] just been a natural fit for me."[8] Lyle has provided the Patriots with stable and consistent leadership throughout the club's existence.

The 1999 Patriots were an immediate hit at the box office, drawing 335,056 fans for an average of 5,235 a game. This ranked them near the top for attendance not only for independent professional baseball but also for minor-league affiliated baseball nationwide. First-year success in a location is not unusual. The concern of every baseball front office is whether interest would decline once the novelty of having a team in an area wore off. Through 2007, there has been no decline in attendance whatsoever for the Patriots.

The team solidified the roster for the 2000 season, adding hard-hitting outfielders Kevin Dattola, Greg Blosser, and Michael Warner to an already talented lineup. Second baseman Billy Hall also joined the club, and contributed 104 stolen bases. The pitching remained solid, not spectacular, and Sparky Lyle molded the Patriots into an Atlantic League powerhouse, winning both the first- and second-half divisional championships in both 2000 and 2001. After qualifying for a first-round bye, the Nashua Pride swept the Patriots in the 2000 league championship series. Third baseman Escandon, destined to become team captain, was added to the roster along with first baseman Mike Glavine, the brother of major-league pitcher Tom Glavine, for the 2001 season. The Patriots responded with a combined 83-43 won-lost record for both halves.

The 2001 Atlantic League Championship Series was notable for New Jersey fans as for the first time, the Somerset Patriots met their northern New Jersey rivals, the Newark Bears, in a best-of-five league championship series. What followed was sheer baseball drama for northern and central New Jersey fans, who were still reeling from the September 11 attacks two weeks earlier. The series opened in the shadow of lower Manhattan, at Bears and Eagles Riverfront Stadium in Newark, on September 29.

The Patriots had been swept out of the postseason in their two previous appearances in 1999 and 2000, failing to win a game in either year. When they dropped the first two games of the 2001 championship series by scores of 8-4 and 6-2, it looked like it was going to be more of the same and yet another postseason failure for the Patriots. Back in Bridgewater for game three, the Patriots trailed 2-1 going into the eighth inning and were six outs away from elimination. In that eighth inning, an RBI single by DaRond Stovall and a two-run double by Glavine revived the Patriots' hopes as they defeated the Bears 4-2, keeping the series alive. Once again, in game four, it was heroics by Glavine that saved the day. With the team trailing by two runs in the bottom of the ninth inning, Glavine tied the game with a dramatic two-run home run off Newark pitcher Calvin Jones. Greg Blosser added a three-run home run in the bottom of the tenth inning, giving the Patriots a 7-4 victory and tying the series at two victories apiece. The Patriots and Bears returned to Newark for the deciding game five.

Left-handed pitcher Robert Dodd co-led the Patriots with ten wins during the 2001 regular season, but by the end of the playoffs, his arm was tiring. Lyle called on him with only two days' rest since his last start, and Dodd responded by shutting out the Bears for six and two-thirds innings before giving way to relievers Luis Arroyo and closer John Briscoe. Fittingly, Briscoe, one of the last of the remaining original 1998 Somerset Patriots, recorded the final four outs for the Patriots. The 4-0 shutout clinched the Patriots' first Atlantic League championship, and even Lyle, who had been through the miraculous Yankees world championship run in 1978, admitted that this victory was "something special."

The box-office success for the Patriots also continued, with the club drawing more than 350,000 fans in both 2000 and 2001. Despite narrowly missing the playoffs in 2002 by losing out to the Bears on a tiebreaker, the 358,000 spectators who came through the Commerce Bank Ballpark's turnstiles assured the club of their fourth straight season of averaging more than 5,100 fans per game. There would be no letup in 2003, as Lyle's club put together another championship run. Glavine and Blosser, heroes of the 2001 club, were no longer with the Patriots. They were ably replaced by catcher Robinson Cancel, outfielders Edgard Clemente, Norm Hutchins, and the hard-hitting Ryan Radmanovich. Ex-Yankee Brett Jodie anchored the pitching along with Jason Dickson. After eliminating the Camden Riversharks in two straight games in the first round of the Atlantic League playoffs, the Patriots squared off against Butch Hobson's Nashua Pride in the championship series. Like 2001's, this one did not come easily. The Patriots fell behind in the series, two games to one, but Justin Jensen scattered five hits over eight innings in game four, leading the Patriots to a 10-3 victory. A fifth and deciding game in Nashua was necessary. The Pats won game five, 8-4, behind four hits each by Radmanovich and Hutchins, giving them their second Atlantic League title in three years.

The success of the team caused them to be embraced by the central New Jersey fans. They came to Commerce Bank Ballpark in 2004 in record numbers; 376,315 paid attendees for a whopping 5,376 per game average. Despite missing the playoffs, stellar performances by Clemente, Jeff Nettles, and the Atlantic League's Most Valuable Player, Victor Rodriguez, helped the Patriots welcome their two-millionth fan to Commerce Bank Park that season. Rodriguez's season was especially noteworthy, as he led the league with a .371 batting average, adding 25 home runs and 111 runs batted in. His success enabled him to sign a lucrative contract to play professionally in Taiwan in 2005, which was good for Rodriguez if indeed an unfortunate loss for the Patriots.

The Patriots treated their fans to a strong start in 2005, winning the South Division first-half championship by three games over the Camden Riversharks, which qualified them again for the Atlantic League playoffs. Pitchers Dave Elder, Brad Clontz, Brian Tollberg, and Derek Lee all signed contracts to return to affiliated organizations during the first half, leaving the Patriots scrambling for pitching in the second half. Sparky Lyle and former player-procurement director Adam Gladstone did a remarkable job replacing them. Tim Christman and championship series MVP Mark DeFelice were capable newcomers, and the Patriots prevailed in the 2005 playoffs despite struggling in the second half of the season. Much of the credit was given to Gladstone for his keen eye for talent.

"When looking for players to play for the Somerset Patriots, I always ask the prospect one question: Where do you want your career to go?" explained Gladstone. "If they say that this is the end of the line, then they are not a desirable option. I have always wanted players that were hungry and wanted to utilize the league as a showcase back to major-league organizations. Not only was it important to Gladstone to attract talented ballplayers to Somerset, they also needed to fit into Steve Kalafer's philosophy of fan friendliness and be the type of people who could be counted on to interact with the local community. Gladstone views the roster flexibility in the Atlantic League as a benefit in attracting the best available talent. "The Atlantic League differs from any other independent league for many reasons. Our roster limit is twenty-five, but we have no restrictions in signing players. Every other [independent] league has guidelines on the makeup of their rosters. They need to have a certain amount of rookies, a certain amount of veterans, and so on." In keeping with Frank Boulton's ambition of having the Atlantic League be a boutique league in the Northeast, a team's roster could consist of all players with major-league baseball experience. Thus, the talent and level of play is greater than most other independent leagues. Besides not having rookie versus veteran quotas in its roster makeup, Atlantic League players are signed to one-year contracts and become free agents at the end of every season. However, most players, if not picked up by affiliated clubs, are eager to return to their Atlantic League teams because of the quality of the stadium facilities and the ability to showcase their talent against better competition. "Our belief is that the Atlantic League will always be able to replenish our players, and we pride ourselves on promoting our players back to affiliated teams," explained Gladstone. "Those promotions make my job easier when selling an Atlantic League opportunity."[9] Gladstone left the Patriots at the end of the 2006, forming Baseball and Sports Associates (BASA), a venture with Joe Klein, the executive director of the Atlantic League. They formed the company to assist a group of four Atlantic League clubs to procure players in 2006. This partnership is unique in independent baseball, and it seeks to leverage the skills of Klein and Gladstone in finding Atlantic League–caliber players while freeing up club management to concentrate on other business operations. In 2006, this group included the Patriots, but not having the full resources and attention of Adam Gladstone was noticeable in the Patriots' performance. The team fell to barely a .500 won-lost record and failed to qualify for the league playoffs, just one year after winning the league championship. The Patriots sought to rebound in 2007 with pitching coach Brett Jodie now in charge of player procurement and manager Sparky Lyle lending his familiar helping hand.

The Somerset Patriots are firmly established as a New Jersey professional baseball success story. Was it the good brand of baseball that brought the people out? This probably has something to do with it, as surely it is more fun to sit and watch a competitive club night after night instead of one being continually beaten. But when you walk around Commerce Bank Park, you get a sense that the baseball game on the field is only a small part of the story behind this franchise. A closer look into the operations of the Patriots reveals the real reasons for their continued success at the box office.[10]

Arriving at Commerce Bank Park on the afternoon of a night game, I'm greeted at the entrance to the parking lot by a simple sign that read "Baseball Game Tonight, 7:05 PM." I cannot help but notice the large group of cars parked in the outer reaches of the lot. This is a result of the ballpark lot's function as a daily park-and-ride facility for the Bridgewater station of the New Jersey Transit Raritan Valley Line. The commuter trains, visible coming and going outside the right-field fence, add to the atmosphere inside the ballpark. Before preparing the operation for tonight's game against the Long Island Ducks, staff members take time out from their work to gather in a conference room to sing "Happy Birthday" to one of their coworkers and to share in some birthday cake. This type of closeness is demonstrated time and time again among the staff that Patrick McVerry has assembled. McVerry has been the president and general manager of the Somerset Patriots since the beginning of the franchise. The Penn State graduate, who also received a master's degree in sports administration from East Stroudsburg University, has assembled a young and passionate group which he refers to as "a fine oiled machine." Most of McVerry's operations team has been in place since his arrival in 1999, which contributes to the spirit and dedication evident on a game day. "We all know our duties, they [the staff] all know what they need to do, and they all have such pride in this ballpark, the team, and how people view us that they want to do the best job they can." McVerry credits the Patriots' fan-friendly and family philosophy to "this vision . . . of how the county wanted this ballpark, how Steve [Kalafer] wants this ballpark, and how I want this ballpark." The vision is a combination of friendliness, attention to detail, positive public image, and just plain fun.

At 5:00 PM, two hours before the game, both regular and game-day staff gather below the press level to prepare the ballpark for the arrival of the fans on this very hot and humid July afternoon. This includes setting up the concession areas, preparing the field, and paying great attention to the cleanliness of the park. Pride is a major motivator among the young people working at Commerce Bank Park. At 5:45 PM, an hour and twenty minutes prior to the game, the sky grows extremely dark and it becomes apparent that a late-day thunderstorm is about to hit. Suddenly, Patriots front-office staffers appear en masse, running down the aisles of the stands and entering the field to help pull the protective tarpaulin over the infield. They all seem to know their role, and the field is covered in plenty of time to protect it from becoming unplayable from the pouring rain. When questioned later, public relations director Marc Russinoff explained, "yes, everybody does that [pulls the tarp], from the general manager on down. And, you know, it's obvious that everyone has to be flexible in a job like this only because you're going to be asked to do a lot of different things." The sky clears at about 6:30 PM, and appropriately, a vivid rainbow appears in the sky, stretching across the outfield from left field to right. The fans begin to enter the park and are welcomed by the staff employees, still cleaning the remnants of infield dirt off their shirts and shoes after putting the tarpaulin away.

In an era where the public image of some professional athletes has taken on such a negative tone, the Patriots strive for exactly the opposite. "We have a very positive image, and we make sure that the players we have are very positive and have strong impacts in the community around us," explained Russinoff. "Our players are really good guys and very accessible to our fans. Sparky Lyle has been fantastic since the beginning, going out there and making sure our sponsors are taken care of, our group leaders, our season-ticket holders. . . . [F]rom the very beginning, our message has been of just being very accessible." Patriots players expect to be called upon to be community friendly. Retired team captain Emiliano Escandon explained his role as he understood it. "Mr. Kalafer envisioned a team that not only produced on the field but became intertwined with the community, getting out there, getting involved with the schools, going to the malls, just really being very recognizable faces, not just during the season, but during the off-season," explained Escandon. "So, when they approached me last year [2004] and named me team captain, obviously it was an honor. . . . [A]nytime a man like Mr. Kalafer thinks enough of you to represent his whole organization, it is definitely an honor and something I don't take lightly at all." A California native and ex-schoolteacher, Escandon recently became a full-time New Jersey resident so that he could continue his community work all year round. Utilizing his teaching skills, he's a full-time spokesman for the club's Strike Out Drugs program and has visited more than thirty schools and other locations, teaching kids to make the right choices when it comes to drug, alcohol, and tobacco use. Escandon also teaches young players the art of hitting and fielding a baseball at Zoned Sports Academy in Bridgewater. It is a connection made possible by Escandon's style of play. "A lot of the parents come down to Zoned and say we like the way you play the game.

That's how we want our son or daughter to learn the game. Giving lessons and having the kids who come to watch you play come and learn from you, that's even a bigger thrill. You can't ask for anything more. People have told me, you should coach in college. Well, if I have a college team, I can only help twenty-five guys every year, where, if you're an instructor, you can help thousands of kids. Teach them the game and help them learn the game. That is much more rewarding." Tonight, Escandon, who is nursing a sore leg muscle and is not in the starting lineup, spends a good deal of pregame time at the railing along the first-base stands, signing autographs for youngsters holding caps, baseballs, and scorecards. He greets them all with a smile and a few words. The excited expressions on the kids faces tells it all. It is a scene that many of the Patriots players repeat at the park before every game.

Brian Bender, who broadcasts the Patriots games on WCTC radio in New Brunswick as well as via the Internet, puts the Patriots' image consciousness into simple terms. "That has always been the Patriots' motto," explains Bender, "to have good players in the clubhouse and good people, not just good players." Walking through the stands prior to tonight's game gave me an opportunity to check with some fans to see if they agreed with this assessment. A couple from Spotswood, New Jersey, bedecked in Patriots jerseys, caps, and t-shirts, when asked why they keep coming out to Commerce Bank Park, explained, "Because it feels like family here. It's good baseball, and they play hard. It's an atmosphere like old-time baseball." When asked the same question, another couple, from North Plainfield, put it succinctly; "Good view, good seats, no traffic!" David Reyes, a Raritan Borough resident in his twenties, attends almost every home game and travels to some games on the road. Why? "I love the play in the Atlantic League," said Reyes, "It's good baseball. Everybody has a fair shot." A couple of sections over sat a mother with her young daughter, from Long Hill, who had a triple-header of reasons for being at the ballpark. "It's Dukes of Hazzard Night, my daughter is having a birthday party here tonight, and we love baseball."

Unaffiliated professional baseball is no doubt a serious business, but the bottom line at a Patriots game is family and fun. "My favorite part?" asks Bender. "It's just the fun. Being able to sit up here [in the broadcast booth] every night and seeing the families down on the field. Watching the game, there's a lot of laughing going on, whether it's at a prank between the innings or something that's happening on the field, there's just a lot more fun at this game. Major-league baseball to me seems too much business, and that is a big thing for me. This is just more fun!"

This type of fun and entertainment has even made fans out of people who cared little for baseball before. Yvonne Selander is an adult reference librarian for the Somerset County Library System at the Bridgewater branch. Before the Patriots came along, she had attended only five or six professional baseball games in her life, all at the major-league level. By chance, she and a couple of her friends decided to attend a Patriots game three years ago, and she has been hooked on the experience ever since. Yvonne now attends upward of twenty-five games per season. "It's like, wow, you can see the people!" she explains. "It's not like you're in these seats in Oshkosh somewhere. You can actually see the people. The baseball players look like they're having a great time. . . . [E]verybody's just so nice, from the people that run the place to the players. It's just such a nice, family, happy atmosphere." Selander also admits to becoming well versed in the game of baseball and into how the team is performing on a daily basis. "I do check the Web site every morning to see if they won or not." She has attended games both by herself and with groups of up to twenty people. When she was working at Rutgers University, Yvonne convinced her work group to have some outings at the Executive Party Deck at the ballpark. "During the winter, I count the days until opening day."

The local business community has also embraced the Patriots. Central New Jersey is home to the sprawling office complexes of pharmaceutical companies and telecommunications and technology giants, retail centers and stores, large commercial and private banks, and real estate companies. Rutgers, the State University of New Jersey, is centered in neighboring New Brunswick, and the thousands of students, faculty, and staff make for a very large and inviting target audience. Many of the companies and organizations take advantage of the park's luxury suites and picnic areas for their company and group outings, partnering with the Patriots for the entertainment of both their employees and their clients. The location of the ballpark in Bridgewater lends itself to easy access for after-work activities.

As long as the Patriots maintain their standards, there is no reason to believe that they cannot be successful for years to come. Truth is, aside from the movies, there really is not much competition for the family entertainment dollar in Somerset County and its close environs. The beaches and the boardwalks are miles away, as are New York City and Philadelphia, with all that those cities have to offer. The Great Adventure Amusement Park in Jackson and the State Aquarium in Camden are also lengthy drives on congested roads if driven during peak hours. Even the Atlantic League—professional baseball that is unaffiliated with a major-league franchise—has caught on and captured the fans' imagination. "The fans really don't care," explained Kalafer. "The only affiliation that means anything is the New York Yankees. When I looked at the Trenton Thunder when they were affiliated with the Boston Red Sox, and I polled their fans, 85 percent of the fans didn't know that they were affiliated with anybody, let alone the Red Sox. People who went to five games or less could not name three players. What I really found in my research is that they love the affordable family entertainment aspect, they love seeing their neighbors at the ballpark and they love all the between-innings activities. This is why people come to the ballpark, not because they're affiliated with somebody."

The velvet-toned voice of the public-address announcer and local television veteran Paul Spyhalla welcomes the fans to the game and announced the starting lineups. Mascots Sparkee and General Admission, the patriot soldier in full colonial uniform, entertain the fans behind home plate and between the dugouts. A young student from a local middle school performs the national anthem. Sparky Lyle takes his usual place at the corner of the dugout and looks out at another impressive crowd. The Patriots take the field, and the fans settle in for another night of baseball along Interstate 287 in Bridgewater. If only the other teams in the Atlantic League could achieve this perfect blend of success both on and off the field. In the upcoming chapters, we will take a look at the unique challenges faced by other New Jersey Atlantic League teams. Unlike the Patriots, who fit seamlessly into the fabric of Somerset County suburbia, these other teams each have had their own unique identity challenges. In the case of the Newark Bears, the subject of the next chapter, reconciling the nostalgia of Newark's baseball days gone by with current-day demographics is the ball club's primary challenge.

7

Newark and the Bears

Combining the Past and the Present

The present was not living up to the past. After an absence of fifty years, the Bears returned to the city of Newark in 1999 amid great fanfare and expectations. It did not matter that it was no longer the 1940s, that venerable, old Ruppert Stadium was torn down in 1967, or that the Bears were an independent professional team instead of the Triple-A affiliate of the New York Yankees. None of this mattered to Bears owner Rick Cerone or to Newark and Essex County officials. The history of baseball in Newark made it appear only logical to them that "if we build it, they will come"—meaning fans, by the thousands. Tales of the old Newark Bears, the Yankees farm club from 1932 through 1950,

Bears and Eagles Riverfront Stadium, Newark. Photograph by Bob Golon, 2005.

became bigger than life over the years, as did the expectations for the successful return of their new namesake. In 2003, it became obvious that there must have been some kind of miscalculation. The politicians came through, even though they had a tough time finding a suitable site for the new ballpark. Besides having its own population of 275,000 (according to the 2000 census), Newark was surrounded by the heavily populated towns of Kearny, Elizabeth, Irvington, and East Orange. The demographics looked good. Or did they? In reality, what Cerone and Newark officials experienced was more in a series of predictable growing pains of a city and an area struggling to establish a new identity. These growing pains are evident everywhere in Newark as the past gives way to the present, and not just at the new Bears and Eagles Riverfront Stadium. Establishing a new identity often takes time. One simply has to travel through the area to see how Newark is seeking to reinvent itself by combining tangible investment and intangible hope in forging this new identity.

Traveling north on Broad Street after exiting Interstate 78 brings me feelings of nostalgia for Old Newark. These feelings are embodied in the buildings and landmarks that I pass. I move north from Lincoln Park, so named because Abraham Lincoln once made a speech at the South Park Presbyterian Church there. Newark Symphony Hall is on the right, a neoclassical auditorium that was originally built to be a Shriner's temple in the 1920s. Benny Goodman, Frank Sinatra, Judy Garland, and Mick Jagger all performed there when it was known as the Mosque Theater.[1] Farther down on the right is Newark City Hall, the magnificent stone structure that opened in 1908, currently encased in scaffolding as it undergoes a major renovation. The City Hall facelift is not the only big construction site in the area, as one block to the north, just beyond Lafayette Street, the imposing steel skeleton of a 700,000-square-foot indoor arena rises above the neighboring buildings. The 17,000-seat arena will become home to the New Jersey Devils National Hockey League team in late 2007 and will host other sporting and entertainment events. Beyond the arena site is the famous Four Corners Historic District, at the intersection of Broad and Market Streets. The Four Corners was the original business and retail crossroads of Newark. Prior to the 1967 race riots, an event that devastated the economy of the city, big department stores named Bamberger's, Hahnes, Orbach's, and S. Klein's dominated Broad Street from Market Street to Central Avenue. Shopping in downtown Newark was a "happening." The riots changed all of that, as both residents and visiting shoppers fled the center of Newark, leaving it to decades of decay that the city is still recovering from. The big retailers left, too. You can still see the "S. Klein on the Square" sign hanging from its old former storefront at Broad Street across from Military Park. Across from Klein's is a public plaza where the massive Public Service Electric and Gas Company bus and streetcar terminal once stood. After the terminal was demolished in 1981, a modern headquarters for the utility was built on the land behind it as part of the Gateway Center business district. This complex of office buildings was the first post-riot initiative designed to start the revitalization of Newark's economy. Farther north, the New Jersey Performing Arts Center sits where Broad Street and Park Place meet. Opened in 1997, NJPAC is the cultural center of Newark, hosting the New Jersey Symphony Orchestra, Broadway-style shows, and numerous concerts and entertainment events. Evidence of corporate commitment to Newark is everywhere as Prudential Insurance, Verizon, and IDT Telecommunications have major office buildings along Broad Street. At Washington Park, the Newark Public Library, Newark Museum, and Ballantine House provide a public connection to Newark's historical past. As I make my way to the northernmost section of Broad Street, a train station that used to serve the Erie-Lackawanna Railroad now functions as the Broad Street commuter station of New Jersey Transit's Morris and Essex and Boonton-Montclair lines. Across from the station is the abandoned Westinghouse manufacturing plant, where thousands of employees worked years ago when electronic products such as radios and televisions were manufactured in the United States. That plant, the "Westinghouse" sign still visible and hanging on it, represents the best and the worst of Newark today. It is evidence of a glorious past as well as being a present-day eyesore of abandonment and decay, but it also represents the future since it is only a matter of time before the building is razed and the property transformed as the northern Broad Street area is being redeveloped.

Dr. Clement Alexander Price, professor of urban history, public history, African-American studies, and New Jersey history at Rutgers University–Newark, has lived in Newark since 1968 and is the foremost expert on its history and culture. His documentary "The Once and Future Newark," which aired on New Jersey Public Television in late 2006, shows viewers not only a look at Newark's past but also the city's efforts to reinvent itself through capital projects like those envisioned for the northern Broad Street area.[2] "There are two major capital developments well planned for that area of Newark. The Newark Museum is going to create a new main entrance to the museum at the intersection of Washington and Central Avenues," explained Price. "There will be a grander and a more compelling entrance to the museum. The Newark Public Library has plans under way to build a major addition to the main building there on Washington Street. [O]ne would think that these projects would serve as economic generators for commercial development along Orange Street [where the Westinghouse building sits], along Broad Street, and perhaps creating a greater expanse of commercial [and] residential establishments along James Street and as far west as Martin Luther King Boulevard." Additionally, Rutgers–Newark announced in September 2006 that it would be relocating its business school to One Washington Park, a building on the corner of Broad, Washington, and Orange Streets that until recently housed offices for Verizon Communications. Additionally, the site of Rutgers' old business school at Fifteen Washington will be redeveloped for student housing as well as mixed-use options such as retail, market-rate housing, and parking.[3]

Price is optimistic about what the future holds culturally for the northern Broad Street area. "It is my sense that in another five or ten years, the northern end of Broad Street will be much busier, will be richer in respect to new buildings, and will also be very urbane in a sense that you will have an intersection of students, of upwardly mobile singles, and married couples, not to mention the middle-aged empty-nesters who will probably come to Newark," said Price. Diagonally across Broad Street from the old Westinghouse plant and the Broad Street station is another example of Newark's effort to redevelop the area: a baseball park, Bears and Eagles Riverfront Stadium, home of the Newark Bears of the Atlantic League.

The new ballpark's name was given to invoke memories of Newark's glorious baseball past when the original Bears and the Negro League Eagles dominated the city's sports scene in the 1930s and 1940s. Once inside, the park has all of the amenities of a modern professional park for independent and minor-league baseball clubs. Like the city of Newark itself, the modern-day Bears are trying to marry the past with the present and the future by appealing to a whole new generation of Newarkers while not forgetting Newark's baseball heritage.

In the exterior of the customer concourse of the park, in the area between home plate and first base, is the new Newark Baseball Hall of Fame Room, dedicated to Newark's baseball past and present, which is open to fans that attend ball games. When the park first opened in 1999, the room was used as a video arcade, where children who came to the games gathered when they became bored with baseball. John Brandt, a former general manager of the Camden Riversharks who took over as general manager of the Bears in 2006, and Mike Collazo, the Bears' corporate partnerships director, had other ideas for the arcade room. Out went the video games, and in came visual history. Collazo has been the driving force behind the campaign to make Newark's baseball history come alive. "We'd like to make this as formal and interactive [a] place as possible, like any museum or memorabilia kind of area," explained Collazo. "The support from the community has been immense. Increasingly, fans have been donating items that they have because they want to see this history preserved and see it in a place where they feel it should be displayed, which is our ballpark. They feel the connection that we have to that legacy. We don't even display all of the materials we've gotten in the very short time we've had the room." Despite his lack of a professional museum exhibition staff, Collazo intends eventually to display as many of the donated artifacts as possible.[4]

Inside the entrance to the history room, two large photographs hang on the right side wall. One is a team photo of a Newark Bears club, circa 1930s, in their pinstriped home uniforms, posing in front of the stands at Ruppert Stadium. The other is an action shot from the same time period, looking from behind home plate to straightaway center field. The large, manually operated scoreboard in the picture shows that the Bears are playing their International League rivals from Rochester on this day. Farther down is a display case that contains items dedicated to the memory of the Newark Eagles, in particular New Jersey natives Monte Irvin and Larry Doby, who both starred for the Eagles before moving on to Hall of Fame careers in the major leagues. Above this case is a framed photograph of Effa Manley, the pioneering co-owner of the Eagles, along with a story telling of her exploits that resulted in her being the first woman ever to be inducted into the National Baseball Hall of Fame in Cooperstown. Another display case contains more photographs and documents from the old Bears, as well as other pieces of memorabilia from Newark's baseball history. A photograph of Harrison Field, where the Federal League Newark Peppers played, is displayed, as well as pictures of ex-Bears and Yankees Yogi Berra, Charlie Keller, Tommy Henrich, and Joe Gordon.

As rich as the display of old Newark baseball history is, Collazo takes care to include the history of the new Bears in this setting as well.

A grandstand seat from the current ballpark is displayed, as well as a photo collage of the 2002 Bears, who won that season's Atlantic League championship. Ex-major-league sluggers Jose and Ozzie Canseco played for the Bears in 2000 and 2001, and a photograph of Ozzie surrounded by the Westfield, New Jersey, little-league team is prominently displayed. There is a special poster dedicated to Rickey Henderson, who played for the Bears in 2003 and 2004. Henderson, the all-time major-league leader in stolen bases, provided Newark fans with considerable excitement and professionalism during his stay with the Bears. Proclamations and gifts from politicians welcoming the club back to Newark in 1999, along with a front-page spread from the *Newark Star-Ledger* with a banner headline proclaiming "Welcome Back Bears," from their 1999 opening, round out the collection. The *Star-Ledger* spread is indicative of what drives this historical collection. Below the headline welcoming back the new Bears is a photograph of old Ruppert Stadium along with a memory-filled article by the legendary sportswriter and Newark native Jerry Izenberg. Even though there was a forty-eight-year gap between the old Bears and the new, the *Star-Ledger* united the two eras in print. "We, too, want to connect the old with the new," said Mike Collazo as we exited the Hall of Fame Room.

The current management of the Bears is not the first Bears management team to use Newark baseball history as a tool to try to attract fans. Their original owner and founder, Rick Cerone, also saw history as a primary motivational force in his effort to bring professional baseball back to Newark during the 1990s. A Newark native, Cerone grew up in the North Ward and starred on the Seton Hall University baseball team before embarking on a seventeen-year major-league career. Cerone's time in the majors is primarily remembered for the period he spent as a catcher with the New York Yankees. In 1980, Cerone appeared in 147 games as the first full-time replacement for the popular Yankees captain Thurman Munson, who was killed in an airplane crash the year before. Cerone, nicknamed "the Italian Stallion" by Yankee broadcaster Phil Rizzuto, possessed a fiery demeanor, notably demonstrated by a sharp and some say profane exchange between him and Yankees owner George Steinbrenner in the Yankees' clubhouse during the 1981 playoffs. True to his New Jersey roots, Cerone never backed away from a challenge, and this trait drove him forward when he left active playing after the 1992 season. Determined to stay in baseball, he became a part owner of the Wilmington (Delaware) Blue Rocks, a Single-A farm club of the Kansas City Royals.

Frank Boulton, the founder and principal owner of the Blue Rocks, had attempted to put a minor-league club in Long Island but was rejected by league executives because the necessary permission could not be obtained from the New York Mets, who controlled the Long Island territory. Undaunted, Boulton decided to pursue his own independent professional league, the Atlantic League, and he sought influential baseball names to help in his quest to place franchises in northeastern locations. He found a willing participant in Rick Cerone.

While growing up in the North Ward, Cerone constantly heard stories from his father, Aldo, about the old Bears and Eagles and the legendary Ruppert Stadium in the Ironbound section of Newark. These stories never left Rick Cerone, and out of this sense of nostalgia and history grew his desire to bring a Newark Bears club back by building a brand new ballpark in the city. He also saw firsthand how the new minor-league park in Wilmington became a resounding success, and he envisioned the same happening in his hometown.[5] This vision coincided with Newark's effort to revitalize its waterfront with projects like the New Jersey Performing Arts Center and the Gateway Center either already built or in progress. Professional sports would be another way of attracting visitors to the city, and mayor Sharpe James became supportive of the project. Short on business experience but nonetheless determined, Cerone lobbied long and hard, and finally convinced Mayor James and the Essex County Executive James Treffinger to have the Essex County Improvement Authority sell $22 million dollars in bonds to finance a new ballpark. Treffinger saw potential for the venture, since, in his view, if the presence of a ballpark improved surrounding real estate values by 20 percent, it would generate an additional $1.2 million yearly in tax revenues for Newark.[6]

The city chose Riverbank Park as the location for the new baseball park in April 1996. The Atlantic League set a goal of the 1997 season to begin play, so Cerone had to move fast to have the new ballpark ready in time. He embarked on an energetic public campaign to garner additional support for the project, but he soon met determined neighborhood opposition. Local residents did not want to lose their parkland, and they formed the Save the Park at Riverbank (SPARK) movement. The ten-acre park, located along the Passaic River, was one of only two public parks in the Ironbound neighborhood of 50,000 residents. SPARK was relentless in its opposition, and a combination of legal and environmental efforts delayed and finally stopped Cerone's effort to build at Riverbank

Park. A new site was found between McCarter Highway and the northern tip of Broad Street, and the city and county set out to acquire the land. The steep price of the land, plus higher construction costs, pushed the estimated bill for the ballpark up to $34 million, approximately 50 percent above the normal cost of $20 million that a minor-league facility typically cost. Cerone, who invested $2 million of his own money in the project, and the public officials who were staking their reputations on this project were taking a risk but moved forward. Observers doubted the wisdom of the plan because of the cost overruns. A *New York Times* writer, Ronald Smothers, in his July 4, 1999, article expressed doubt about building such a costly ballpark for an unproven team like the Bears. Also, he cited an area parking shortage (the current outdoor parking deck would not be built until 2005) that had the potential to cost fans six to seven dollars to park their cars, with some of the spaces being blocks from the ballpark. Yet, Mayor James told Smothers, "The cost overruns have been overblown and misinterpreted," and he insisted that "this investment in affordable, family entertainment will change the image of Newark forever." The plan proceeded, albeit with delays.

Similar delays in ballpark construction at other locations forced the Atlantic League to postpone its initial season until 1998, at which time the new parks in Atlantic City and Bridgeport, Connecticut, were ready to open. Cerone's Newark ballpark was not among those ready in time, and the newly minted Bears, under manager Tom O'Malley, played their entire 1998 home schedule at the Ballpark at Harbor Yard in Bridgeport in front of mostly empty seats. The Bears stumbled to a 35-65 record, the worst in the Atlantic League, and O'Malley cited the nomadic existence of the club as a reason for their dismal performance. Keith Thomas led the club in most offensive categories, batting .326 with 103 hits and 75 runs batted in while playing in eighty-nine of the club's one hundred games. Eight of those RBIs came in an August 16 game at Atlantic City, which is still a single-season club record. Tim Cain, who won forty-three games for the Bears from 1998 through the 2001 season, won ten of the club's thirty-five wins that initial season, but little else went well for the homeless Bears. The Bears looked forward to playing in their new home ballpark in 1999.

Bears and Eagles Riverfront Stadium, nicknamed "the Den," remained a construction site as the 1999 season opened, and Cerone was forced to relocate the Bears' first twenty-two home games to Skylands Park in Sussex County. Former Yankee Hensley "Bam Bam" Meulens joined Keith Thomas in the lineup, along with ex–Seton Hall player and Texas Ranger farmhand Ryan Gorecki. The Bears played the entire first half of the season at Skylands, winning twenty-four games against thirty-five losses. Finally, Bears and Eagles Riverfront Stadium, still unfinished and barely operational, opened for the long-awaited return of the Newark Bears, after the Bears had played the equivalent of 182 consecutive road games.

On July 16, 1999, an opening-night crowd of 6,101 saw the Bears play in their new white-and-violet home uniforms for the first time. Film clips of the old Bears and Eagles played on the video board in right field prior to the game. Cerone reached back to his Yankees connections and hosted ex-Bear and Yankee Yogi Berra, as well as Hillside resident Phil Rizzuto, both members of the Baseball Hall of Fame, to throw out the ceremonial first pitches. The Bears' opponent on this evening was the Lehigh Valley Black Diamonds, and the fans were treated to plenty of offense, with the game tied 8-8 after nine innings. In the bottom of the tenth inning, first baseman Doug Jennings hit a home run over the right-field wall to give Newark an extra-inning 9-8 win, sending the crowd home happy. Having a home of their own agreed with the Bears, and they finished third in the second half of the Atlantic League season, five games behind the first-place Somerset Patriots. Even though they failed to make the playoffs for the second straight year, better days seemed to be ahead, at least on the field, now that the Bears had their own home field. Cerone set out to build the type of roster that he felt would attract more fans to the park.

In the next three seasons, ex–major leaguers Ozzie and Jose Canseco, Rickey Henderson, Jose Lima, Jack Armstrong, Lance Johnson, Jim Leyritz, and Pete Incaviglia all wore the Newark Bears uniform. Bobby Hill, the second-round draft choice of the Chicago Cubs in 2000, decided to play the season with the Bears before eventually signing a Cubs contract, and he led the Bears in games played, stolen bases, and runs scored. The Bears improved their record to 74-66 in 2000, then followed it up by winning the Northern Division first-half title in 2001. This success qualified the Bears for the Atlantic League playoffs for the first time in their history. After sweeping the Nashua Pride, two games to none in the opening round of the playoffs, the Bears faced their closest New Jersey rivals, the Somerset Patriots, for the league title. The Bears won the first two games of the best of five series, but the Patriots came roaring back, winning the final three games of the series, including game five in Newark, to defeat the Bears and win the league championship. In 2002, the Bears, in their first season under new manager Marv Foley, rode the bat of first baseman Jimmy Hurst to another Atlantic League playoff appearance. This time, the Bears prevailed, defeating the Atlantic City Surf in the opening round, then sweeping the Bridgeport Bluefish in three games to win the championship.

Despite the team's success on the field, however, Cerone found the business of running the Newark Bears more troublesome and challenging than he ever imagined. In 2003, the Bears were not drawing as many fans to Riverfront Stadium as Cerone had hoped. The city of Newark and the Essex County Improvement Authority, which split the cost of building the stadium, forecast that an average of 4,000 fans per game was needed in order for the stadium to turn a profit and pay for itself. In 2000, the Bears averaged 3,200 fans per game. That number decreased to barely over 3,000 fans in 2003. On some midweek evenings, it was hard to count even 1,000 fans in the ballpark. Cerone felt that his time in Wilmington as a minor-league owner had prepared him properly for the business responsibilities of running a baseball franchise. He assumed that the storied history of the Bears and Eagles would drive attendance at the park, based on nostalgia. The truth was that even though baseball historians wax poetic about the old Bears and Eagles, there were not too many people still alive in Newark who actually remembered them playing there. Cerone then tried to go to the neighboring suburban communities to create interest in the club, but he had trouble developing a realistic marketing plan to do this. Some elements that he considered critical to the club's success in Newark, like nearby indoor parking facilities, a light-rail system running to the ballpark, and the widening of Route 21 all happened—but not until after he sold the club. The Bears were struggling, as was Cerone in making sense of it.

Cerone views his relative lack of success in drawing more fans to Bears games in Newark as a personal failure more than a business failure, and his efforts left him emotionally and physically drained. "I gave up many things, personally, to try to make this go well. I gave up a major-league broadcasting career that was progressing nicely because I felt I had to be at the park all of the time," recalled Cerone. He could often be seen leaning over the railing behind the stands down the first base line, talking to the fans who recognized him. "It was tough to be looking at 4,000 empty seats most of the time, and I took it personally." Yet, Cerone does not feel a total lack of accomplishment in bringing the Bears back to

Newark. "I was disappointed for Newark in the way we did. Regardless, we accomplished something great in Newark," Cerone explained. "We built a beautiful ballpark. There was nothing but dilapidated buildings in the area when we got there. There were hypodermic needles on the ground. We sought to change that." Cerone pointed to the positive feedback he received from fans who came from Essex and Morris Counties. "It changed the way they looked at coming to downtown Newark," said Cerone proudly. "We just needed more of that to happen."

Jim Cerny, the Bears' assistant general manager for operations and public relations director, is very careful not to criticize Cerone. "Rick got this built," exclaimed Cerny during a 2005 interview. "He did an amazing job as a politician to get this stadium built to bring baseball back to Newark. He had a fire and a passion to make this happen. And the easy part was the first couple of years, because so much goodwill had been generated, people came."[7] Along the way, Cerone engaged in some very public spats with Essex County over the raising of ticket prices and the county's failure to sell luxury box rentals to capacity, as well as its inability to find a sponsor for naming rights to the stadium. The franchise was staggering, but Atlantic League CEO Frank Boulton believed that Newark could be as strong as any team in the league. It was time for Cerone to take a step back and, as he told the *Star-Ledger* in January 2003, "let businesspeople run the business."

Cerone reached agreement with Steve Kalafer, the owner of the highly successful Flemington Car and Truck Country chain of automobile dealerships, to sell him controlling interest of the Bears in early 2003. Kalafer already owned the Somerset Patriots of the Atlantic League and had great success with them since entering the league in 1998. After a season of sharing ownership responsibility with Kalafer in 2003, Cerone sold his remaining portion of the club to Marc Berson, Millburn-based real estate developer and Newark native. After operating the Bears for three years, Kalafer stepped back and Berson became the majority owner of the Bears.

Berson came to the Bears with a strong reputation of involvement in projects that benefit overlooked urban areas. He was instrumental in the creation of the New Jersey Performing Arts Center in Newark and remains on the executive committee of that organization. Berson is also chairman of the board of trustees of the Newark Beth Israel Medical Center. His investment firm, the Fidelco Group, is actively engaged in the northern Broad Street revitalization effort, including the redevelopment of the One Washington Park building across from Bears and Eagles Riverfront Stadium. He has the connections and ties to Newark necessary to work within the city to make the Bears successful, but more effort is needed. Better ties to the community and neighborhoods must be created to gain the support of Newark's population for the Bears.

Clement Price favors an approach that would bring the Bears more in touch with Newark's community leaders. "Newark is a city that over the last fifty years became increasingly disjointed," stated Price. "Its civic culture was extremely compromised. The riots took its toll on the city with respect to neighborhoods and a sense of cohesiveness in the city. When you start something in Newark, you really must introduce yourself to the city through interaction with the clergy, educators, foundations, people who have long affiliations with the city, and also not-for-profits. The fact that the Newark Bears, up to now, have not created a community advisory council or community advisory board, or some organization that puts a human face, and a civic face, on the Bears organization and the Bears team—that really is problematic."

Connection with Newark's two predominant neighborhood constituencies is mandatory for the Bears to achieve success, those being the black and Spanish-speaking populations. The Bears lost some points with the black community a couple of years ago when a mural depicting the history of black baseball in Newark was abruptly taken down from where it hung above the playing field. That particular act affected some black leaders like Price the wrong way. "That was just the dumbest thing," said Price. "The current Bears should represent the longer history and memory of baseball across the color line in Newark." In fairness to the Bears, Price was unaware of Mike Collazo's new historical gallery being assembled in the ballpark. When informed of the gallery and the prominent place of the Eagles and Newark black baseball history in it, Price was genuinely pleased.

Attracting the Spanish-speaking community to Bears games might turn out to be more of a challenge, one that might be difficult for the Bears to address, since this local community does not have a tradition of watching baseball, favoring *futbol,* or soccer, as its sport of choice. Newark's Ironbound section is inhabited mainly by people of Portuguese, Brazilian, Central American, and Ecuadorian decent. No one knows the neighborhood's passion for soccer better than Kim DaCosta Holton, professor of Portuguese and Lusophone world studies at Rutgers–Newark. Ironbound's passion for soccer, according to DaCosta Holton, was particularly evident during last year's World Cup matches. "So much passion," said DaCosta Holton. "People just poured into the streets after the games, literally thousands of people. There was what is called *engarrafamentos*, or bottlenecks, where cars couldn't get through at times. That display of emotion and passion really gives a good sense of how important soccer is within that community. In the Ironbound, the Portuguese, Brazilians, and Ecuadorians were dressed in their national team shirts, even on the off days during the World Cup. It was, it seemed, like a nonstop soccer celebration and consumption during that time." Baseball has a strong presence in Spanish-speaking countries like Cuba, Puerto Rico, the Dominican Republic, and Mexico. These areas traditionally are not well represented in the Ironbound. With this in mind, can the Bears have hope of attracting Ironbound patrons to their games? DaCosta Holton said, "I don't think they're going to change the . . . sports consumption patterns of folks who are middle-aged, folks that are established in their affiliations. I think it's more the up-and-coming generation, the younger kids who, as the Portuguese community becomes wealthier, will have more opportunity to spend one to three nights a week at sports practices and at games. I think that is the generation that can really embrace baseball to a greater extent and become fans of the beautiful [ball]park that's just down the street."[8]

Both Price and DaCosta Holton agree that the Bears' future fan base must be cultivated by giving attention to today's youth population of Newark. Price sees the need for an increase of the baseball culture in Newark and urges the Bears' involvement in local little-league programs. "When you're driving through Newark," explained Price, "you don't see a lot of baseball being played. That certainly is the case in the main area of Newark, west of Route 21." Inviting local little-league and youth soccer clubs for a night at the ballpark is something the Bears aim to continue.

The Bears already promote youth activities in many ways. During the 2006 season, the Bears partnered with the Rutgers–Newark Scarlet Raiders baseball team to hold two free youth clinics at the ballpark, where up to two hundred children participated at each clinic in three-hour instructional sessions on the field. All participating youths received a free Bears game ticket, t-shirt, hot dog, and soda for their efforts. The ball club has also participated with Newark and other area schools in programs such as Scholarship Superstars, Rip'n Ruppert's Reading Program, and a "Swing for the Fences" writing program and rewards youth participants with free tickets for their academic achievements. Even though it will take years for these kids to become paying customers, the seeds are being planted now for the Bears' future fan base.

The one lasting major problem facing the Bears is the never-ending perception that the area around Bears and Eagles Riverfront Stadium is unsafe, particularly for a night game, and that the ballpark is difficult to get to and from. Nothing is further from the truth. The ballpark is easily accessible from either Interstate 280 or Route 21 (McCarter Highway). A multistory parking deck is located immediately outside of the right-field corner of the ballpark. The northern Broad Street area is filled with activity and development, including, in 2006, the opening of a trolley line connecting Newark's Pennsylvania Station with the Broad Street Station. For those who prefer public transportation to a game, the trolley stops right at the ballpark. The park is roomy, clean, and well appointed, with ballpark food and beverages and a picnic area for large gatherings. Spectators can enjoy close-up views of the Newark skyline and the William H. Stickel drawbridge as well as a vista of lower Manhattan from their seats inside the park, not to mention their proximity to the ball field. And, prior to the 2006 season, the Bears took steps to improve the quality of play so that the fans watching from the nearby seats would enjoy it even more.

John Brandt was brought in by Marc Berson to be the Bears new general manager in 2006 after he served successfully in that post with the Camden Riversharks. Under Brandt, the Riversharks had the best Atlantic League regular-season record from 2002 to 2005. A hard worker and good judge of baseball talent, Brandt immediately took steps to bring some of his Camden magic to Newark. He reached out to his longtime manager at Camden, Wayne Krenchicki, to come north and lead the Bears on the field starting in 2007. Concerning Krenchicki, Brandt told writer Mike Ashmore of the *Atlantic League Baseball News* in December 2006, "[W]e wanted someone who had previously managed, managed with success, and had independent player personnel experience. We feel very good with our selection." Brandt explained his player-procurement philosophy and also assured the Newark fans that his goal was to put a good team on the field. "Finding talent is a process," said Brandt. "Unfortunately, it doesn't happen in one year. We have a core of players in Newark now that I feel we can build around. In Camden, we had a great core that also happened to live in the local area, and that worked real well. In finding a team, you start with a budget. Within any budget, you can build a team, if you start with pitching and defense. We had that in Camden and will get there in Newark. Hours, we all work a lot of hours. Both Wayne and Jim Cerny will do a lot of this [player personnel work] this season as well."

Brandt brings to Newark years of experience in working with inner-city neighborhoods both in Camden and, previously, as part of the Bridgeport Bluefish staff. However, he realizes that the Bears need to do more to market to the outlying suburban areas of Newark, particularly the more affluent communities along the Morris and Essex New Jersey Transit rail line. Brandt recently told Ashmore, "We are trying to expand our NJ Transit marketing program for 2007 for that area. I would love to be able to offer and market route-specific programs, through station signage, seat drops, ticket offers for riders who attend our games, etc. We will get there. We have a good relationship with those towns [Summit, Chatham, and Madison] but we need those towns to consider a Bears game as an option for their entertainment dollar."[9]

In the coming years, Newark and the surrounding area will be providing the Bears with more professional sports neighbors to compete with for those entertainment dollars. Across the Passaic River in Harrison, a 25,000-seat outdoor soccer stadium for the Red Bull Club of New York (previously the New York–New Jersey Metrostars) is scheduled to open in 2009. The stadium will be part of the multimillion-dollar Harrison MetroCentre corporate and retail complex that is planned for the south side of the New Jersey Transit and Amtrak Northeast Corridor railroad tracks, very near to the site where the Newark Peppers played their only Federal League baseball season in 1915. There is conjecture that a soccer stadium cannot possibly help the Bears, as it will only draw potential fans from the Ironbound section away from them. However, an aggressive co-marketing campaign can benefit both clubs and potentially bring more out-of-towners into the area for sports, business, dining, and entertainment.

In October 2007, the Prudential Center arena is scheduled to open, primarily as the home of the New Jersey Devils hockey club. The arena will also be home to the Seton Hall University basketball team as well as a new professional indoor soccer team. Dr. Price is optimistic about the arena's impact in Newark, as long as it is positioned properly. "The better-run arenas in the country, the arenas that create a clientele beyond hockey and, for that matter, basketball, are arenas that become sports emporia as well as entertainment emporia that [have] nothing to do with sports," explained Price. "The Prudential Center should in part be an [emporium] for hockey but should also be for big-ticket rock shows, pop entertainment, as well as a convention center. There has been more talk than planning that the arena might create more of a need for hotel space in the central business district." If the talk becomes action, downtown Newark will become more of an attraction for out-of-towners, and if they market themselves properly, the Bears can also become a part of the new Newark cultural scene.

Establishing their name in front of the business power brokers in Newark continues to be a challenge for the Bears. An example of this is the Newark Regional Business Partnership, an organization of influential Newark business and cultural leaders dedicated to bringing the city back to prominence. On April 18, 2007, the NRBP held a breakfast meeting and presentation at the National Newark building on Broad Street, attended by more than one hundred influential Newarkers. The topic of the day was "Marketing Newark as a Destination," with a focus on the marketing initiatives and projects designed to bring tourist dollars into the city, particularly in the sports and entertainment areas. During the meeting, Nick Sakiewicz, the president of AEG NY-NJ, which is building the Prudential Center and the Red Bulls soccer stadium, talked about a "three-part sports and entertainment triangle" in Newark consisting of the arena, the soccer stadium, and NJPAC. He did not include Bears and Eagles Riverfront Stadium in that context. Dan Biederman, the president of BRV Corporation and founder of entities in New York City such as the 34th Street Partnership, talked of his plans for improving the streetscape of downtown Newark in the Prudential Arena area by designing new signage and sidewalk landscaping. Unfortunately, the current plans did not reach up to the northern Broad Street area of the ballpark. When questioned about it after the meeting, one Bears official expressed frustration to me. "This is typical," he said. "We constantly have to fight for our fair share of recognition." The Bears actively promote themselves in publications such as *GoNewark*, a business community newspaper that highlights entertainment and sports attractions in the area. They reached out to the Newark Regional Business Partnership to celebrate the opening evening of the 2007 baseball season by offering special discounts on tickets to partnership members. Half-price tickets that are already inexpensive shouldn't be necessary to attract people like the NRBP members, who are touting the gourmet dining in the luxury suites of the new arena and million-dollar condominiums across from NJPAC. A consistently packed Bears and Eagles Riverfront Stadium would help the NRBP further market Newark as a destination city and would certainly be worth their small investment to do this.

Patience for this organization is key. Frank Boulton, CEO of the Atlantic League, is committed to Newark. "I think as Newark continues to improve, so will the Bears," said Boulton. "Is it slower than we probably want and [than] the ownership would probably want? Yes. But, Newark can be as strong as any team in our league. I have always been sure that Newark can get the corporate support. I think that they (the owner and staff) work very hard at trying to capture that Essex County group of people that work in Newark or work in Manhattan and come through Newark." Price is also bullish on the future of Newark. When asked to compare Newark with other cities in New Jersey undergoing similar redevelopment, Price counts only New Brunswick as being ahead of Newark. "Newark is a city that has assets that others can only dream of. The fact of the matter is that although this town had a long period of decline, it never lost its stature as New Jersey's largest city, as New Jersey's most energetic city, as the city that had a corporate infrastructure and a higher educational infrastructure and a not-for-profit infrastructure that [were] almost duty bound to help stabilize the city and to ultimately grow the city, which is what you're seeing now." Professor Kim DaCosta Holton also takes a positive view of what is transpiring in the city. "For a while, Newark was losing, having a negative population outflow. That trend has been stabilized, and it looks like it's going the other way now. The fact that there is a new mayor [Cory Booker] with new ideas promises change. I'm hoping for an economic upturn for the city of Newark, and [there are] some positive indicators that this is on the way."

The Bears prepared to open the 2007 season, their tenth as one of the original members of the Atlantic League, hoping to become a model of success in urban redevelopment initiatives. As Clement Price said, the city has a strong foundation to build on, both from an economic and historical basis. The Bears and other entertainment venues in Newark will prosper once Newark regains an identity of being a safe and vibrant city for people to spend time in.

The Bears are not the only baseball club trying to build new business in urban redevelopment areas in New Jersey, and the Bears' task might eventually be easier than that of their two urban counterparts, the Atlantic City Surf and the Camden Riversharks. The Surf are struggling for an identity in their own right as they seek to capitalize on and form a synergy with the casino industry by tapping into the tourist dollars that come into Atlantic City daily. But no team has faced bigger challenges to succeed than the Camden Riversharks. By the early 1990s, the city of Camden suffered from rampant poverty, decaying streets, and a high crime rate as the result of both businesses and longtime residents fleeing the city. Camden had to start from virtually nothing to create an environment appealing enough to attract people from its surrounding suburbs back to the city. Fortunately, a waterfront area existed in Camden that needed redevelopment. Public agencies and politicians shared a vision of a new waterfront tourism industry, along with some high-risk-taking individuals like Steve Shilling who were willing to open their own wallets to see it happen.

Discovering Camden
with the Riversharks

One Wednesday evening, I sat amidst a crowd of approximately 3,500 fans at Campbell's Field in Camden—an impressive number considering that across the river, the Philadelphia Phillies were also playing at home on this evening. The luxury suites on the second level of the ballpark were all occupied, showing corporate and group support for the Riversharks. From my seat on the first-base side of the park, I viewed what is probably the most important aspect of what the Riversharks have brought to Camden: the community itself coming together. Directly in front of me was an African-American father, who appeared to be in his seventies, and his middle-aged son, enjoying the game and discussing its every aspect. Families with children were evident all

The Campbell's Kids greet fans at the entrance to Campbell's Field, Camden.
Photograph by Bob Golon, 2005.

throughout the ballpark. To my left sat an interracial group of ten teen-agers who were talking, giggling, eating hot dogs and ice cream, drinking sodas, and enjoying their night out together at the ballgame, even though the game was not their primary focus. When you're sitting alone in the stands as I was that evening, you get to do a lot of people watching. In this particular case, I was thoroughly taken by watching this array of people united for a summer evening in this spectacular ballpark. This is what developer Steve Shilling had in mind when he invested a personal for-tune and brought professional baseball to Camden. Although the city is undergoing redevelopment similar to what's happening in Newark, this south Jersey ball club draws more fans than the Bears. The people who fled Camden for the nearby suburbs have come back to support the Riversharks, joining their inner-city neighbors on nights such as these. Suburban Camden embraces the Riversharks more than suburban Newark does the Bears. Why? Perhaps it is the lure of the many water-front activities that have been created in Camden since redevelopment began in that area. Perhaps the serenity of the river gives a feeling of safety to those who go there, as opposed to downtown Camden just a few blocks away. The city is one of contrasts. Yet, there is evidence that the diverse populations of people, business and educational organizations, and government agencies are willing to cooperate and invest big money to bring Camden back to its former glory. The waterfront redevelopment and the ballpark at the foot of the Ben Franklin Bridge is evidence of such efforts.

Like any riverfront city, Camden had its roots in manufacturing and commerce. It originally was a ferry hub for travel to Philadelphia, and goods grown on the nearby New Jersey farms were shipped to Philadel-phia from Camden's ports. The creation of the Camden and Amboy Rail-road in 1834 connected Camden to the newly developing shore resort of Atlantic City, with connections up the New Jersey coast to Newark and New York City. The railroad caused the first major boom in population in the city, and heavy industry spurred the second. The greatest period of growth for Camden's population occurred between 1870 and 1920, when it rose from 20,000 to 116,000 residents. This growth was due to new immigrants—primarily Poles, Jews, and Italians—moving to the area to take advantage of the new industrial job opportunities being created in Camden's factories.[1]

Years ago, on the southern end of Cooper Street, sat the Richard Easterbrook steel writing-pen factory. At its height, the Easterbrook factory employed more than 450 people and produced 600,000 pens per day.[2] The New York Shipbuilding Company opened in Camden in 1900. The company was so named because it was originally intended to be located in Staten Island, but the land needed for it could not be secured there. Instead, its founder, Henry G. Morse, decided to locate in Camden for its suitable land, rail facilities, and the availability of experienced shipbuilding labor. More than five hundred ships were built there, mostly for the United States Government, including the nuclear ship *Savannah* and the aircraft carrier *Kitty Hawk*. During the peak of its production during World War II, the shipyard employed 35,000 Camden area residents.[3] At the same time that Morse's firm was establishing itself, an engineer named Eldridge R. Johnson opened the Victor Talking Machine Company in 1901 in Camden, seeking to improve upon Thomas Edison's cylinder sound recordings by advancing recorded disc technology. The modern recording industry was thus born in Camden. Johnson's company became known for its famous "His Master's Voice" logo. The logo consisted of a dog named Nipper listening to sound coming from the horn of an Edison gramophone. Johnson purchased the rights to the logo from the Britain-based Gramophone Company in 1901, and it has adorned the tower of the Victor factory on Market Street since 1909. Major artists, including Enrico Caruso, recorded their music at the Camden factory complex. In 1929, Johnson sold the company to the Radio Corporation of America where, as RCA Victor, it flourished for many years as one of the leading employers in the Camden area into the 1980s.[4] The company can be compared to one of today's Internet startup firms, as the idea of portable recorded music was revolutionary for its time. As famous as the RCA Victor product line would become, however, the consumer good manufactured in Camden that found its way into most American homes was as simple as a can of condensed soup.

In 1869, fruit merchant Joseph Campbell and icebox manufacturer Abraham Anderson partnered to produce canned beefsteak tomatoes. By 1900, the company had figured out how to produce a condensed soup, increased the product line to twenty one varieties, packaged them in distinctive, bright red-and-white cans, and the Campbell's Soup Company became one of Camden's most visible and prolific manufacturers. For most of the twentieth century, the company's water towers in the shape of Campbell's soup cans were a landmark on the city's waterfront. To its credit, the Campbell's Soup Company did not totally abandon Camden later in the twentieth century, when most others did.

After World War II, Camden underwent the same type of demographic shift that affected the larger cities in America. Returning servicemen, now armed with low-interest GI mortgage loans, were taking advantage of new, affordable suburban housing and moving away from the city. New roads were built to accommodate this shift, and the automobile became the primary source of transportation. Local railroads, like the Camden and Amboy line, suffered. The big retailers followed their newly upwardly mobile customers to the suburbs by relocating to sprawling new shopping malls located outside of the city. Finally, industry followed their traditional employee base to suburbia—where land was available along the new highways to build modern, updated factories—instead of rebuilding their older ones in the city. As the middle class moved out of Camden, minorities replaced them, typically at much lower income levels than their predecessors. The remaining stores closed and businesses moved out. Jobs became scarce. The waterfront decayed. Suburban flight turned into economic blight, and no city in America suffered more than Camden.[5]

RCA moved some of its manufacturing to Camden's outskirts. New York Shipbuilding closed down in the mid-1960s. Even Campbell's was slowly reducing its manufacturing capacity in Camden, even though it kept its corporate headquarters there. Camden's population shrunk from 125,000 in the 1950s to less than 80,000. Racial tensions increased, and in 1971, three days of rioting tore apart whatever remained of the city's soul. Camden became known for unemployment, drugs, AIDS, and one of the highest violent crime rates in the country. Fortunately, for Camden, public officials and the remaining business interests were paying attention to waterfront revitalization projects going on successfully in other cities, including those in Baltimore and across the river in Philadelphia.

In 1984, the Cooper's Ferry Development Association (CFDA) was created by city and state leaders—in partnership with Campbell's, RCA, and other private companies—to organize the redevelopment of the Camden waterfront. The CFDA joined forces with the Delaware River Port Authority (DRPA) of Pennsylvania and New Jersey in this endeavor. The DRPA owns the four major bridge crossings into Philadelphia, and improvements to the waterfront would create additional traffic and revenue for them. To this end, the Port Authority provided more than $200 million of funding for waterfront projects. The New Jersey State Aquarium opened in 1992, followed by the Children's Garden horticultural center. The Tweeter Center, formerly known as the E-Center, an open-air 25,000-

seat theater and concert venue, opened in 1995 and has attracted large audiences from both sides of the river. The battleship *New Jersey* took up permanent residence as a museum on the Camden waterfront in 2001. Finally, north of all these attractions, at the foot of the Ben Franklin Bridge, the redevelopment agencies, along with a visionary local real estate developer, were making plans to bring professional baseball to the city of Camden.[6]

In 1990, the Campbell's Soup Company closed its remaining production facility on the Camden waterfront, putting approximately 900 employees out of work. The buildings were imploded in spectacular fashion and the land cleared. Campbell's then sold the twenty-six-acre site to the Delaware River Port Authority for $5.2 million in 1998. Bordered by Delaware Avenue, Federal Street, the eastern abutment of the Ben Franklin Bridge, and the Delaware River, the site immediately became a prime target for a waterfront redevelopment project, catching the interest of Camden area developer Steven R. Shilling. A native of Freehold, New Jersey, and 1980 graduate of Susquehanna University in Pennsylvania, Shilling worked in the banking industry before joining the Quaker Group in 1986. Shilling quickly rose to the rank of president and CEO of the construction, real estate, and mortgage company, as well as becoming its primary investor. He formed another company, Camden Baseball LLC, and set about the task of bringing baseball to Camden.

His first approach was toward the local major-league club, the Philadelphia Phillies. Shilling envisioned the Phillies setting up a local affiliate across the Delaware River and sought their help in building the ballpark. The Phillies had other priorities, however. Their home stadium, Veterans Stadium, was quickly becoming obsolete and the object of criticism from fans and players alike. The Phillies were determined to get a new ballpark of their own built in Philadelphia, and chose to concentrate their efforts on their park rather than in a minor-league park. Knowing that he would have difficulty getting the Phillies' permission to put another organization's affiliated minor-league club so close to Philadelphia, Shilling realized that he had to go in a different direction if his hopes for a ballpark in Camden were to become a reality. Fortunately, this was a period of growth for independent professional baseball, particularly the Atlantic League, and league CEO Frank Boulton recognized the opportunity in Camden along with Shilling. "He [Shilling] is a bright guy, a good listener and a great businessman," Boulton told the Camden *Courier Post* in 2001. "He's been a good student of the sport and has learned a lot by carefully watching baseball projects other than his own."[7] Duly impressed by Shilling, Boulton offered Camden Baseball LLC an Atlantic League franchise for $550,000. With the promise of a club, Shilling was now free to navigate his way around the agencies and local entities whose involvement was necessary to create what became a private-public partnership in the building of the ballpark. He found one such entity willing to assist just a few blocks away from the ballpark site: Rutgers University.

Rutgers–Camden was established in 1950 when the College of South Jersey merged with the South Jersey Law School. As it prepared to celebrate its fiftieth anniversary in 2000, it had grown to a twenty-five-acre campus with 5,300 students and 700 employees, including 235 educators. "Years ago, Rutgers–Camden had a fortress mentality," community activist Frank Fulbrook told the *Philadelphia Inquirer* in 2000. "Today, the campus has adopted an integrated approach to its neighborhood. It's vital to our revitalization strategy. We're working together on a lot of initiatives."[8] In 1990, the university established the Center for Strategic Urban Community Leadership program. The mission of the program is to "foster the understanding of the importance of providing new organizational environments and strategies while building partnerships between urban communities and academia to improve race relations and spur urban development."[9] The program has raised more than $20 million in grant assistance, $2 million of which was used as part of the deal to build a baseball stadium in Camden.

The Rutgers–Camden Scarlet Raptors NCAA Division III baseball team spent years roaming the surrounding area looking for suitable fields to play its home games, playing in Cinnaminson, West Deptford, and South Camden. It wanted to upgrade its program to a facility of its own in Camden in order to attract more and better student-athletes to its program. The proposed ballpark provided the school an excellent opportunity to do this. In keeping with their spirit of community involvement, Rutgers–Camden pledged $2 million in community-development grant money to build the Rutgers–Camden Community Park along Linden and Delaware Avenues, one block away from the proposed stadium site. The park is a combination of tennis courts, soccer fields, and softball fields not only for use by Rutgers–Camden athletic teams but for neighborhood use as well. In return for its investment in the community, Rutgers–Camden was given the title of ownership to the new baseball park once it was built, and the university would then lease it back to Shilling's Atlantic League club, as well as using it as the home for the Scarlet Raptors baseball club. The pieces were falling into place for the private-public partnership.

By late 1999, the Cooper's Ferry Development Association took control of the land from the Port Authority for the ballpark project and, along with Steve Shilling, put in place the financing plans for the new park. Camden Baseball LLC took the lead in building the park for an estimated $20.5 million, on a $9 million line of credit from Sovereign Bank, a $6.5 million low-interest loan from the Delaware River Port Authority, $2 million from the New Jersey Economic Development Authority, plus the involvement of Rutgers. Because the park would be owned by Rutgers and thus exempt from property tax, Shilling agreed to charge a fifty-cent surcharge on each ticket sold, giving the revenue from the added charge to the city of Camden. On a good year, that could provide anywhere from $150,000 to $200,000 of revenue for the city, depending on ticket sales. The park was also expected to generate $360,000 in sales tax revenue per year, and one-half of that amount would also go to Camden because the ballpark area is in an urban enterprise development zone. The complicated arrangement to get the ballpark built demonstrated the commitment of all the parties involved to the revitalization of the waterfront. Steve Shilling's willingness to dip into his own personal checkbook was also a driving force behind the project. With all the details in place, it was time to actually build the ballpark—and complete it in time for the 2001 season.

The design for the park indicated that this would potentially be the largest physical plant, by far, of any park in New Jersey. Besides the 6,450 seats, the plans called for twenty luxury boxes, four hundred exclusive "club" seats in the upper level, and a sixty-seat "super suite" that would rent for $1,200 a night. A planned café with bar and wait service and two other private meeting suites were also included in the second-level design. The fan concourse on the main level would be exceedingly wide, allowing patrons the maximum comfort when walking to and from their seats. A picnic area stretched down the left-field line, and a children's play zone resided in the right-field corner. Of course, the biggest feature of the park, the view beyond the outfield fences, could not be duplicated anywhere. The span of the Ben Franklin Bridge loomed large and imposing outside of the right- and centerfield areas, and a clear view of the Philadelphia skyline could be seen by those sitting on the first-base line by looking beyond the left-field stands. One more financial piece was necessary to complete the complex arrangement for building this baseball park, and an old friend and neighbor came forward to provide the corporate financing and support necessary to assist Shilling in his efforts to bring baseball to the city.

Even though Campbell's kept its corporate headquarters and 1,200 employees in Camden, the last view of its logo on the Camden waterfront was when the large water towers were carted off on flatbed trucks after the 1991 implosions of its old manufacturing plants. The company continued to support the Camden community, however, and announced in late 2000 that it was paying in the vicinity of $3.5 million dollars for the naming and sponsorship rights for the ballpark, to be known as Campbell's Field. A large, illuminated Campbell's Soup logo would again be visible to Philadelphians from atop the Campbell's Field structure. The two Campbell's Kids characters, a staple in Campbell's advertising, would be in evidence both outside and inside the ballpark. The slogan "M'm! M'm! Good!" would flash on the scoreboard for every home-team home run. Campbell's president for North America, F. Martin Thrasher, told the *Philadelphia Inquirer* in early 2001, "Our Campbell's brand is an icon on Main Street, U.S.A., and I can't think of a sport that has more Main Street appeal than baseball. This is a terrific opportunity to associate Campbell's with a fun and very affordable family attraction in our hometown."[10]

The new team held a contest among Camden's school students to name the club, and in July 2000, it announced that the name Riversharks was chosen by more than 5,000 area kids, each of whom was given a free ticket to a Riversharks game. The name reflected the club's home on the river as well as the presence of the state aquarium on the waterfront. The Riversharks also pledged $10,000 worth of athletic equipment to the neighborhood school with the greatest participation in the naming contest. With a new mascot named Finley, the stadium steelwork rising along the river, and a new team name, final preparations were made for the 2001 season. It then remained to be seen if the skeptics who doubted the club's ability to be financially successfully would be proved wrong.

By opening day, the Riversharks had sold half of the four hundred club-level seats for the season, as well as thirteen of the twenty luxury suites, at $33,000 each. Advance ticket sales were close to 100,000. More than 120 jobs at the ballpark were filled by Camden residents. On May 11, 2001, the team played its first home game at Campbell's Field in front of an overflow crowd of 7,192 fans, and manager Wayne Krenchicki's club did not disappoint them. It defeated Lehigh Valley, 9–5, on a fifth-inning home run by first baseman Dan Held. Ex-Phillies infielder Kim Batiste was in the Riversharks' lineup, and he received the loudest ovation from the fans during the pregame introductions. On the field, the club had a difficult season, winning only forty-nine games while losing seventy-seven and failing to qualify for the Atlantic League playoffs. It didn't seem to matter to the local fans, however. The Riversharks played before 280,000 fans in 2001, and that number was kept somewhat lower than what it would have been if the September 11 attacks had not caused cancellations and otherwise suppressed the late-season attendance. The team turned things around in 2002, winning its way to the Atlantic League's best regular-season record with seventy-one wins versus only fifty-four losses. Even though it lost in the first round of the playoffs to the Bridgeport Bluefish, the club's success was not lost on Camden as more than 313,000 fans paid their way into Campbell's Field, the third-best attendance in the Atlantic League. Krenchicki was named the 2002 Atlantic League Manager of the Year and general manager John Brandt the 2002 League Executive of the Year. Pitcher Lincoln Mikkelsen, by winning sixteen games against only six losses, won the Atlantic League's Pitcher of the Year award.

It would be a nice story if the chapter ended on this note, with Steve Shilling, the Riversharks, and Camden all prospering from the presence of the team and Campbell's Field under nothing but sunshine and blue skies. But, this is hard-luck Camden, where nothing since the 1960s has come easy. Tragedy struck the Riversharks in 2003, revealing financial shortcomings of Camden Baseball LLC that challenged the continued existence of the club.

During the last days of the 2002 season, team owner Steve Shilling was diagnosed with an aggressive form of brain cancer. The forty-four-year-old Shilling, an avid golfer and marathoner, succumbed to the cancer nine months later, just one week after the opening of the 2003 season. He left the financial running of the club to the trustees of his estate, while the day-to-day operation of the team fell to general manager John Brandt. Despite the loss of Shilling, Brandt and the Riversharks persevered in 2003, again drawing 300,000 fans to Campbell's Field. Brandt was able to stay focused on running the club, despite the financial problems that were beginning to engulf it. "I'm just blessed to have him in charge of the team," Shilling's widow Doria told the *Camden Courier-Post* in December 2003. "With John in charge I never have to worry about what's going on with the team. He's such a hard worker and has done such a great job building it that I know I can leave him alone and he will continue doing what's right for the Riversharks." A Connecticut native and former baseball player for Yale, Brandt had previous experience selling professional baseball to inner-city areas. After spending some time as assistant general manager of the major-league-affiliated New Haven Ravens of the Eastern League, Brandt became the assistant GM of the Atlantic League's new Bridgeport Bluefish in 1998 and helped launch the Bluefish at their new home at Harbor Yards on the Bridgeport waterfront. "The city of Bridgeport, although similar [to Camden], is also very dissimilar," Brandt explained at Campbell's Field in 2005. "Bridgeport had residential areas that people would move into. Camden did not have that, but it will get to that point. In Bridgeport, we'd be on the news every night and on the sports front page every day. The buzz is very different here. There are so many people in this area, this is not your normal minor-league market." Brandt looks to coexist not only with the Philadelphia professional clubs but with the Camden waterfront attractions as well. "We're not going to be on the front page of the *Philadelphia Inquirer* or *Daily News* sports page, but the *Courier-Post* does a great job for us, the local southern New Jersey newspaper," said Brandt. "There's a balance that we've had to mix in here with, with Philadelphia's museums and exhibits, the New Jersey State Aquarium, and the battleship *New Jersey*. There is a lot here for people to do. The benefit is that the waterfront has given us a chance to attract people to Camden. Hopefully, once they come here, they will come back a number of times."[11]

The Riversharks' performance on the field in 2003 was an inspiration to their fans. Riding the .331 batting average of Brad Strauss and fifteen wins by pitcher Ben Simon, the Riversharks finished thirty games over .500, with a 78-48 regular-season record. Again, they were defeated in the first round of the Atlantic League playoffs, this time by the eventual league champion Somerset Patriots. It appeared that the Riversharks had weathered the storm of their owner's death in good fashion. That optimism was short-lived, however.

On February 19, 2004, Sovereign Bank announced that the club had defaulted on its $9 million loan. This was followed by the shocking announcement from John Brandt that the club had broken even the previous three years only because of the deep pockets of Shilling, who wrote million-dollar checks out of his personal funds each of those three years to help pay down the debt of Camden Baseball LLC.[12] "Steve cared so much for this project, and he didn't want to see it fail," Brandt told the *Courier-Post*. "We've been very successful in terms of ticket sales, fans and advertising. But our operating costs are so much higher than [they are for] similar teams, it is impossible for us to break even cash-wise." In retrospect, the reasons for the financial problems were obvious. Shilling took on an enormous amount of debt in the creation of the ballpark. Only the $2 million in grants from Rutgers did not have to be paid back. The remaining $19 million was all debt as the result of the various loans. Rumors were rampant that the Camden Riversharks were about to fold, leaving Campbell's Field empty.

The administration of governor James McGreevey became involved in working with all of the agencies that were owed money to assist in restructuring the debt. This enabled Camden Baseball LLC to survive in the short term. Additional help was needed, as the Shilling estate could not legally write the checks that Steve Shilling himself had. With the team a losing proposition for it, the estate sought to sell the club in February 2004, when most clubs were already in the serious planning stages for the upcoming season. This news caught league CEO Frank Boulton completely by surprise. "I was actually on vacation with my family and I got a call that they decided to sell the team," explained Boulton. "Well, you don't sell a baseball team in February. You're a little too close to rolling out the bats and balls." In early March, rumors again circulated throughout the Atlantic League that the Riversharks might forfeit the entire 2004 season if they could not afford to begin signing players. Again, the club found itself in dire straits, wondering who and what would save the season.

Since the inception of the Atlantic League, Boulton had surrounded himself with owners who cared as much about the league as they did their own teams. A trio of such owners, including Boulton himself, jumped in and saved the Riversharks before the bank foreclosed on the Campbell's Field mortgage. Somerset Patriots owner Steve Kalafer and Peter Kirk, who owned affiliated minor-league clubs in Maryland as well as a planned Atlantic League club in Lancaster, Pennsylvania, joined with Boulton and purchased the team from the Shilling estate in late March 2004. John Brandt could now pursue ballplayers and otherwise go about his business of operating a baseball team.

The 2004 Riversharks took up where the 2003 club left off, playing well under manager Wayne Krenchicki while leading the Atlantic League in regular-season victories (seventy six) for the third season in a row. The team was led by thirty-seven-year-old Lincoln Mikkelsen, a right-handed pitcher who won twelve games versus only four losses during the regular season, and by catcher Chris Widger, a native of Pennsville, New Jersey. Drafted in the third round by the Seattle Mariners in 1992, Widger, a 1989 graduate of Pennsville High School, reached the major leagues with the Mariners in 1995. He also played for the Montreal Expos, New York Yankees, and the St. Louis Cardinals but was released by the Cardinals in June 2003 when he refused a trade to the New York Mets. Widger took the remainder of the 2003 off and returned to Pennsville. Still feeling the urge to play baseball, he called Brandt about playing for the Riversharks as a way to restart his baseball career. He joined the club in late June, and helped lead it to the postseason for the third season in a row, contributing as a catcher and designated hitter. His time with the Riversharks was well spent. A couple of days before Christmas 2004, Widger signed a contract with the Chicago White Sox and became their backup catcher for the 2005 season. This rags-to-riches story concluded with Widger running out of the dugout to congratulate his teammates as the White Sox won their first World Series since 1917.

For the first time in team history, the Riversharks won a playoff series in 2004 by sweeping the Atlantic City Surf in the first round. The biggest offensive contributor for Camden in the two-game series was the usually light-hitting shortstop Tony Rodriguez. Batting ninth in the order, Rodriguez had six hits in eight at-bats, including a home run and six runs batted in.[13] The Riversharks' luck ran out in their first Atlantic League Championship Series appearance as they were swept by the Long Island Ducks, three games to none. A crowd of 5,458 came out to see game three at Campbell's Field, but it went home disappointed after ex–New York Mets pitcher Bill Pulsipher settled down to shut down the Riversharks after giving up three runs in the first inning, enabling Long Island to come from behind to win the game. Camden's biggest win of all, however, was announced on October 15, three weeks after the team lost the championship series.

Frank Boulton, Peter Kirk, and Steve Kalafer announced that the team was placed on firm financial footing, due to the restructuring of the debt service with Sovereign Bank, the Cooper's Ferry Development Association and the Delaware River Port Authority. Kirk told the *Camden Courier-Post* that the triumvirate of experienced baseball owners lent an overwhelming expertise to the running of the franchise. "It [the Riversharks] had a much larger staff doing things than a typical ball club would have. The three owners have operated a dozen ball clubs. We were able to organize in a way that was most beneficial."

"I would have been crushed, following Steve's death, if this thing was not able to revive," John Brandt said late in the 2005 season. "I think, in some ways, I forgot how far we've come. We've made some great impacts with the community, and I think that's what Steve's opinion of this venue was. You got to the point [in 2004] that looked bleak in a lot of ways, but the benefit of two years later, in looking at it, is pretty rewarding."

The 2005 Riversharks began the season as a temporary home for two high-profile clients of the big-league players' agent Scott Boras. Top prospects Stephen Drew and Jered Weaver were unable to reach deals with the clubs that drafted them in 2004, and decided to sign with the Riversharks to keep in playing shape while Boras negotiated for them. Drew, a shortstop from Florida State University and the brother of major leaguer J. D. Drew, was drafted fifteenth overall by the Arizona Diamondbacks. Weaver, a right-handed pitcher who was drafted twelfth overall by the Los Angeles Angels, also had a high-profile brother in the majors, Jeff. Brandt knew that the Riversharks were providing only a temporary arrangement for these two young stars, but the publicity they netted the team was worthwhile. Both players needed to sign contracts with their drafting clubs by May 31, otherwise they would have to reenter the amateur draft. Boras worked out the deals just under the deadline. Drew's stay at Camden was exciting. He led the Atlantic League with a .427 batting average and hit a grand-slam home run in his final game as a Rivershark. Weaver, who joined the club later than Drew, pitched only a few practice sessions for the Riversharks under the watchful eyes of major-league scouts. He was scheduled to pitch one inning of relief for the club on the day that he signed his contract, but he was held out of the game when it became apparent that a deal was in the works.

The 2005 season started slowly, but the Riversharks caught fire in August, when they won twenty out of twenty-seven games en route to an eighty-victory season, the fourth consecutive year that Camden led the league in regular-season wins. The slow start in the first half meant that the club would have to win the Southern Division outright in the second half to gain the playoffs once again. The Riversharks fell just short of their goal as Atlantic City finished strongly to win the division.

Changes to the organization are not unusual in independent baseball, and the Riversharks were no exception. After running the club since its inception in 2001, Brandt decided to move to another challenge, accepting the general manager position in Newark with the Bears for 2006. The Riversharks named Adam Lorber to replace Brandt as general manager. Lorber was the Riversharks' director of corporate sales from 2002 to 2005 and had a successful record of cultivating relationships within the community. One of the new owners, Steve Kalafer, scaled back his involvement, with the club being run mainly by Peter Kirk's Keystone Baseball LLC, the group that also runs the Lancaster Barnstormers of the Atlantic League. Boulton remains an owner but is willing to change that if the right opportunity comes. "We are looking to put a local face on it," explained Boulton. "We've got the ship righted, it's going where we want it to, and we would like to encourage somebody from the area who could be a hometown face [to be a co-owner]. We want the right person, because it is important that we get the right person in there to make sure the club prospers for decades to come."

The Camden Riversharks appeared to be the steady ship that Boulton spoke about as they headed into the 2007 season with the major-league veteran Joe Ferguson as manager. Attendance remains solid, and the club is profitable. The club is poised to enter a new period of growth, which can only be good news for Camden and the waterfront. There is other good news for the beleaguered city. Campbell's Soup Company announced, in February 2007, its intention to build a $98 million office complex on 110 acres bordering Admiral Wilson Boulevard. The office park plans include a new world headquarters building for Campbell's, maintaining the 1,200 jobs there. The rebirth of Camden is a slow and sometimes agonizing process, but projects like the waterfront redevelopment, Campbell's Field, Rutgers–Camden, and the new Campbell's office complex give the city hope for more investment in the future.

It is tempting to lump the redevelopment efforts going on in Newark and Camden with those that have taken place in Atlantic City after casino gaming was legalized there. After all, each of the three cities has seen the infusion of billions of dollars in an attempt to bring tourist and entertainment dollars to what were run-down, decaying urban areas. The similarities end there, however. The nature of the investment in Atlantic City and the types of tourists it attracts, as well as its location, makes the situation of the Atlantic City Surf baseball club far different than that of both the Newark Bears and the Camden Riversharks. Nothing can demonstrate this better than a trip to an Atlantic City Surf game on a late August evening.

9

The Atlantic City Surf

Searching for a Niche

The days are still hot, the surf is warm, and the boardwalk is alive with vacationers on any given day in late August. However, Labor Day is approaching, and everyone knows the beach season is about to end, lending a sense of urgency to all activities, including Atlantic League baseball all across the state. Division pennants and league championships are being won and lost. The laziness of warm afternoons and evenings at the ballpark is replaced by the anticipation of the wild

The twin spires of Bernie Robbins Stadium, which was built to resemble a sandcastle, Atlantic City. Photograph by Bob Golon, 2005.

pitch, the overthrown ball from the outfield to home plate, or the strike-out that could mean the difference between winning a championship or packing up for the season.

But Atlantic City seems immune to the climactic energy felt by summer vacationers and baseball fans alike. In this city of 41,000 people, the festive mood inside the casinos does not lessen. Gambling, drinking, and hard partying are not affected by early sunsets and cooler weather. Perhaps this is why the Atlantic City Surf have struggled to be financially successful in this city, despite having proved themselves time and time again on the baseball field. Most city visitors don't seem interested in the fact that their hometown team is in a desperate race to make the playoffs. On August 22, 2005, the Surf are playing against the Nashua Pride, the first-place club in the Atlantic League's Northern Division. Even though both clubs are number one in their respective divisions, fan attendance tonight barely reaches 1,200. While looking at the impressive casino sky-line in the distance and the sea of empty seats in front of me, the contrasts of the baseball situations in Newark, Camden, and Atlantic City comes into sharp focus.

As mentioned in the previous chapters, Newark attempted to recon-nect with its storied baseball past with a population that not only does not remember it but, in some cases, cares little about it. Camden's desire to rebuild its waterfront into a major tourist destination led to an over-aggressive funding arrangement for the ballpark that forced the late Steve Shilling to dip into his own pocket in an attempt to repay the debt, almost causing the bankruptcy of the ball club in the process. Despite this, Camden and the surrounding areas have accepted the Riversharks and support them far better than Newark did in the Bears' case. In At-lantic City, the tourist industry has been well established. There are the boardwalk and marina areas that lure customers from miles away. For-tunes are spent daily in the Atlantic City casinos among the bright lights and the continuous entertainment. A bombardment of sensory glitz is aimed at casino patrons, with each casino trying to out do the other. Nearby are the Atlantic Ocean and the beaches of the New Jersey shore, which attract their own legion of tourists during the summer months. The shore scene provides a serenity that is perhaps as powerful to the senses as is the excitement of the boardwalk. Yet, the ballpark is, for the most part, sparsely attended. Perhaps it is a case of sensory overload for those who visit and live in Atlantic City, and the Surf struggle to find their place in the midst of it.

On this late-August day, the Atlantic City boardwalk is occupied by the usual crowds of excitement seekers trying to change their luck by moving from casino to casino. Some look happy, some sad, and some even look desperate. The afternoon boardwalk casino crowd is dominated by senior citizens, who came in great numbers when legalized gaming in Atlantic City arrived in the 1970s. They arrive by the busload or in their automobiles, carrying their complimentary ten-dollar slot machine coupons given out by the casinos and bus companies as an incentive to draw them in. They wear their casino promotional club cards around their necks like jewelry, to have easy access to them when a tempting slot machine comes a calling. They spend money, but given their limited incomes, they don't spend much. They come for a few hours, have their fun, maybe enjoy an inexpensive lunch, then board the buses or get into their cars and head home, normally before dark. There is hardly a child or a young family to be found among them.

At dusk, another distinctly different group takes over the casino scene. This mostly younger and more affluent group is evidence of the success Atlantic City has been experiencing since the Atlantic City Convention and Visitor's Authority shifted the resort's marketing focus in 2003. This tourist group seeks the excitement of a Las Vegas–type experience. For a while, Las Vegas had tried to market itself as a family entertainment destination. It built pirate ships and roller coasters into the newer resorts. Yet, it found there is really no way to reconcile casinos with families and children, and a "bring your kids" message quickly turned into a message of "what happens here stays here." Atlantic City casino executives took notice. Encouraged by the building of a new convention center and the rock-and-roll-focused Borgata Hotel Casino and Spa, as well as the renovation of the Tropicana Resort into a modern and upscale reincarnation of Old Havana, the Convention and Visitors Authority quickly scrapped the "America's Playground" slogan for a more Vegas-like "Always Turned On." In a January 2006 interview in the *Atlantic City Press*, Jeffrey Vasser, the executive director of the Convention and Visitors Bureau, said, "Our visitors are younger, more affluent now and that plays into the 'always turned on' theme. Look at places like the 40/40 Club [a trendy sports bar and lounge at the Walk, a retail center]; that place doesn't start cranking until late. It helps get the word out, this is the place to be."

But it has become apparent that the casino scene is not the place to be if you're a young family with children. That group aims for the more traditional style of Jersey Shore resorts, which are miles away by car from the center of Atlantic City. And those resorts are also miles away from the Atlantic City ballpark.

On this beautiful late-August afternoon south of downtown, at the Sandcastle ballpark (later renamed Bernie Robbins Stadium after a local jewelry retailer), in a section of Atlantic City dubbed "downbeach" by the locals, pitcher Ryan Schurman of the Atlantic City Surf is preparing to face the Nashua Pride. Schurman, originally a tenth-round draft choice of the Atlanta Braves in 1995, is trying to resurrect a career that seemed to be all but over just five shorts weeks ago. He bounced around both the Braves and Cincinnati Reds organizations for five years, with little success. After recording ten wins for the Camden Riversharks of the Atlantic League in 2001, he was signed by the St. Louis Cardinals organization and pitched for the Double-A New Haven Ravens of the Eastern League. Schurman was released from the Ravens after posting no wins, three losses, and a bloated ERA of 7.06. It was back to the Atlantic League, where he pitched for both the Riversharks and the Bridgeport Bluefish during 2003 and 2004. After being released by the Bluefish due to a salary dispute, and nearing his twenty-ninth birthday, Schurman went home to Oregon, wondering if he would get another call. Lincoln Mikkelsen, his teammate in Camden, was spending the 2005 season in the dual role of pitcher and pitching coach for the Surf, and he remembered Schurman when the Surf pitching staff needed help in early July. Luckily, Schurman had kept himself in pitching condition during his layoff, and when the call from the Surf came, he had an immediate positive impact on the club. His 4-1 won-lost record helped the Surf get back into the Southern Division pennant race. Tonight, against the Pride, Schurman has been called upon to pitch against Denny Harriger, who is the Atlantic League's leading pitcher with a 13-5 record and an ERA of 3.63. It figures to be quite a pitching matchup, but it remains to be seen if anyone among either the tourists or local population will care enough to come out to see the game.

As the clubs gather for their pregame warm-ups, the casinos glisten in the sunlight beyond the outfield fence. Casino gambling and professional sports have always had a very uneasy relationship, due to the unwillingness of sports management to allow the perception of interaction between gamblers, oddsmakers, and their clubs. Yet, it was casino money that indirectly led to the building of the Atlantic City Sandcastle baseball park.

According to its Web site, the Atlantic City Casino Reinvestment Development Authority (CRDA), established in 1984, "is responsible for maintaining public confidence in the casino gaming industry through the reinvestment of a portion of gaming revenues to revitalize Atlantic City and other areas throughout New Jersey. . . . [T]he CRDA has used casino reinvestments as a catalyst for meaningful, positive improvement in the lives of New Jersey residents statewide. In doing so, the CRDA has dramatically changed Atlantic City's residential, commercial, cultural, and social landscape." Casinos have a simple choice. They can either pay a tax of 2.5 percent of their gaming revenues directly to the state of New Jersey or reinvest 1.25 percent of those revenues through the CRDA in community or other economically viable projects. The casinos mostly choose to reinvest through the CRDA, because it gives them a potential return on their investment in the form of public recreation and entertainment facilities that assist in promoting tourism. In the mid-1990s, a baseball park in Atlantic City seemed like a good way to promote tourism to the region by providing a family entertainment alternative, not only for out-of-town visitors but for nearby residents as well. Through the efforts of mayor James Whelan and state senator William Gormley, a deal was cut with the CRDA to finance $11.5 million of the $14.5 million cost of the ballpark, with the remaining $3 million financed by city taxpayer bonds, to be repaid at $280,000 per year for twenty years.

The city attracted a new Atlantic League franchise as part of Frank Boulton's initiative to create the league. Boulton received a very generous and favorable deal from Atlantic City. The new club, nicknamed the Surf, would be responsible only for paying the city $75,000 a year in rent, to be used for stadium improvements and repairs. The ballpark was scheduled to be built in time for the beginning of the 1998 Atlantic League season. Boulton has positive memories about dealing with the Atlantic City area politicians. "Senator Gormley got us the state money, and Jim [Whelan] got the city money," explained Boulton. "Jim Whelan was very public, and [he] put himself out front on the project. We had done a lot together. I had gone down at their invitation to speak to many of the casino owners and local businesses. Atlantic City is a city that swells during the summer, along with the whole south Jersey region. The beachfront area grows by at least a million folks. So, you have an interesting situation where you have a couple of different lords and masters and a couple of different places to market to. You have the people that live there all year round, who are going to be your core fans, you have the people that visit in the summer that you have to teach to incorporate an Atlantic City Surf game as part of their vacation when they come down to the shore, and then you have the visitors in the casinos." It was a deal that Boulton felt would come up aces for a long time.[1]

It seemed to be a can't-miss proposition. The park would be visible from the Atlantic City Expressway, the main highway that carries thousands of tourists daily to and from downtown Atlantic City from points north and south via the Garden State Parkway. All it would take was the addition of a simple, clearly marked exit from the expressway to direct fans to a two- or three-hour diversion from gambling at the casinos. Also, the local residents are familiar with Route 40, otherwise known as the Black Horse Pike, which connects local communities like Mays Landing and Pleasantville with the downbeach area. The suburbs of Northfield, Linwood, and Somers Point connect to the pike from Route 9, then to Bernie Robbins Stadium at the eastern end of the pike. For those residents, it is a toll-free ride of no more than twenty minutes to and from the ballpark. However, the section of the Black Horse Pike that connects the outlying suburbs to downbeach is alien to most of the people who live in the outlying areas, and few care to drive that stretch of road. The seven miles from the parkway area to the ballpark can be described as seedy at best, downright depressing at worst. The residential areas cry out their poverty, with the small, mostly early- to mid-twentieth-century homes in need of some serious repair work. Fuller's Shangri-La Lounge, abandoned and overgrown with weeds, sits as a testament to perhaps a previously better era gone by. Once through the residential and commercial area of Pleasantville, the Black Horse Pike takes on the aura of a 1950s highway that never made it to 1960. Smaller motels dot the road, some abandoned, some needing to be. Then come the automobile dealerships: five, six, seven in a row. More motels are scattered in between. Once into West Atlantic City, newer motor hotels like Hampton Inn and Comfort Inn markedly improve the surroundings. The waters of Lakes Bay border the pike on the right, and as you cross into Atlantic City proper, you're greeted by a large yellow-and-black lighthouse, a leftover from the days when Atlantic City was the queen of the shore resorts. Atlantic City High School, a relatively modern structure, strikes an imposing figure on the right-hand side. As you approach Bernie Robbins Stadium on the left, the downbeach casinos loom large in the distance. The roadside is lined with the latest casino billboards advertising their slot-machine jackpots. A McDonald's restaurant sits directly across the street from the stadium, and a small, now closed airport, Bader Field, sits right outside the left-field wall. A few small private planes sit on the runway, with little landing or takeoff activity taking place.

The ride to Bernie Robbins Stadium is a relatively easy one, and once you reach the parking lot, there is absolutely nothing to suggest that you should be afraid of this neighborhood. The lot is well lit at night, safe, inexpensive, and easily accessed from both sides of the highway. Still, the residents look at this area with suspicion.

Bernie Robbins Stadium was designed to look like an actual sand castle. The staircases of the park's main entrance are flanked by two large red-brick towers, topped by spires in the shape of two small pyramids, mimicking what a child might build on the beach with his or her plastic sand toys. The entranceway itself is adorned on both sides by large murals painted by Galloway Township artist Michael Irvin. The twenty-two-foot-high by fifty-foot-wide murals illustrate baseball history, showing young boys choosing up sides for a baseball game superimposed on pictures of the game's great players, including Babe Ruth, Hank Aaron, and Ty Cobb. After climbing up the stairs to the main concourse inside, patrons are directed to their seating sections by a sign that hangs above the gift store. Besides employing a traditional numbering system, all sections are named after the Atlantic City streets made famous in the Monopoly board game—for instance, section 217 is named States Avenue. The concourse is roomy, with concession stands around the outer perimeter, and when you first look out at the field and grandstand areas, you're immediately struck by the unusual color scheme used for the seating. The lower seating sections closest to the field are a bright and cheery sea-foam green, with the upper sections contrasting in navy blue. Game time tonight is scheduled for 6:30 PM, and when the gates open an hour before the game, a small gathering of people make their way up the stairs and into the concourse.

The Surf opened their stadium on May 20, 1998, with an 8–5 loss to the visiting Somerset Patriots. At that time, the park, then known as the Sandcastle, was one of only three completed home fields for Atlantic League clubs, along with Bridgeport and Nashua. Frank Boulton had high hopes for the new venue, and his faith seemed to be rewarded when a capacity crowd of 5,470 filled the ballpark for the opening game. However, only 1,906 showed up the following evening, and an even smaller crowd of 1,606 attended the game on Friday, May 22, which also happened to be the first evening of the long Memorial Day weekend. Surf president and general manager Ken Shepard voiced his displeasure about the small turnout to the *Atlantic City Press* when he said, "I wish we had a little bigger crowd, but I'm not going to make any excuses. It's the first day of a holiday [Memorial Day] weekend, and we should have more people out here." Even though it was only three days into its existence, the pattern of poor attendance at the Sandcastle was already being set.

The Surf needed to draw an average of 3,000 fans per game to turn a small profit, but in their eight seasons in the Sandcastle, the closest they have ever been able to get to that figure was 2,718 per game in 1999, an improvement from the 2,466 average of their first season in 1998. After slumping to 2,337 and 2,262 in 2000 and 2001 respectively, they attempted to capitalize on their southern New Jersey Philadelphia Phillies fan base by bringing in Mitch "Wild Thing" Williams to replace Tommy Helms as manager midway through the 2002 season. The unpredictable Williams, best known as a sometimes successful but always colorful relief pitcher for the Philadelphia Phillies, led the Surf to a first-place finish in the second half of the season as well as a playoff berth, and attendance rebounded to more than 2,500 fans a game in 2003. Williams grew tired of managing an independent club and left after 2003. Even though his replacement, the low-key Jeff Ball, took the Surf to the playoffs from 2004 through 2006, attendance once again spiraled downward, to a low of 1,984 per game during the 2006 season. This late-season 2005 game was indicative of the lackluster sales plaguing the Surf, especially on weeknights.

As Ryan Schurman takes his warm-up pitches, the starting lineups are being announced against a backdrop of the Beach Boys' "Surfin' USA" playing over the loudspeakers. It seems a fitting musical selection in a stadium that has a beach volleyball court, complete with sand, outside its picnic area. The public-address announcer makes an unusual request for fans at a baseball game, asking them, "please do not feed the sea gulls while sitting in the stands." Former major-league outfielder Darren Bragg digs in at home plate to bat leadoff for Nashua as the small crowd settles into their seats. The ballpark looks and feels empty. Schurman gets Bragg, David Francia, and Kevin Haverbusch all to hit into easy outs, each met by a smattering of applause. The Surf's third baseman Dario Delgado, who would end up with two hits in three at-bats on this evening, doubles in the bottom of the first inning, but right fielder Ozzie Timmons, who played for the Mets Triple-A affiliate in Norfolk as recently as 2004, grounds out to short, ending the threat. Both Schurman and Harriger take control of the game, skillfully trading shutout innings through the fourth. Even though it is only nearing 7:30 PM, darkness is already falling on Bernie Robbins Stadium. Spectators in the club seating area, located in the upper level directly behind home plate, are treated to a wondrous sight developing beyond the outfield fence. The Atlantic City casino skyline shimmers and illuminates like a modern-day Oz at the end of the yellow brick road. The paradox is just as striking: the stunning view of the skyline of the gambling hot spot of the East Coast in the distance with only about six people in the club seats on this beautiful evening to enjoy it.[2]

The local press plays a role in trying to increase the visibility of professional sports in Atlantic City. Pete Thompson is the nightly sports anchor for WMGM-TV, channel 40, in Atlantic City. Every evening that the Surf are home, Thompson hustles from the station's studios in Linwood to Bernie Robbins Stadium, handheld video camera in tow. He shoots some highlight footage, formulates a story line from reporters covering the game in the press box, then hustles back to the station, where he prepares his segment of the late-evening newscast. Because TV-40 is the only local noncable network affiliate in the greater Atlantic City area, Thompson likes to differentiate his sports reports from those on the Philadelphia stations by "leading local," as he puts it. During the baseball season, this means leading with the Surf, regardless if they're home or away. "We certainly try to get video of almost every home game. There's very few home games that we miss. Every so often there's a conflict, but for the most part, if they're home, we're there," explained Thompson. The only limitation that Thompson has is the lack of a live truck to do remote broadcasting from, which he says he would make use of at Surf games if he had it. "You work with the tools you're given," he lamented, "and I think we do a pretty good job given what we have."[3]

Chuck Betson, the former director of marketing and media for the Surf, agrees that channel 40's coverage is good for the Surf. "The television coverage, I'd give an A to," said Betson. "The Surf is their lead story every night." Not so, however, with the local newspaper, the *Press of Atlantic City*. "I heard a very accurate assessment about the *Press:* they don't help you and they don't hurt you," explained Betson. "They cover us. Could it be better? Yes. It's not the coverage like the Somerset Patriots get from the *Courier News*, but we do get covered every night. We don't make the lead page, which bothers me because we are the professional franchise in town. But, I guess I always want more. The TV coverage I'd give an A, and the newspaper coverage, I'd give it a C-plus."[4]

Is it fair to say that getting casino executives, employees, and patrons to drive the one-to-two-mile distance between the casinos and the ballpark is key to the Surf's eventual success? Betson was not so sure about the role that the casino industry can play. "It's a casino town, with very little corporate [climate]. We have no white-collar climate. Our population base is fueled by casinos. The majority of the people who live here work in the service industry, whether that be a dealer, a waiter, a waitress, et cetera. I wish we had more of a white-collar industry, but we don't. Now, the casinos have supported us, but it hasn't been what we've wanted, it's never what you wanted, but they have stepped up and done marketing, and they do buy tickets for employees, but this is not a project that the casinos have to sustain. We want them to support us, but their job is not to sustain us." A look at the casino advertising on the outfield wall confirms what Betson says. Out of all the casinos profiting in Atlantic City, only two, the Borgata and the Trump Casinos, bought advertising space at the Sandcastle in 2005. Ironically, one other casino, the Mohegan Sun Casino in Connecticut, advertises in the ballpark, obviously in an attempt to get tourists to leave Atlantic City for the casino in the Connecticut woods. Sitting in the upper tier of the stadium, taking in the breathtaking view of the casino skyline made Frank Boulton understand why the casinos did not advertise more with the club. "Sitting on a summer night in the ballpark, looking at the Atlantic City skyline is one of the best seats in baseball. It's kind of funny because as we sat there, I realized why the Tropicana Casino doesn't have an outfield sign; because they already have one right out there," noted Boulton, pointing to the view of the casinos in the distance. The casinos are smart enough to realize that their best advertising vehicle is that spectacular view of the skyline.

Chuck Betson's observation that the Atlantic City area has no white-collar culture is borne out by the fact that only one luxury box in the upper level is occupied on this night. Luxury boxes or suites are popular after-work outing venues for companies and their customers at other New Jersey professional baseball locations. Not so at the Sandcastle, at least for this evening. It's too bad, because tonight they're missing a very good ball game developing on the field.

In the top of the fifth, with the game still scoreless, the Pride's Orlando Miller leads off with a double down the left-field line. Tom Creighton then reaches first base safely on an error by Surf shortstop Rayner Bautista, moving Miller to third. Darren Bragg grounds out to second, scoring Miller and giving the Pride a 1-0 lead. Schurman settles down to retire the side without any further difficulty, but when Harriger retires the Surf in order in the bottom of the fifth, including two strike-outs, it seems the one Pride run might be enough to win the game.

Thirty-six-year-old Denny Harriger was enjoying a comeback season in 2005. Drafted by the New York Mets in the eighteenth round of the 1987 amateur entry draft, Harriger pitched for twelve seasons in the minor leagues for the Mets, San Diego Padres, and Detroit Tigers organizations before finally making it to the big leagues with the Tigers in 1998. Unfortunately, Harriger did not impress the Tigers enough to stay in the majors, winning none and losing three with an ERA of 6.75 in four appearances. He moved to the Cincinnati Reds organization with Indianapolis of the International League in 1999, where he posted a career-best record of 14-6 at the Triple-A level. Harriger signed with the Korean Baseball League and had two successful seasons there, winning seventeen games in 2000 and eight games in 2001, despite pitching with a sore shoulder that was originally diagnosed incorrectly as tendonitis. While he was in the Pittsburgh Pirates' minor-league training camp in 2002, his shoulder continued to hurt, and doctors finally diagnosed the injury as a torn labrum. He needed shoulder surgery, which forced him to be inactive until 2003. After rehabilitating his shoulder, Harriger returned to baseball by signing with the Long Island Ducks in the Atlantic League. Although he posted a 5-10 record, his shoulder was strengthening and he felt he could still be an effective pitcher. Moving on to the Nashua Pride in 2004, Harriger won four games while losing three, and finished the 2005 season with a strong 16-8 record and the title of ace of the Pride's pitching staff.

In the bottom of the sixth inning, with the score still 1-0 in favor of the Pride, Harriger retires Tom Goodwin and Bautista quickly for the first two outs. He appears to be getting stronger as the game goes along, then, as happens often in baseball, the unexplainable takes place in the form of four straight Surf base hits. Third baseman Dario Delgado legs out a broken-bat double down the right field line. Ozzie Timmons follows with a ground-rule double, tying the game at one run apiece. First baseman Jose Velazquez hits a line drive up the middle for a base hit, scoring Timmons and giving the Surf a 2-1 lead. Harriger suddenly seems vulnerable, even more so when designated hitter Al Benjamin follows with a single of his own, moving Velazquez to second. A big hit here would expand the Surf's lead, but Harriger gets center fielder Gary Johnson to hit a pop fly to Joe Kilburg at third base, stranding both Velazquez and Benjamin and ending the inning. The small crowd applauds as the inning ends with the home team leading by a score of 2-1. Three innings remain in the game, which in baseball can be an eternity. Neither of the managers, Butch Hobson of the Pride and Jeff Ball of the Surf, had any intention of taking his ace pitcher out of the game unless he completely lost his effectiveness. It was the pitchers' game to win or lose.

As tonight's game moves into the seventh inning, pitchers Ryan Schurman and Denny Harriger toss the dice and somehow figure out how to make them come up zeros. Harriger gives up a leadoff double to the Surf's Kevin McDonald in the bottom of the seventh, then easily retires his next six batters. Back in the Pride's seventh, Schurman retires Orlando Miller on a fly ball to right but walks the number nine batter, Tom Creighton. Up next, Bragg hopes to call on his major-league experience to move Creighton over in an effort to manufacture what could be the tying run. Instead, he pulls the ball too hard toward first baseman Velazquez, who fields the ball and quickly fires it to shortstop Bautista, for the force-out. Bautista then straightens and delivers a bullet back to Velazquez, just nipping Bragg and completing an inning-ending double play. Schurman cuts through the final six Pride batters in order and with ease, finishing a masterful 2-1 Surf victory in a game that neither pitcher deserved to lose.

A quick look at the clock reveals that it is now only 8:40 PM. This game was played in an incredibly short two hours and five minutes, unheard-of in these days of three-hour-plus baseball games. It was the type of exciting, well-played baseball that the Atlantic League touts itself for. There was even plenty of time to jump in the car and go back to the casinos for a full evening of fun seeking. Paid attendance was an announced 1,280. It seemed lower, and it was too bad, because those who did not come missed a whale of a baseball game.

Down in Camden that same day, the Riversharks needed eleven innings to defeat the Newark Bears, 7-6. Both Camden and the Surf finished the evening tied with records of 24-14, to remain deadlocked for first place in the Southern Division. Camden faded in September while the Surf won twenty-four out of their final thirty-two games to win the division by seven games, securing a first-round playoff berth against the Somerset Patriots. In the playoffs, the Surf's luck ran out. After losing the first game of the series, 5-2 at the Sandcastle, the series moved to Somerset for game two. The Surf received two RBIs each from Ozzie

Timmons, Julian Yan, and Melvin Rosario to defeat the Patriots, 7-3, forcing a deciding game three. Pitcher Mark Persails held the Patriots hitless through five innings and scoreless through six, but the Surf could only manage one run off the four Patriots pitchers. Persails tired, and the Patriots scored one run in the seventh inning and four in the eighth to earn a 5-1 series-clinching victory and a berth in the Atlantic League Championship Series. The postseason was over for the Atlantic City Surf, and time was rapidly running out on Frank Boulton's ownership of the club. Change was in the air for the Surf, and many changes took place from 2006 to 2007.

In January 2006, Boulton announced that he leased the team, with an option to sell it, to Mark Schuster of Magnolia, New Jersey. Schuster came to the Surf with an impressive baseball resume. He was the vice president and general manager of the Fort Myers Miracle, the advanced Single-A level affiliate of the Minnesota Twins, when they set franchise attendance records from 1994 through 1996. Schuster then moved on to the Charleston RiverDogs, the South Atlantic League low Single-A affiliate of the New York Yankees, which, under his guidance from 1997 through 1999, also set attendance records. Then it was on to Portland (Oregon) Beavers, the Triple-A affiliate of the San Diego Padres. The Schuster-led franchise set that club's season attendance record when 454,197 entered the ballpark in Portland in 2002. It is little wonder that Mark Schuster has earned a reputation as "a turnaround guy."

Schuster then focused his attention on independent professional baseball. He is currently the principal owner of the El Paso Diablos and the president of the St. Joseph (Missouri) Blacksnakes, both of the American Association. The common tie between the American Association and Schuster's previous clubs in both Fort Myers and Charleston is the Goldklang Group, headed by Marvin Goldklang. In 1989, Goldklang led an investment team that eventually acquired controlling interests in the Fort Myers, Charleston, and Williamsport (Pennsylvania) affiliated franchises. That would be followed in 1993 by Goldklang's initiative, along with Mike Veeck, Miles Wolff, and Van Schley, to establish a new independent professional league in the Midwest—the Northern League—which became an extremely successful venture stressing affordable family entertainment.

Schuster explained his rationale for becoming involved with the Surf to writer Lori Hoffman for *Atlantic City Weekly* in June 2006. "I've been in this career for a long time now, and I've followed the situation in

Atlantic City, and knew that it might be available for purchase. I thought [the franchise] had underperformed. That is my M.O., to take companies that have been underperforming and take them to new levels. It was a challenge that people told me I was crazy to take on. The town loves this team but it has struggled." Schuster's strategy sounded good, but even he could not influence the size of the drawing population of the Atlantic City area to create large numbers of new fans. "Our goal is not to go out and create new customers," Schuster explained. "Our goal is to take those people who are coming here now and have them come back more often. How do you do that? You do it by creating a fun environment [with] great promotions, great food, and great customer service. We really only need to take that customer who comes five or six times a year and have them come nine or ten times over a five-month period."[5]

Schuster took on a greater challenge than even he might have realized. Despite the Surf being the only New Jersey–based Atlantic League team to make the postseason playoffs in 2006, ticket sales fell below the 2,000-average-per-game mark for the first time. It became clear that more changes needed to be made if the club was to survive. In 2006, the Nashua Pride transferred its affiliation from the Atlantic League to the Can-Am League run by Miles Wolff. It had long been rumored that the Surf might seek a shorter-season league like the Can-Am League to play in, figuring that the Memorial Day to Labor Day schedule of that league might better align itself to the summer tourism season. With the relationship between the Atlantic and Can-Am Leagues now firmly established, the time was right to transfer the Surf. On October 21, the two leagues announced the transfer of the club to the Can-Am League, effective beginning with the 2007 season.

Looking back, Atlantic League and Surf founder Frank Boulton was reluctant to call his experience in Atlantic City a failure. "I will by no means ever put it in the category of a failure. Atlantic City and the people of Atlantic City and the people of south Jersey have enjoyed Atlantic League baseball. We set record crowds in Atlantic City with fireworks shows. We had 7,000 fans in that ballpark, and they've been playing baseball with the same name for ten years, so to me it is a success. Is it the most successful team in the Atlantic League? No. But if you lay it against the tapestry of all of minor-league baseball teams across America, it holds it own. So, I never want the people of Atlantic City to feel like it failed. I want them to feel good. This is not a demotion. Moving the club to the

Can-Am League is intelligent, forward thinking." Bob Wirz, an independent-baseball expert and longtime Can-Am League operator, called the transfer a smart move for both the Surf and the league. "If I were looking at the good of the Can-Am League, Atlantic City gives the league another franchise that has a good chance of doing well in Can-Am terms. I think the length of season obviously was a factor in the minds of the people in Atlantic City. They've got good operators down there. They've done OK [in the Atlantic League], but they couldn't quite measure up to Somerset or Long Island, and so they see that they're better equipped to be in a shorter season with a little better economics for them. I think the Can-Am League sees Atlantic City as potentially another decent-to-strong franchise for it."[6]

For now, the Atlantic City Surf franchise continues for its fans. The cutting of expenses by shortening the season should benefit the bottom line for Mark Schuster. The Can-Am League provides a hustling brand of baseball that the team hopes will appeal to those fans who love spending a lazy summer day or evening at Bernie Robbins Stadium, enjoying the shore air, the seagulls, the breathtaking casino view, and, of course, the baseball. Questions still remain about the future of the club, however. Questions that remain to be answered.

The Bader Field airport, whose runway sat directly behind the stadium in left field, closed in late 2006. The 130 acres of land now sits idle. Even though it will probably take many years of politics, proposals, and counterproposals, redevelopment eventually awaits the site. The Las Vegas casino mogul Steve Wynn reportedly is interested in acquiring the land for a massive, new casino and entertainment complex. Some people favor new, publicly funded housing for the site. Others talk about creating a massive theme park there, to cater to the family crowd and truly bring family entertainment to Atlantic City. At times, it is speculated that the redevelopment of Bader Field might also include razing Bernie Robbins Stadium and relocating professional baseball to elsewhere in the area. One rumored site is land adjacent to the modern Atlantic City International Airport near Mays Landing, west of the Garden State Parkway. Many people feel that would make sense, as it would encourage more year-round residents to attend games without needing to venture down the Black Horse Pike.

Regardless, for the immediate future, it is business as usual at Bernie Robbins Stadium. As the 2007 season approaches, the Surf get ready to join their New Jersey counterparts, the Sussex Skyhawks and the New Jersey Jackals, in the Can-Am League. Unlike the Atlantic League, the Can-Am League is an independent professional league that had its origins in smaller towns in the Northeast, far away from the sensory overload of that which is Atlantic City.

10

Youth Must Be Served

The Can-Am League in New Jersey

Young New Jersey baseball players. They all could have made it, if not for the accident of birth. After all, in New Jersey, they could not play ball all year round like the fortunate kids in California, Florida, and other warm-weather areas of the country. If only they could have had that chance to practice and compete in winter leagues like those West Coast kids, they could have been just as successful. At least they all think that way. The dream dies hard, and for many young men who played baseball in New Jersey or other northeastern colleges and universities over the years, their careers typically ended on graduation day

The entrance gate to Yogi Berra Stadium on the campus of Montclair State University. Photograph by Bob Golon, 2005.

because their exposure to scouts was limited by both geography and poor playing conditions in cold weather.

Zach Smithlin and Josh Ury are two New Jersey boys who typify the local kids with a dream of being professional baseball players. Their careers seemed stalled after collegiate baseball, only to be revived in a league that features hungry, young players who still have that dream. Furthermore, the pair have the added benefit of playing in front of family and friends in New Jersey, something that their fellow northeasterners did not have until the advent of independent professional baseball. The New Jersey Jackals, Sussex Skyhawks, and as of 2007, the Atlantic City Surf are members of the Can-Am League, an independent baseball league where youth is definitely served well and where dreams can still live.

The Can-Am League arrived in New Jersey in 1998 as a relatively obscure league. Then known as the Northeast League, it placed a club in a new, picturesque ballpark nestled underneath and adjacent to the Yogi Berra Museum and Learning Center on the campus of Montclair State University in Little Falls. The opening lacked the fanfare of the efforts being made in the larger cities like Newark to establish their own independent professional clubs. Also lacking were the major-league affiliations enjoyed in Trenton and, in 1998, Sussex County. The Northeast League's season started later (end of May) and ended earlier (Labor Day) than most of the other minor or independent professional leagues in New Jersey. Its players tended to be younger, most of them lacking the professional experience of their Atlantic League counterparts. The New Jersey Jackals represented the Northeast League's first attempt at a club in New Jersey, and without a Sparky Lyle in the dugout or a Rick Cerone in the owner's box, skepticism about their ability to survive had to be expected. Nine years later, the Northeast League, now named the Can-Am League, has grown to three clubs in New Jersey. The new Sussex Skyhawks joined the league in 2006 when they replaced the New Jersey Cardinals in Augusta after the franchise moved to State College, Pennsylvania. The Atlantic City Surf switched from the Atlantic League to begin play in the Can-Am for the 2007 season. The Can-Am League now boasts the same number of clubs in New Jersey as the Atlantic League, and judging by the support exhibited by the Jackals' fans in Little Falls and the Skyhawks' faithful in Sussex County in 2006, the league has succeeded in establishing an identity of its own in New Jersey.

The Northeast League, created in 1995, was the predecessor of the Can-Am League. Its founder was Jay Acton, a New York–based literary agent who once had baseball author Roger Kahn as a client. The original six clubs were based entirely in small communities in New York State. The league branched out geographically in 1996 with additions in Rhode Island and Maine, followed in 1997 by clubs in Connecticut and Pennsylvania. By this time, Mike McGuire had replaced Acton as director and CEO, and McGuire is credited with stabilizing the Northeast League. In 1999, the league merged with the Midwest-based Northern League to form a larger league with two divisions. Miles Wolff, "the father of independent baseball," who founded the Northern League in 1993, brought his expertise and skill in running independent operations to the Northeast. This arrangement of combined leagues lasted for four years. In 2003, the leagues separated once again and the clubs in the east re-formed the Northeast League, with Miles Wolff remaining as its commissioner.[1] The independent-baseball pioneer and expert Bob Wirz, who followed Wolff's career from his days with the Thunder Bay Whiskey Jacks in the early Northern League, has an appreciation of what Wolff brought to the Northeast League. "I think it brings you a lot of credibility when Miles is involved, and it also brings in certain other people that Miles has been involved with," explained Wirz. "The Goldklang Group, with Marv Goldklang and Mike Veeck, has been managing the Brockton [Massachusetts] team. They come to the league, part and parcel, because of Miles—because they are friends who have built the Northern League. Miles put the Quebec team in place, and that's one of the stronger franchises in the Can-Am League now, too. He's a gifted guy, and his reputation certainly helps."[2]

Seeking to strengthen relationships between the club owners and the league, Wolff renamed the league the Can-Am League in 2004, after a class-C minor league that had its roots in the 1930s. This name change gave him a legal opportunity to restructure some of the leagues rules and bylaws to reflect the strengthening of the franchise agreements. The original Can-Am League franchises in 2004 included Bangor (Maine); Elmira (New York); Brockton, Lynn, and Worcester (Massachusetts); New Haven (Connecticut); Quebec City (Canada); and Little Falls (New Jersey). The league added Nashua (New Hampshire) and Augusta (New Jersey) for the 2006 season and Atlantic City (New Jersey) for 2007.

Whereas the Atlantic League sought to entice ex-affiliated players and former major leaguers to their rosters to attract fans to their targeted metropolitan areas, the philosophy of the Northeast–Can-Am League suggested a more conservative approach. In the Northeast and Can-Am

Leagues, undrafted college players aspiring to play professional baseball were welcome. Bob Wirz elaborated about this player philosophy. "I think one of the nice things is that the Can-Am League is giving the younger player who has been overlooked in college an opportunity. Maybe he's a late developer, or he played in a northern school or a small school, did not get drafted or did not get signed by an affiliated club. Yet he has a lot of talent, so I think that's a nice opportunity," said Wirz. "I believe there's over 500 new jobs a year in independent baseball for the young player just coming out of college, and for every independent league that's added, those numbers go up." The Can-Am requires that a minimum of five players per team be rookies—players with less than one year of professional experience. Out of a twenty-two-player roster, only a maximum of four players could be classified as a veteran having five or more years of professional service. The rest of the roster spots can only be filled with players with two to four years of professional experience. The league aims to substitute hungry, younger players seeking professional exposure for big-name players. The result is a hustling brand of baseball that appeals to the local audiences in the smaller, Can-Am League communities. One such community is Little Falls.

Professional baseball in Little Falls happened due to the convergence of three forces. Three diverse entities had a major impact in the creation of the ballpark and the team. These entities were a university, a famous ex-major-league baseball player, and a corporate mogul with a philanthropic flair.

Montclair State University traces its roots back to 1908 as a "normal school," dedicated to the education and training of secondary school teachers. It was originally known as Montclair State Teachers College until an expanded enrollment and curriculum enabled it to become a multidisciplinary college in the 1960s.[3] Under athletic director Greg Lockard, Montclair State College became a powerhouse in NCAA Division III baseball, winning the division championship in 1987 and 1993. Lockard convinced Montclair State officials to include new athletic facilities, including a new field for the baseball team, as part of the master plan as Montclair State achieved teaching university status in 1994. Lockard explained, "The stadium made sense for the University's facilities master plan, and it just so happened that professional baseball was part of the mix. We were trying to put together the best facility in Division III in the country, and even considering the possibility of moving to Division I, so it was facility driven." Today, Montclair State University is New Jersey's

second-largest university, behind only Rutgers, with a student enrollment goal of 18,000 by 2008. The university engaged in an active building campaign in the mid-1990s to enable it to expand and accommodate
the planned increased enrollment. Montclair State University is also very
fortunate to have one of the most beloved figures in United States sports
and popular culture as its neighbor and as one of its benefactors. Baseball
legend Yogi Berra and his family played a key role in the development of
the stadium area on campus.[4]

Originally from St. Louis, Lawrence Peter "Yogi" Berra made Montclair his home when he was playing for the New York Yankees. Berra and
his wife, Carmen, raised their family in Montclair during his career as a
major-league player, manager, and coach. He first came to New Jersey as
a member of the Newark Bears in 1946 before joining the Yankees full-
time. Known for his unathletic appearance and his unique use of the En-
glish language through sayings known as "Yogi-isms," Berra became one
of the most recognizable faces in America. Combining a Hall of Fame
baseball career with a flair for business endeavors made him extremely
successful, not only in sports, but financially as well. Over the years,
Berra's reputation for charitable giving grew, and his annual golf tour-
nament, also held in Montclair, raised considerable funds for youth and
educational activities throughout the area. Montclair State University
recognized his efforts by conferring him with an honorary doctorate in
humanities in 1996. When the stadium was being proposed for the campus in the mid-1990s, the university approached Berra to ask him if he
would lend his name to it. He agreed, and the new ballpark for the Montclair State baseball team became Yogi Berra Stadium.

A more permanent memorial to Berra took shape in 1997 in the
form of a museum containing his baseball artifacts. Known as the Yogi
Berra Museum and Learning Center, it gave Berra and his family the
continued opportunity to focus on youth and educational programs.
Dave Kaplan is the director of the Museum and Learning Center as well
as the coauthor of two of Berra's books, *When You Come to a Fork in the
Road, Take It!* and *Ten Rings: My Championship Seasons.* Kaplan explained the genesis of the Yogi Berra Museum this way: "Rose Cali, a
trustee of the University, proposed to build a gallery adjoining the stadium as a tribute to Yogi. She was the founder of what ultimately became
the Museum, getting some other folks to incorporate Friends of Yogi,
Inc. in 1997 as a non-profit organization. Carmen Berra got extremely involved to make it more into a learning center with programs for children,

and the Yogi Berra Museum and Learning Center opened its doors to the public in December, 1998, with the first public visitors being the Bradford Academy, an elementary school in Montclair. It is important to note that the Berras do not benefit financially from the Museum and Learning Center [a 501(c)(3) organization] but are active participants in fundraising and championing the programs and camps we operate."[5] This type of selfless philanthropic activity typified the building of the entire stadium and museum complex. The final force for its creation came from a lesser-known Montclair resident in the form of an unprecedented gift to the university: $13 million for the construction of the baseball stadium. The name Floyd Hall became synonymous with the development initiatives at Montclair State University.

Hall is an Oklahoma native who spent his formative years in California. A master of the art of retailing, Hall became the chief executive officer of the Minneapolis-based Target chain in the mid-1980s. He moved to Montclair with his family in 1985 after leaving Target to take over the Grand Union chain of supermarkets, based in Wayne, New Jersey. Hall engineered a successful and profitable turnaround of Grand Union. His mission there accomplished, he left Grand Union in 1989 to create another retail operation called The Museum Company, a chain of mall-based shops that specialized in selling museum art reproductions. In 1995, the Kmart Corporation, near bankruptcy, convinced Hall to work his turnaround magic for them. Working out of his New Jersey office, Hall introduced the "Big K" store concept, leading the company successfully until 2001.

During his time with Kmart, Hall became acquainted with the president of Montclair State University, Irvin Reid, and athletic director Greg Lockard. The university originally asked Hall to lead a fund-raising campaign for a new baseball stadium to house the MSU Red Hawks. Having always been interested in owning a baseball team, and feeling a strong sense of wanting to give back to his community, Hall viewed this as an opportunity to accomplish both while providing Montclair State with its long-needed baseball facility. He contributed $13 million of his own money in a unique private-public partnership to construct the baseball stadium and a two-rink ice arena on university land in Little Falls. "I've always been enthralled with professional baseball, and I just thought that it [the stadium] would give us an opportunity to do two things at one time," said Hall, "build the baseball stadium for the university and fit in with the master plan of the university." In explaining his commitment to the surrounding neighborhood, Hall stated, "I was fortunate enough to do well in business and I really wanted to give something back to the community, and I specifically wanted to do something nice for kids and their families. I just think it's so great to have a wholesome place to go to and watch professional baseball and to be able to have a good time. It's a wonderful way to spend a summer evening. That was my main goal."[6] Upon the completion of the facilities, Hall gifted them to the university, and his company, Floyd Hall Enterprises, was granted a long-term lease to operate both the ice arena and the ballpark.

"I have nothing but admiration for Floyd Hall and the New Jersey Jackals," said Bob Wirz. "They built a beautiful ballpark, and one of the things that I really like about Yogi Berra Stadium, which I think is a tremendous lesson for people in most independent leagues is: don't overbuild. The park is cozy, it's comfortable, and you're in close to the action." Indeed, the ambiance of Yogi Berra Stadium is different than that of any of the other ballparks that have been built in New Jersey since 1990. The complex is located at the northernmost section of the Montclair State University campus. Set off at the end of a large section of university parking lots is the Yogi Berra Museum and Learning Center, a modest, cream colored building with red trim. To the left of the museum is a gated area with a large sign, in the shape of a baseball, with the words "Yogi Berra Stadium" in script written on it. To the left of it stands a small building with ticket windows. Your first reaction when you arrive in the area is "where is the ballpark?" There is no large brick-and-steel building rising above this entrance. You don't see any evidence of a ballpark until you approach the gate area below the stadium sign and look in. There below you, down a long flight of concrete stairs, is a quaint little ballpark, its bright red seats contrasting against the green of the grass and the brown of the base paths. Once down these stairs, you are surrounded by the coziest of ballparks, in what appears to be a country setting. Except for a large brown-and-green office building rising beyond the outfield, the park is surrounded by lush green trees and a grassy slope down the first-base line. The open-air stands hold 3,784 permanent seats, about half the amount of other New Jersey professional baseball parks. The grass hill area alongside the right-field line can accommodate extra fans on blankets, and often does for popular events like fireworks nights. The limited seating capacity makes every seat an intimate location, very close to the action on the field. The stands, on any given game day, contain numerous families with children. Sometimes smaller is better, and in the case of Yogi Berra Stadium, the well-planned layout gives the fans a feeling of being involved in the action before them. The Jackals averaged approximately 2,300 fans per game since 2002. The crowds, considered large by Can-Am League standards, seem to enjoy the baseball as much as the afternoon or evening of family entertainment. The Jackals participate in all of the typical minor-league and independent baseball entertainment features, with activities for kids and between-inning contests. The short season of the Can-Am League means that all of the Jackals home games are played while the university is not in session, making parking easier for those attending the games.

"I'm sure that Floyd Hall must have had a vision of what he wanted to see," explained Bob Wirz. "He also has a quality guy in Greg Lockard, who oversees the operation." Lockard left his position at Montclair State to join Floyd Hall Enterprises as president. Along with Larry Hall, Floyd's son and executive vice president, the partners set out to build their new Jackals baseball team once the franchise was granted to them.

The independent-baseball veteran Kash Beauchamp became the Jackals' first field manager in 1998, and was given the responsibility of assembling the roster. Beauchamp put together an immediate winner. "I give Kash Beauchamp the lion's share of the credit," explained Wirz. Wirz is familiar with the early days of the Jackals, as he owned part of the Waterbury, Connecticut, club at the time. "Kash is an aggressive type of manager and recruiter and successful in most of the places he's been because of his nature. He put together a tremendous team." Led by first baseman D.C. Olsen's .327 batting average, outfielder Keith Gordon's seventy runs batted in, and the pitching of Paul Magrini (nine wins) and Mike Hartung (seventeen saves), the new Jackals won fifty-three games while losing only thirty-one to advance to the Northeast League playoffs. In those playoffs, Beauchamp's Jackals rolled over the Allentown Ambassadors and the Albany-Colonie Diamond Dogs in consecutive two-game series sweeps to give the Jackals the 1998 Northeast League championship in their very first season. Beauchamp led the Jackals to the playoffs again in 1999, this time in the newly expanded Northern League. After winning the divisional series over Allentown, the Jackals lost the Northern League East series to Albany, three games to one, depriving them the opportunity to play in the first combined Northern League championship series. After the Jackals slipped to a 31–53 season in 2000, Kash Beauchamp left to manage the Lincoln Saltdogs in 2001, handing the Jackal's managerial reins to former Minnesota Twins pitcher and Waterbury Spirit manager George Tsamis.

Tsamis inherited a club that looked mediocre at best, and their 2001 regular season record (45-45) seemed to bear that out. Yet, the Jackals managed to qualify for the Northern League playoffs as a wild-card team behind the hitting of Aaron Fera (.355 average with eighteen home runs) and the pitching of Joel Bennett (ten wins). Bennett played for the Jackals for six seasons (2001–2006) and set many of the club's all-time pitching records. In the 2001 playoffs, Tsamis's team caught fire and played well, particularly outfielder Trey Beamon. Beamon achieved a .585 batting average in winning the league's Most Valuable Player award for the postseason. The Jackals swept Albany in the division series, defeated the Elmira Pioneers in five games in the Northern League East series, and then defeated the Midwest Division's Winnipeg Goldeyes, three games to one, for the overall 2001 Northern League title. The momentum of the 2001 Jackals carried into 2002, when the Jackals set a club record for regular-season wins (sixty-two) in coasting to their second consecutive Northern League championship under George Tsamis. Outfielders Travis Bailey and Billy Rich led the offense, while Joel Bennett led the pitching staff with fourteen wins. Tsamis moved on to St. Paul, Minnesota, to manage the Northern League Saints in 2003. His two-season winning percentage of .598 (107-72) is the highest in the history of the club, giving the new Jackals manager, Joe Calfapietra, a record to strive for.[7]

Joe Calfapietra established a reputation in independent baseball as an excellent player-personnel evaluator, spending five seasons as director of baseball operations for the Allentown Ambassadors, including two seasons as field manager. After spending one year helping to develop the expansion Northern League Gary (Indiana) Railcats in 2002, Calfapietra moved east to the Jackals in 2003. He immediately took his club to the Northeast League playoffs, losing to the Brockton Rox in the divisional series. In 2004, led by ex-major-league infielder Wilton Veras, the Jackals made the playoffs again with a 54-39 regular season record. After defeating the Bangor Lumberjacks in the divisional series, the Jackals rode the pitching of Joel Bennett to come from two games down in the final series to defeat the North Shore Spirit, three games to two, for the 2004 Northern League Championship.

The club did not make the Can-Am League's playoffs in 2005 and 2006. Regardless, they have firmly established themselves as part of the northern New Jersey baseball scene. One Jackals player who is thoroughly familiar with that scene is Fair Lawn native Zach Smithlin, who began his professional baseball career with the New Jersey Cardinals in Sussex County in 2003. Not having been drafted after playing collegiate baseball at Penn State University, Smithlin was invited to try out for the St. Louis Cardinals organization, and was released after playing a moderately successful season with the New York–Penn League Cardinals. The Jackals quickly signed Smithlin, who, like other young baseball players hoping for another chance at affiliated ball, was grateful for the opportunity. A fleet-footed outfielder, Smithlin batted .300 with fourteen stolen bases in 2004, and his energetic style of play has endeared him to the Jackals fans. After a brief stay at spring training with the San Diego Padres organization in 2005, Smithlin returned to the Jackals and played for them through the 2007 season. "Personally, I get a lot of support, being from the area, so I really like to playing around home," explained Smithlin during batting practice at Yogi Berra Stadium in August 2005.[8] Like most minor-league and independent professional players, Smithlin, at age twenty-six, knows that the clock is ticking on his baseball career, and he needs to keep advancing. "Guys realize that if you're starting to get to twenty-six, twenty-seven, twenty-eight years old in independent ball, your time is starting to pass. You never know when it's going to happen [being re-signed by an affiliated organization]. You just have to be seen by the right person on the right day," said Smithlin. "You hear it all the time, and it sounds like a cliché, but you have to go out and hustle and give it 110 percent, and that's what the scouts are looking at, not the numbers, but the type of player you are." It is this type of hustle and desire that typifies independent baseball. In affiliated, minor-league baseball, player development and advancing through the organization are the primary motivators. In independent ball, showing hustle and winning games count the most. For fans, winning games is more meaningful, especially when some of those wins come at the expense of a local rival.

The Jackals had no local rival for the first eight seasons they played in Little Falls. The closest ball club to them is the Newark Bears, and the different season lengths of the Can-Am and Atlantic Leagues make it virtually impossible for the two clubs to even consider playing each other in exhibition games. Floyd and Larry Hall, Greg Lockard, and the Can-Am League commissioner, Miles Wolff, found an ideal opportunity to rectify that situation in creating some local competition for the Jackals for the 2006 season.

In Augusta, the patience of New Jersey Cardinals' owner Barry Gordon with his strained relationship with the owners of the park finally ran out in 2005. Ticket sales for Cardinals games leveled off to an average of 3,100 fans per game, even though some detractors dispute that total as being inflated and in fact not reaching 2,000 on most days. The parent St. Louis Cardinals asked that some improvements be made to Skylands Park, and the New York–Penn League told the club that it had to bring the field lighting up to higher league standards. Millennium Sports Management, the owner of the ballpark, hesitated to put more money into the facility. Gordon, tired of losing on his investment, sold the franchise to a group who moved it to a new 6,000-seat, state-of-the-art facility on the campus of Penn State University. In early October 2005, it was officially announced that the New Jersey Cardinals, a fixture in Sussex County since 1994, would be leaving New Jersey. Skylands Park faced a bleak future unless another club could be found to play there.

Rumors about the park's future began immediately. The stadium and the Cardinals still had a contractual arrangement in place for use of the park through 2006, and a new club could not move in until the contract could be resolved. Given the rocky past relationship between Gordon and Millennium, a buyout of the contract would not be easy. Also under discussion, separate from the stadium issue, was the development of land surrounding the ballpark at Ross Corner, most notably by a ninety-unit mixed retail and residential complex called Sussex Commons. This project provided two schools of thought for the future of the property. One school noted that the Sussex Commons development would bring additional retail traffic to the area and make the ballpark more visible to potential fans, which would be good for baseball attendance. The other alternative, less positive for baseball, was that Millennium could choose to knock down Skylands Park and sell the land to the highest-bidding developer. In late October 2005, Can-Am League commissioner Miles Wolff stepped into the discussions.[9]

Wolff believed that Sussex County was attractive for a Can-Am League team, as attendance in the smaller Can-Am markets was similar to what the Cardinals were drawing. The league also had an all-road-game club called the Grays playing in 2005. A team playing a complete road schedule is common in independent baseball, as it enables leagues to maintain an even number of teams, which makes scheduling games more manageable. It also supplies jobs for those players seeking them. It is ideal, however, for all clubs to have a home of their own, and this fueled the league's desire to find additional territories. Wolff wanted both Nashua and Sussex County in the Can-Am League, but he was running short on time to arrange it for the 2006 season. He was fortunate to have a willing New Jersey partner in Floyd Hall Enterprises.

Floyd Hall was immediately bullish on placing a club, to compete with his Jackals, at Skylands Park. "I think it's a good area to have a baseball team and it could succeed," Hall told the *New Jersey Herald*. "A good organization could come in and bring the kind of good baseball and family activities that Sussex deserves," Hall promised to lower ticket, concession, and parking prices at Skylands and to otherwise create a more fan-friendly environment. He also felt it was mandatory to put a club in Skylands in 2006, because he felt that if the park sat empty for the season, the goodwill of the local fans would be lost and it would be twice as difficult to reestablish a franchise there. Bob Wirz had his own view on why Floyd and Larry Hall were interested in Sussex County. "I think they care so much about their league," speculated Wirz, "that when they saw an opportunity for the league, and they saw that the ballpark was available, I think they probably got involved in Sussex as much for the benefit of the league as anything." Negotiations continued through late 2005, and on January 9, 2006, Wolff and Floyd Hall Enterprises announced that Sussex County would be in the Can-Am League in 2006, saving Skylands Park and baseball for Augusta, New Jersey. The new club was named the Sussex Skyhawks. "It's a Whole New Ballgame!" immediately became the club's marketing slogan as plans proceeded to field the club for the first time in May 2006.

On Memorial Day, May 29, the Skyhawks opened their first season at Skylands Park with an evening game against the North Shore Spirit from Lynn, Massachusetts. Improvements were already evident in the ballpark. The press box area was newly repainted and the ceiling, which had been in disrepair, fixed. The restrooms were clean and in operating order. Yet, an hour and a half before the game, Floyd and Larry Hall could be seen scurrying around the fan concourse, tending to last-minute preparations, at a frantic pace. "We're not sure what we have here as of yet," Floyd Hall said to me as I greeted him in front of one of the new concession stands. "I still see lots of things that need to be done. We're sticklers for details." Hall seemed optimistic overall about his prospects in Sussex County and his new relationship with Millennium Sports Management. "I'm okay with Millennium," Hall said. "They've done okay by us, so far," meaning that the initial business relationship between the Hall group and Millennium was going somewhat smoother than it had with the Cardinals. Hall also felt sure that the fans would accept the Can-Am League style of baseball.

How different was Can-Am baseball from New York–Penn League affiliated baseball for the Sussex County fans? Realistically, the play is not that much different at all. A similarity between the leagues is that both focus on younger players, some fresh out of college, and play a short-season schedule. There are no big established stars in either league. Nobody is more qualified to speak about the differences and similarities in the leagues than the Jackals' outfielder Zach Smithlin, who played in both. "Well, the obvious difference," explained Smithlin, "is with an independent club, there's a little more room to do your own thing, and there's a little more lax on team rules. With an affiliated club, you have to come to the park dressed in a collared shirt and slacks every day, but here you can show up in sandals and shorts, and I think both situations have their benefits. It's a little bit more of a player's game in the independent leagues. There is always the chance that there are scouts at these [independent] games anyway. It is still professional baseball, and you are still getting paid, and everybody's got that dream, whether you're in independent ball or affiliated ball, to get to the big leagues. On the field, I would say the two leagues are very, very comparable." Lee Deuser, a fan from Wharton, New Jersey, who attended an average of fifteen New Jersey Cardinal games per year, wasn't so sure what he would find. "It was kind of disappointing when the Cardinals left, and I don't know what this is like [the Can-Am League] so we came out tonight to find out," Deuser said as he sat in the stands at Skylands Park awaiting the first pitch on opening night. When asked what the Skyhawks had to do to keep him a fan, Deuser responded, "the game has got to be exciting, it has to be a good atmosphere like it was before. They lowered the prices, and that's a big plus."

The box seats were full on opening night, the reserved seats above the middle aisle half-full, as a crowd of 3,240 came to witness the first game in Sussex Skyhawks history. Most of the cheers were reserved for Skyhawks outfielder Josh Ury, a native of nearby Parsippany, who did not disappoint his fans when he doubled during the opener.

Ury became a sentimental favorite of the local fans during the 2006 season. He typified the dedication of a professional baseball player in the independent leagues. A 1997 graduate of Parsippany Hills High School in neighboring Morris County, Ury broke the school's hitting records that were held previously by ex-major-leaguer Johnny Orsino. Ury entered Winthrop University in South Carolina, where he continued to refine his baseball skills. Undrafted by a major-league organization out of college, Ury tried out for the independent Frontier League in 2002. He played four seasons in the Frontier League, in small communities like Johnstown, Pennsylvania; O'Fallon, Missouri; and Chillicothe, Ohio. Nearing twenty-seven years of age and tired of the travel, Ury decided to return to his New Jersey home, where a teaching and coaching career awaited him in the Parsippany school system. Then the Sussex Skyhawks were created, and the opportunity to play one more year of baseball, in front of local friends and family, was too good to pass up. Ury made the most of the opportunity. Batting mostly in the third position in the Skyhawks batting order, he averaged a robust .269 with fourteen doubles and thirty-seven runs batted in. In 2007, the Parsippany Hills High School baseball team will benefit by having Josh Ury as their coach. But, on the opening night of the 2006 baseball season, Ury was very much a Sussex Skyhawk. Coaching would have to wait one more year.[10]

Unfortunately for the Skyhawks, the North Shore Spirit banged out twenty-four hits on opening night to win the game, 18–11. The outcome was the only negative of the evening, as the Skyhawks seemed adept at the usual pregame and between-innings entertainment, contests, and giveaways. Except for the most die-hard baseball purists, most in the crowd probably didn't realize the difference between the affiliated Cardinals and the independent Skyhawks based on the entertainment provided for the fans. "That's an area where there's not one iota of difference between independent and affiliated baseball," explained Bob Wirz, who helped operate the New Haven County Cutters of the Can-Am League. "It's the same show, and if it's done right, you go away from the park, and you may not know who won the game or the score of the game, or you may not know who the home team was playing, but you had a good time, and what's wrong with that?" added Wirz.

The Skyhawks were competitive in the season's first half, winning twenty-three while losing twenty-two and finishing only two and one half games behind the first-half winner, the North Shore Spirit. Two player losses hurt the club as it moved into the second half of the season. Pitcher Kevin Olsen, who started the season with four straight victories for the Skyhawks, was signed by the Oakland A's organization and returned to affiliated baseball at the end of June. Left-handed pitcher Chris Zallie, who had three wins against two losses with a low earned run average of

2.48 in forty innings pitched, sustained a season ending injury and could not return. The club, under first-year manager Brian Drahman, did not sustain its momentum in the second half, as the Skyhawks only won nine games against thirty six losses.

Despite the dismal won-lost record, the first season of the Sussex Skyhawks is considered a success. The team averaged 2,183 fans over thirty-nine home games for the season, ranking them thirtieth out of the fifty-five independent professional teams in the country. Considering that the Skyhawks did not have a full off-season to implement marketing plans and group sales strategies, the support they received was solid. Special events were a big draw, as the Skyhawks filled the park to capacity for all of their scheduled fireworks shows. A more favorable holiday schedule and some better luck with the weather should have a positive impact for the Skyhawks attendance in 2007. The Skyhawks lost six of the forty-six scheduled home dates in 2006 due to rain. Besides the games to be played against their northern New Jersey rivals, the Jackals, the Skyhawks will have another New Jersey club to compete with in 2007. The Atlantic City Surf, formerly of the Atlantic League, transferred to the Can-Am League and will begin play in the league in May.

The Surf still play at the 5,500-seat Bernie Robbins Stadium at the southern end of Atlantic City. The Surf became the southernmost area reached by the Can-Am League, stretching the league from Quebec City, Canada, to Atlantic City. Bob Wirz thinks that the move makes sense for the Surf and for the league. "If I were looking at the good of the Can-Am League, Atlantic City gives them another franchise that has a good chance of doing well in Can-Am terms," said Wirz. "I think the length of the Atlantic League season [early May through September] obviously was a factor in the minds of the people in Atlantic City. They've done okay, but they can't quite measure up to Somerset or Long Island in attendance, and they see that they are better equipped to be in a shorter season with a little better economics for them. I think the Can-Am League sees Atlantic City as potentially another decent-to-strong franchise for it in the years to come."

The Can-Am League expanded to ten clubs for the 2007 season, with the addition of Atlantic City and the continuance of the Grays, the all-road team. Home schedules for the clubs have been expanded to fifty-six games each, beginning on Memorial Day weekend and running through Labor Day. Having three teams in the Can-Am League gives New Jersey a good balance of affiliated and independent professional clubs.

The Trenton Thunder and Lakewood BlueClaws provide the affiliated action, the three clubs in the Atlantic League (Camden, Somerset, and Newark) provide a longer-season, higher level of independent ball, and the three Can-Am League clubs provide shorter-season competition with younger players, much like the lowest levels of the minor leagues. There's something for everyone in New Jersey baseball.

So, let's experience what millions of New Jersey fans have since 1994. Let's go to a ball game!

11

Nine Innings with the
Lakewood BlueClaws

In the preceding pages, we have traveled throughout the New Jersey
baseball landscape. From the cornfields of Sussex County to the
Camden waterfront, we've looked at both minor-league and independent professional clubs from a working perspective. We have visited
front offices in the different yet similar worlds of the eight New Jersey
clubs who work to appeal to both the family entertainment and baseball
fan markets. After visiting ballparks, conducting interviews, and doing
research, it is now time to take a well-deserved evening of rest. What better way to relax than by going to a ball game? It is getting late in the 2006
season, so we'd better hurry up and get to a game or else we will have to
wait until next season. We might as well witness a little bit of history, too.

The Boardwalk Food Court at FirstEnergy Park, home of the Lakewood Blue-
Claws. Photograph by Bob Golon, 2005.

Tonight, for a $6.00 general admission ticket, we can bring our blankets and sit on the grassy outfield embankments and watch the first Lakewood BlueClaws playoff game ever at FirstEnergy Park with fellow "sod squad" fans.[1]

The Lakewood BlueClaws were one of the last teams to come to New Jersey, beginning play in 2001. A lower-level Single-A minor-league affiliate of the Philadelphia Phillies, BlueClaws players are typically in their second or third season of professional baseball. Even though the BlueClaws have had future Phillies stars like National League home run champion Ryan Howard and promising young pitchers like Gavin Floyd and Cole Hamels play for them, these stars rarely stayed for more than one season. The team never attained the South Atlantic League championship playoffs until this, the 2006 season. That is why it may be surprising to many readers that the BlueClaws have never had trouble attracting fans. As we've seen about New Jersey baseball though, field victories are not closely related to team popularity. In the Garden State it seems it is more about location, investment in the community, and community support than about a playoff berth or a championship ring.

This Wednesday evening, September 6, happens to be one of the first school nights of the new school year. This circumstance, combined with the fact that midweek minor-league playoff games don't usually draw large crowds, poses a real question of whether there will be a large turnout of fans at tonight's game. Drawing fans during the regular season has never been a problem for the Lakewood BlueClaws. They have parlayed great local fan demographics with the influx of summer shore vacationers to become, by a large margin, the attendance leaders of New Jersey baseball. The BlueClaws averaged more than 6,600 fans per game over the past two seasons, outdrawing the nearest competitor, the Trenton Thunder, by approximately 600 fans per game. Most fans attend minor-league games not because they are die-hard fans of the team but because they enjoy the inexpensive entertainment. Tonight's crowd would prove to be unique in this respect, and they begin to arrive at the park early.

An hour before game time, at 6 PM, cars are lined up at the ballpark entrance on New Hampshire Avenue, their drivers waiting to pay the $1.00 parking fee for a spot in the spacious parking areas. Young parking attendants, resplendent in their red-and-blue Hawaiian shirts, direct the cars to the various lots. FirstEnergy Park looks out of place in the industrial park section of Lakewood. The ballpark is not in downtown Lakewood, nor is it even in an outlying residential area. Yet, not a single warehouse or factory can be seen from its parking lots. What rises in the distance is the pointed, sloping roof and the slate walls of FirstEnergy Park, designed to mimic the Victorian-era construction of old Lakewood. When it was first announced in 1999 that the Lakewood area would be hosting minor-league baseball, the idea was met with skepticism that would be proved incorrect. The demographics were favorable. A total of 200,000 residents lived year-round in Lakewood as well as in the surrounding towns of Brick Township and Toms River. Construction of housing for the year-round residents had yet to peak in the Monmouth and Ocean County areas. The ballpark property was within one mile of the busy New Jersey Routes 70 and 9 as well as the Garden State Parkway. Construction of a new parkway exit that would empty cars onto nearby Cedar Bridge Avenue began shortly after the ballpark opened. Building the park in Lakewood also made good economic sense, as Lakewood had been designated as an urban enterprise recovery zone in 1994. This was done in an effort to attract new businesses and residents to Lakewood by having the New Jersey state sales tax reduced to 3 percent in the urban enterprise area. As part of the enterprise zone agreement, Lakewood also receives approximately $3 million per year in sales tax rebates from the state to help fund economic development projects, enough to repay the bonds necessary to fund the building of the ballpark without costing Lakewood's taxpayers a penny.[2] These details are the furthest things from the BlueClaws fans' minds as they make their way to the entrance gates one hour before game time tonight. They have their BlueClaws shirts and hats on, as well as their game-faces. There is a serious nature about this crowd that is much different than the typical minor-league crowd on a lazy summer evening.

After buying our general admission tickets at the ticket window, we pass by the Claw's Cove apparel shop on our way to the main entrance gate. The store is doing a brisk business. Besides all sorts of BlueClaws apparel and memorabilia, Ryan Howard Philadelphia Phillies jerseys are a featured item. Howard played with Lakewood in 2002, on his way to eventual stardom with the Phillies. He hit nineteen home runs for the BlueClaws, considered a high amount for a lower level minor-league player. By 2005, the big first baseman was the National League Rookie of the Year, and in 2006, he led the National League with 58 home runs and

149 runs batted in. The BlueClaws dedicated bobble-head doll nights and other promotions to Howard, who fast became the first famous former player of the franchise.

Moving past the Cove, we make our way into FirstEnergy Park through the entrance directly behind home plate. The size and expanse of the park stand out. Not bounded by any geographic limitations such as small city blocks or a crowded neighborhood, the designers of First Energy Park built outward instead of upward. The 6,588-seat grandstand slopes gently up to a fan concourse that is one of the widest and most comfortable in baseball. The concourse does not stop at the outfield corners like it does in most other parks. Instead it wraps around the outfield in one continuous loop, allowing fans a unique opportunity to walk completely around the playing field. The Philadelphia Phillies, the parent club of the BlueClaws, were so impressed with this feature that they built a fan concourse completely around the lower deck of their new ballpark, Citizens Bank Park, which opened in 2004. The BlueClaws general manager Geoff Brown explained the building of FirstEnergy Park as being a case of lessons well learned from the recent construction of minor-league parks across the nation. "We had the benefit of the stadium-building boom in the early 1990s, and here we were, seven years after that boom. The architects were now more familiar with what minor-league stadiums could offer, so we took the good in a lot of the ballparks across the country and put them all together and made this facility, which is just unbelievable," explained Brown.[3] The BlueClaws were serious in their desire for a unique ballpark design. After the initial cost estimates for the park came in above the $20 million that the township anticipated, the BlueClaws agreed to spend $2 million of their own money to ensure that the walk-around concourse and the elevated picnic areas that extend down both the first- and third-base lines would be built, as well as a third picnic area in left field.[4] The playing surface is built below ground level, making it possible for the outfield to be surrounded by a grassy knoll area below the concourse. This area can accommodate up to 3,000 additional fans carrying blankets or towels into the ballpark to spread out and sit on, much like spending a day on the nearby beaches. The group sitting in this area quickly became known as "the Sod Squad," and it is in this area that we settle in for the game tonight.

Besides the full-time residents of the area, the BlueClaws benefit greatly by the influx of vacationers attracted to the nearby New Jersey shore resorts during the summer months. This is not lost on BlueClaws

management, and evidence of the shore culture is everywhere in the ballpark. In the right-field corner of the concourse, there is a food court designed to look like the boardwalk food stands that are found in Point
Pleasant and Seaside Heights. Boardwalk-style food, from cheesesteaks
and sausage sandwiches to funnel cakes are available here, and fans can sit
at a large area of picnic tables located in front of the food court. At 6:15 PM,
forty-five minutes prior to the throwing of the first pitch tonight, there
are approximately fifty people waiting in line for dinner at the food court.
As is the case at Citizens Bank Park in Philadelphia and Fenway Park in
Boston, it appears that part of the appeal of going to a game in Lakewood
is arriving early to enjoy dinner at the food court before the ballgame.

To the right of the eating area is a boardwalk-style arcade, complete
with a wheel of fortune and Skee-Ball games. BlueClaws staffers hand
out baseball-card sets to those who play and match the number on the
wheel. Large wooden lifeguard chairs line the outfield at the edge of the
concourse, affording those who are able to climb up onto them an elevated
view of the game. In the deepest part of the outfield concourse, in straightaway center field, is the Rat Trap, a tiki bar with a grass roof that serves
beer and other exotic beverages. Here, fans can enjoy their favorite brews
while watching the game from standup picnic tables above the center-
field wall. In the left-field corner of the concourse is a play area for kids,
filled with inflatable rides and attractions. Even the team's name, the
BlueClaws, is in honor of one of the most popular recreational fishing activities at the Jersey shore: the summertime pursuit of the blue-clawed
crab. All that is missing from the ballpark is the sand and the surf itself.

In 2005, the summer tourism industry in Ocean and Monmouth
Counties generated approximately $5.2 billion dollars of revenue, with
$800 million of that revenue being spent on personal and family enter-
tainment.[5] It is little wonder that the Lakewood BlueClaws target this industry for summer customers. "We kind of have a niche for everyone,"
explained Mike Ryan, the club's director of marketing. "I like to think of
us as a shore attraction. I don't necessarily like to use the word 'competition' when I refer to the beach or the boardwalks or Six Flags Great Adventure Amusement Park. I like to think of them as our partners in the
tourism industry. We've done cooperative marketing with businesses like
Monmouth Park Racetrack and Jenkinson's Pavilion in Point Pleasant. A
baseball team just adds to the reasons why it's great to come down to the
New Jersey shore. Now you don't only have the beach, the fishing, and
the bars to go to. I feel that coming to a game here and sitting on the lawn,

you can sit in the sun, lay your blanket down, and you get a baseball game instead of just watching the boats going back and forth. You have a baseball team, with a nice bar in center field, so you get everything."

However, today is September 6, and the summer tourist season unofficially ended last Monday with Labor Day. Yet, the cars keep pouring into the parking lots and the stands are rapidly filling at 6:30 PM. The lack of tourist trade tonight can be seen by the fact that there are only four beach blankets set up on the lawn. With the beach and summer sun time over, these are serious baseball fans filling the grandstand area, most with some sort of BlueClaws apparel on. The appeal of the team obviously extends beyond the summer tourism crowd.

After visiting the food court, we settle on our blankets with our cheesesteak sandwiches, french fries, and diet Cokes. I don't know if there is a more American scene than the one I'm watching tonight. Sitting in the grass in right field, I can see the sun beginning to set over the stands. Some young players toss the ball around in the outfield while others run wind sprints. Families and friends are gathered, chatting and laughing. John Mellencamp music plays on the loudspeakers. Great invention, this baseball game. The seats are beginning to fill in. This is a very peaceful place, pregame. The public-address announcer acknowledges the local businesses that are sponsoring tonight's events and promotions. A company called Blue Water Communications distributed to all of the fans coming into the park tonight a commemorative oversize ticket stub, suitable for framing, as a memento of this first playoff game in BlueClaws history. A quick scan of the advertising billboards at FirstEnergy Park shows the presence of national corporate sponsors like Home Depot and Verizon Communications as well as a number of smaller, local businesses, from delicatessens to regional banks, who have chosen to spend their advertising dollars within the community. As the local politicians make congratulatory speeches to the BlueClaws organization before tonight's first ball is thrown, there is great evidence of community pride in the air.

The BlueClaws play the Lexington Legends tonight in the first round of the South Atlantic League playoffs. The Legends are a Single-A affiliate of the Houston Astros of the National League. Lexington gained prominence earlier in the season when future Hall of Fame pitcher Roger Clemens pitched some games for them in preparation for his mid-season return to the Astros. Clemens's nineteen-year-old son Koby, an eighth-round draft choice of the Astros in 2005, plays third base for the Legends, hoping to emulate his father by playing for the Astros in the future. This first round of the playoffs is in the best-of-three format, so there is little room for error tonight, as whoever loses this game will be facing elimination from the playoffs as soon as Friday night. The league plays a split-season schedule during the regular season. Those teams in first place at midseason automatically qualify for the playoffs, with the remaining clubs battling for two additional playoffs spots in the second half of the season. The Legends won the Northern Division first-half title, and the BlueClaws finished strong by winning the Northern Division second-half title. Whoever comes out victorious in this round will face the winner of the Southern Division playoffs, either the Augusta Green-Jackets or the Rome Braves, for the South Atlantic League championship. Dusk settles on the park as both teams line up along the first- and third-base lines, respectively, after being introduced to the crowd. There's an autumn chill in the air, which adds to the atmosphere and makes the evening truly feel like postseason baseball.

Tonight's pitching matchup is a good one. Twenty-two-year-old Brad James starts the game for the Legends. The right-handed James won six games and lost only two during the season, with a low 1.36 earned run average per nine innings. Taking the mound to start the game for the BlueClaws is nineteen-year-old Carlos Luis Carrasco from Barquisimeto, Venezuela. The Phillies gave Carrasco a $300,000 bonus to sign a contract in 2003. He combines a fastball consistently timed in the mid-90s (mph) with an effective changeup unusual for a pitcher as young as he. The well-respected baseball publication *Baseball America* named Carrasco the number-one minor-league prospect in the Phillies system going into 2007. The lanky right-hander won twelve games while losing only six during 2006, striking out an average of one batter per inning. Carrasco delivers ball one to the Legends' designated hitter Nathan Warrick at 7:05 PM, and the game is under way.

Smaller, auxiliary scoreboards displaying the inning, the ball-strike count, and the line score hang from both the first-base and third-base grandstands, making it easier for those of us on the lawn to view the ball and strike count without having to continually turn our heads to see the big video scoreboard in left field. Carrasco walks the second batter of the inning, and after he attempts to pick the runner off at first base, a recorded voice shouting "don't even try it!" blasts from the loudspeakers. Recorded sound effects—such as glass breaking when a foul ball leaves the ballpark, mimicking the sound of someone's windshield being broken—are a big part of the minor-league atmosphere. A roar goes up from the crowd of 6,410 when Lexington first baseman Mark Ori hits a fly ball out to short left field, ending the scoreless top of the first inning. It is a deep-throated, long-lasting cheer, an indication that the fans are truly into the action on the field as it unfolds before them. The BlueClaws go down quietly in their half of the first, and the pitching duel between James and Carrasco is on.

Koby Clemens lines a hard-hit, clean single into left field for the Legends to lead off the top of the second. Being the son of a major leaguer is not always easy, especially when your dad is Roger Clemens. In spring training this year, the younger Clemens was taking batting practice against his father and surprised Roger by hitting one of his pitches over the fence. Koby immediately found himself where many major leaguers do after taking his dad deep. On the very next pitch he was dusting off the seat of his pants after having to hit the ground to get out of the way from a high hard one. Blood might be thicker than water, but not during batting practice! Koby Clemens batted only .229 for the Legends in 2006, but he showed some power, with five home runs and thirty-nine runs batted in, and is considered a good prospect in the Astros organization. With Clemens on first and after striking out center fielder Mitch Einerston, Carrasco gives up another base hit, this time to second baseman Eric King. With one out and runners on first and second base, Carrasco faces his first jam of the evening, but it would be short-lived when BlueClaws third baseman Welinson Baez catches a hot ground ball off the bat of Pedro Espinoza, beats Clemens to the bag at third for the second out of the inning, then, needing a perfect throw to first baseman John Urick to complete an inning-ending double play, does the job. This brings another great roar from the partisan BlueClaws crowd. The clubs trade zeros through four and one-half innings, and the score stands at 0-0 going into the bottom of the fourth. As a tense hush falls over the crowd between innings, we are treated to the usual entertainment at minor-league ballparks: a dizzy-bat race, tee-shirt tosses, and Buster the mascot racing a young fan around the bases—losing to the youngster, of course, as Buster always does.

A large, orange full moon appears through the smoke from the barbeque pits above the food court, rising in the sky above right field as the game moves into the bottom of the fourth inning. Mike Spidale, a .345 hitter during the regular season, leads off with a hard line drive single to left field—the first base hit of the game for the BlueClaws off James.

Cleanup hitter Jeremy Slayden follows by hitting a prodigious fly to the deepest part of the ballpark. The ball goes over the head of center fielder Joshua Flores, landing just at the base of the wall below the Rat Trap bar. Slayden speeds home from second base to score the first run of the game, touching off a celebration by the BlueClaws crowd. It's the kind of fan reaction normally heard at major-league ballparks when the home team is rallying and the fans are into the game as one. Something is definitely different about this Lakewood BlueClaws crowd tonight than any other crowd that I've ever witnessed at a minor-league game. They care who wins! This is *their* team, and they are here tonight to cheer their Blue-Claws to a win in their first playoff game.

After attending many games since 1994 in New Jersey, going to all of the ballparks throughout the seasons, the fans tonight gave me something new to consider. Why have the BlueClaws developed such a rabid fan base? After observing the operations of the eight New Jersey clubs and seeing how they pursue their different drawing areas, I came to a conclusion. All of the New Jersey teams make a conscientious effort to work with their communities. Most do a very good job. Some do a great job. The Lakewood BlueClaws, however, take it to the next level and do an outstanding job. BlueClaws management put together a team of ambassadors who, through old-fashioned hard work, have made the BlueClaws into an irreplaceable part of the local community during their short existence. Who are these community ambassadors? The mandate from the BlueClaws front office to drive community involvement comes directly from the top via the club owner, Joe Finley.

Finley left his law practice in the early 1990s to become an owner of the Trenton Thunder. Successful with that club, he decided to expand his horizons and sought a club for the New Jersey shore area later in the decade. Minor-league baseball does not prohibit dual ownership of clubs, and the local officials in Lakewood helped FirstEnergy Park become a reality. Finley now owned his second club, the Lakewood BlueClaws. Raised in southern New Jersey as a Philadelphia Phillies fan, Finley sought an affiliation with the Phillies, even though Lakewood lies directly on the imaginary line that divides residents' loyalties between the Phillies and the New York clubs.[6] The partnership he developed with local political officials proved to him that the community was anxious to see baseball in Lakewood work, and Finley sought immediate ties with the community by beginning some joint charitable projects. Finley and fellow Trenton

Thunder owner Joe Caruso started the Grand Slam We Care Foundation, which became the charitable arm of both the Thunder and BlueClaws organizations.

The BlueClaws' director of community relations Jim DeAngelis is the administrator of the foundation for the team. "Every year, the Grand Slam We Care Foundation donates $45,000 to three local charitable organizations in partnership with Wachovia Bank. The Salvation Army, the Ocean County YMCA, and the Big Brothers–Big Sisters of Monmouth County have been previous awardees," explained DeAngelis. "Another part of our Grand Slam We Care Foundation is our Tickets for Kids Program, which allows underprivileged and underserved kids in Monmouth and Ocean Counties the opportunity to come to a game, which they might not have otherwise. Over the last five years, the BlueClaws have donated over 7,000 tickets to local charitable organizations for children." DeAngelis and the BlueClaws actively pursue an alliance with local educators through Buster's Reading Program. He and the team's mascot visit thirty to forty elementary schools during the winter months, teaching children that reading is important. "The most improved student of every classroom in every school that we have an alliance with gets to go to a game, go onto the field, and introduce themselves to the crowd via the public address system. Another program that we have is Buster's Book Pals Program, where if children read fives books during the year, they get a complimentary BlueClaws ticket." Wonderful programs, but is this charity sincere?

It is only natural to cast a cynical eye on such aggressive efforts in the community-relations area, and a further look reveals an intelligent business rationale for conducting these programs. As altruistic as they are, the charitable efforts accomplish another very important goal for the BlueClaws: getting the children's parents to accompany them to the ballpark and, hopefully, generating the repeat family business that is so important to minor-league clubs. It is well worth a free ticket for a child if the parent buys some hot dogs, a couple of sodas, and a baseball cap. The goodwill generated within the Lakewood area by these programs makes adults in the area more eager to spend their entertainment dollars with the team. It is a win-win proposition for all involved, but it takes the motivation and hard work of owners like Finley and his staff to keep conveying the feeling of sincerity to the public. For his efforts, Jim DeAngelis was named the South Atlantic League's Community Relations Director of the Year for the 2005 and 2006 seasons, and he takes his personal ties to the area seriously. DeAngelis not only does the BlueClaws' community work, he also contributes as an individual, serving on the executive board of directors of the Toms River Chamber of Commerce and the Salvation Army of Ocean County and as an appointed member of the Ocean County Tourism Advisory Council. Good business and local commitment are able to coexist in the team's operation. Getting the word out about the BlueClaws via the local media is also an important part of the overall community relations effort.

Ben Wagner was the play-by-play broadcaster of BlueClaws games via the radio and Internet through the 2006 season, after which he took a similar position with the Triple-A Buffalo Bisons. Wagner's play-by-play work was an extension of his overall duties as the club's media and public relations manager. The media and public relations manager's number-one priority during the off-season is maintaining the visibility of the BlueClaws via media and community communications. Wagner was the main mouthpiece of the franchise during his tenure with Lakewood. "It's constant, constant, constant community involvement in letting the community know we're always involved," explained Wagner. "We get involved with silent auctions and donate tickets for them. If something tragic unfortunately happens to a local child or family, the BlueClaws want to be right there to help. If someone has a house fire, we want to host a clothing drive to help out the affected family. We want to carry our message all year round that we are here for the community; we are here for your family. If one family has a concern, we listen to it. We've done it that way all the years we've been here." Wagner also put a high priority on his relationship with the local press outlets, in particular the *Asbury Park Press* and the *Ocean County Observer*, the main daily newspapers that serve the Monmouth and Ocean County areas. "Absolutely, hands down, that's the number-one thing, the local newspapers," said Wagner. Our goal during the season is to have something about the Lakewood BlueClaws in the sports sections each and every day. It is also my role to write something about the team that is community oriented and have it appear in the papers during the off-season at least three times a week, whether it's announcing a theme night, honoring a local little-league team, or teaming up with a local sponsor to give away a $25,000 grant to a not-for-profit local organization." Wagner feels that it is the responsibility of the club to let the community know that it cares about it far more than by just placing run-of-the-mill advertising. "If it's a story, people are going to read the story and identify with the BlueClaws. Through communication, we have developed an incredible following in the Monmouth and Ocean County areas. It's a hand-in-hand combination. We support the community, and the community supports us." The 6,410 fans that came to cheer passionately for the BlueClaws tonight was evidence of the connection that the local area feels with the team.

The Legends and Blue Claws settle in for what was to become a tense nail-biter—a chess match disguised as a baseball game. Each batter becomes important, as every pitch could determine the outcome of the game. The Legends' second baseman Eric King reaches safely on a single to lead off the top of the fifth inning, but Carrasco settles down, striking out the last two batters of the inning. In the bottom half, James strikes out Lou Marson for the first out but walks the number-nine batter, Welinson Baez. James gathers himself and strikes out Matt Thayer, and with two out and a runner on first, it looked as if James might get out of the inning without further trouble. However, Avelino Asprilla hits a double down the left-field line, moving Baez to third, then Mike Spidale walks to load the bases. Sensing that James is tiring, Lexington manager Jack Lind makes a pitching change. He calls on left-hander Chris Blazek to pitch to Jeremy Slayden in an attempt to stop the rally in this critical at-bat. If Slayden gets a hit here, he would drive in two runs, opening up a 3-0 lead and gaining some critical breathing room for the BlueClaws. Slayden brings the fans to their feet by hitting a solid line drive to center field that briefly looks like the key blow, but centerfielder Joshua Flores catches the ball to end the threat. The score remains 1-0 in favor of the BlueClaws through five innings. Carrasco hits Eli Iorg with a pitch to begin the Legends' sixth inning, and after inducing Justin Towles to ground out, Carrasco allows Mark Ori to line a clean single to right field. Iorg, who moved to second on the previous groundout, runs at full speed, and the BlueClaws fans hold their breath as it looks as if he will score easily to tie the game. Right fielder Thayer has other ideas. He charges the ball, gathers it in, and delivers a perfect throw to home plate, forcing Iorg to scramble back to third base, thus saving the lead for the Claws. Right-hander Will Savage begins to warm up in the BlueClaws bullpen, but he sits back down as Clemens hits a ball hard to third base that is converted into a quick double play by the BlueClaws infield, ending the Legends' threat. In the bottom of the sixth, BlueClaws shortstop C. J. Henry strikes out looking, for the second out of the inning, drawing a reaction of boos from the local fans. It is unusual that a BlueClaw is booed by the partisan home crowd in such an important game, but perhaps the high expectations everyone had for Henry had something to do with that. Henry was a first-round pick of the New York Yankees in the 2005 draft, a curious choice considering that the Yankees employ Derek Jeter at shortstop and probably will for the next ten years. After a lackluster year of batting in the .240s for the Yankees' Gulf Coast and Chattanooga farm teams, Henry was traded to the Phillies organization on July 31 as part of the deal that sent Bobby Abreu and Cory Lidle to the Yankees. As Henry returns to the dugout, Marson grounds out to second, and the game goes into the seventh inning with the BlueClaws clinging by a thread to their 1-0 lead.

Carlos Carrasco returns to the mound for the top of the seventh inning, which surprises some in the crowd. Minor-league pitchers very rarely pitch past seven innings as pitch counts are carefully monitored to prevent putting a strain on a young prospect's arm. But these are the playoffs, and Carrasco rewards manager Dave Huppert's confidence by retiring the Legends in order in the inning. It appears that Carrasco is getting stronger as the game goes on. Nick Cavanaugh begins the seventh inning on the mound for the Legends and has a strong inning himself, striking out two while retiring the BlueClaws in order.

Huppert might have pushed his confidence in Carrasco to the limit in the top of the eighth inning. As Carrasco comes out to begin the inning, an uncomfortable buzz in the crowd is heard, as no pitchers are warming up, on standby, in the BlueClaws bullpen. Carrasco immediately validates those fears by walking the leadoff batter, Nathan Warrick. After Joshua Flores sacrifices Warrick to second, Huppert senses the impending danger and has Savage return to warming up in the bullpen. Huppert is taking the chance that Carrasco has one more batter left in his stamina, but Iorg lines a single to left field. Warrick scores, and Iorg goes to second base on the throw, tying the game at 1-1. Savage runs in to replace Carrasco, to the blaring strains of "Disco Inferno" on the loudspeaker, and the home crowd falls silent, as if someone had let all of the air out of balloon. In a midsummer regular-season game, many of the fans would probably start heading to the exits at this point, but not this crowd. They may have been silenced, but their resolve is not broken as they remain in their seats for what looks like the possibility of extra innings. Savage retires the only two Legends he faces, ending the top half of the eighth with the game still tied.

The fans reawaken as Michael Spidale prepares to lead off the bottom of the eighth inning for the BlueClaws. Rhythmic clapping and chanting of "let's go BlueClaws" rock the ballpark. Spidale checks his swing in an attempt to lay off one of Cavanaugh's pitches, but the home plate umpire calls it a strike anyway, bringing a chorus of loud boos directed at the umpire. Spidale walks, and the Legends bring Jacob Hurry out of the bullpen to pitch to Jeremy Slayden. The crowd groans as Hurry appears to have caught Spidale napping and picks him off at first base, but the umpires rule that Hurry committed a balk and award second base to Spidale instead. As Legends manager Lind argues with the umpires about the balk ruling, Huppert senses a BlueClaws rally and has his closer, Brett Harker, warm up in the bullpen in the event that he is needed in the ninth inning. Slayden hits a long rocket to Flores in the deepest part of center field, and the ever-alert Spidale tags up and moves over to third base with one out. The chant of "let's go BlueClaws" is now deafening. Hurry walks Clay Harris intentionally to set up a potential force-out double play at second base. John Urick lines a clean base hit to right-center field, scoring Spidale and putting the BlueClaws ahead, 2-1. The partisan fans are on their feet in the stands. The BlueClaws again load the bases, and the crowd senses the kill. However, Legends pitcher Sergio Perez, who took over for Hurry after Urick's base hit, knuckles down and strikes out Marson and Baez to end the inning. The scoreboard shows BlueClaws 2, Legends 1. Three outs are needed to seal a Lakewood victory in game one of the playoffs.

Closer Brett Harker makes his way to the mound from the bullpen down the first base line as the crowd stand and cheers. All that's missing is the "Enter Sandman" music that accompanies both Mariano Rivera and Billy Wagner's entrances as closers for the Yankees and Mets at the New York stadiums. Clemens leads off the ninth for the Legends and hits a bullet line drive directly at center fielder Spidale for the first out. Ryan Reed, pinch-hitting for Mitch Einerston, sends Spidale back to the warning track in center field with a long drive. Two Legends out, one to go. All the spectators are again on their feet, cheering Harker on. Harker obliges them, striking out Eric King to end the game and setting off a wild celebration in the stands. The victorious BlueClaws players exchange numerous high fives as they leave the field. The high fives extend to the stadium exits also, as BlueClaws staffers, easily identified by their Hawaiian shirts, send off the smiling fans leaving the stadium with the traditional extended handshake as they head back to their cars.

The BlueClaws faithful kept smiling in the days that followed. After a day off, the series with the Legends resumed at FirstEnergy Park on

Friday, September 8. Lakewood ace Matt Maloney, who led the South Atlantic League with sixteen wins and a 2.03 earned run average in 2006, allowed only two runs on four hits in seven innings as the BlueClaws won, 8-2, to sweep the series from the Legends. Next up for the Claws were the Southern Division champion Augusta GreenJackets in a best-of-five South Atlantic League championship series.

The BlueClaws opened the series on the road, but the long bus trip to the Georgia town did not seem to bother them. Harris singled in the winning run in the eighth inning of game one to give the BlueClaws a 2-1 victory on Monday, September 11. The following night, the BlueClaws and the GreenJackets engaged in a classic battle for survival, with the BlueClaws triumphing again by a 2-1 score. This time, it took a home run by Urick in the top of the thirteenth inning to send the BlueClaws home to Lakewood with a commanding 2-0 lead in the series. Whatever hangover the GreenJackets might have had from the disappointing loss two nights before did not affect them as they beat the BlueClaws with ease, 11-1, in game three. Manager Huppert put the ball in the hands of his ace, Matt Maloney, for game four, and the pitcher did not disappoint him. He struck out twelve and scattered seven hits in a complete-game, 5-0 victory to give the Lakewood BlueClaws their first South Atlantic League Championship. As Thayer caught the final fly ball in right field off the bat of the GreenJackets' Pablo Sandoval, another celebration began in the stands and on the field as the BlueClaws players lined up to receive the league championship trophy in a ceremony at home plate.

BlueClaws fans are sophisticated enough to know that this year's success does not guarantee a repeat next season, as the 2007 roster will be totally made over with newer players coming up in the Phillies system. The 2006 BlueClaws who are judged as being talented enough to stay with the organization will move on. Some will go to the advanced Single-A club in the Florida State League in Clearwater. The "can't miss" prospects, if they play well during spring training, might even go as high as the Double-A Reading Phillies in the Eastern League. Lakewood fans will be content to root for their new players while following the exploits of the ex-BlueClaws via publications like *Baseball America* and the Internet. Maybe another Ryan Howard will emerge from the bunch. The players that the Phillies think will never make it to the major leagues will be released from the organization, and some may hook up with other organizations or with an independent club to continue chasing their dream.

The rest will simply go home, knowing that they were good enough at one time to play minor-league ball and be part of the 2006 South Atlantic League champion Lakewood BlueClaws.

Back at FirstEnergy Park, preparations are made for the off-season. Anything that can be moved is put on wheels and taken under cover to protect it from the elements of the winter. The Rat Trap is wheeled to a spot on the concourse under the overhang of the grandstand to protect it from snow and ice. The park is inspected, cleaned, and repaired before going to sleep for the long winter. Behind home plate, however, in the BlueClaws' offices, plans are already being made for 2007 promotions. New sponsorships are pursued, season-ticket packages are advertised, and the off-season community and charitable activities go into full swing.

April will be here in the blink of an eye, when it will again be time to "play ball," not only here in Lakewood, but in the seven other New Jersey ballparks, as well. For New Jersey baseball fans, winter is now a little bit easier to take, knowing that more relaxing afternoons and evenings await them next season. Considering all the years that the state had no professional baseball prior to 1994, it is no minor accomplishment that the game once again is flourishing. Baseball is alive and well in New Jersey!

12

Conclusion

The Community of New Jersey Baseball

I t is March 3, 2007. The late-winter chill is struggling mightily to give way to the brilliant early-morning sunshine on the campus of Montclair State University. There is nothing that looks more lonely than a ballpark in the off-season, and Yogi Berra Stadium is no exception. Viewed down the long stairway entrance, the infield is shielded from the winter cold and ice by a protective tarpaulin, and the uncovered outfield grass is the same shade of brown as the front lawn of my house. But today,

A rainbow settles over Commerce Bank Ballpark, Bridgewater, after a thunderstorm. Photograph by Bob Golon, 2005.

hope springs eternal. In what is becoming an annual rite of spring, the New Jersey chapter of the Society for American Baseball Research (SABR) prepares to hold its annual all-day conference. Named the Elysian Fields Chapter in honor of what many people believe is the birthplace of baseball in Hoboken, approximately seventy-five New Jersey baseball junkies gather for a day of speeches, panel discussions, and research presentations. Spring training is here! You can feel the air getting warmer already.

For most of those dark years between 1950 and 1994, New Jersey was the baseball stepchild of New York and Philadelphia. Even the New Jersey baseball historians who wanted to participate in SABR had to belong to either the New York or Philadelphia chapters and attend their meetings, as New Jersey did not have its own chapter. With the return of professional baseball to the Garden State in 1994, as well as the emergence of institutions like the Yogi Berra Museum and Learning Center, baseball fans here suddenly had places to go to—a community of their own. Surely, during the baseball season, television sets at home are still tuned to the Yankees, the Mets, and the Phillies, as nothing takes the place of major-league baseball for the baseball purist. But New Jersey became proud of its new facilities and its identity as a successful baseball location of its own. New Jersey is a mixture of baseball cultures that mirrors locations nationwide. We have baseball in urban settings, much like the successful minor-league operations in Buffalo and Memphis. We have baseball in rural settings that remind us of the appeal of baseball in smaller independent leagues like the current American Association in the Midwest. Our eight clubs are sandwiched between the major cities of New York and Philadelphia and have furthered the argument that such suburban clubs can exist in the shadow of their big-city brothers, much as Lowell and Brockton, both in Massachusetts, are in the shadow of Boston. Yet, despite all of this commonality, there is an element of competition between the New Jersey clubs that is always evident.

Ask any of the front-office personnel of the New Jersey minorleague and independent professional teams, and they will tell you that all of the teams are in competition with each other, and to an extent, they are correct. They all compete for fans, for families looking for affordable entertainment, for the attention of the press, and for the revenue brought in by corporate and group support that enables their survival. It is an allconsuming, twelve-month-a-year mission for the young men and women who work in the industry. Yet, the overall health of their industry is the underlying factor that drives club ownership and front-office behavior, much different than that seen in major-league baseball.

This concern became most clear to me in the collective decision by the Atlantic League owners to bail out the Camden Riversharks when the team faced financial ruin, as well as in the willingness of Steve Kalafer to attempt to help one of his primary competitors, the Newark Bears, when Rick Cerone was seeking to sell his share. The Can-Am League witnessed this all-for-one attitude when Floyd and Larry Hall brought a replacement team into Sussex County to compete with their own New Jersey Jackals. The affiliated-club owners are no strangers to difficult business decisions, as theirs is a constant struggle to balance the needs of the parent organization with their own while striving to maintain a winning club for their fans. Players come and go in both independent and affiliated minor-league baseball. Players of all-star caliber often leave their clubs in midseason, causing a stress on their organizations to replace them while providing continuity for their fans. Be that as it may, the most important factor that all of the New Jersey clubs need to consider is their respective communities, and those who do this the best will undoubtedly succeed in the long term. The similarities in their operations far outnumber the differences, with local involvement and participation as the common theme.

New Jerseyans have been able to identify and take pride in knowing that the Nomar Garciaparras, Robinson Canos, and Ryan Howards of the world got their early professional experiences in the state. They've enjoyed watching the Sparky Lyles and the Rickey Hendersons bring major-league credibility to their independent clubs. They have taken joy in seeing baseball parks rise in neighborhoods that were long neglected, as part of serious redevelopment projects in an attempt to bring those areas back to wealth and prominence. They've enjoyed watching the younger players pursue their dreams, because, after all, we all have dreams. And, as the years go on, the community of New Jersey baseball gets stronger, as evidenced by the SABR conference in the theater at the Yogi Berra Museum and Learning Center today.

Sam Bernstein, founder and leader of the Elysian Fields Chapter, kicks off the meeting by introducing "Brooklyn" Bradley Shaw, who is dressed in the uniform of the Flemington Neshanock, one of the vintage baseball clubs becoming popular in the state. Shaw entertains the audience with his rendition of "Casey at the Bat," the legendary poem by Ernest Lawrence Thayer. Professor Lawrence Hogan of Union County

College, one of the foremost experts on Negro League baseball and the author of *Shades of Glory: The Negro Leagues and the Story of African-American Baseball*, gives the keynote address about the rich history of black baseball in New Jersey. Hogan is followed by a panel discussion titled "Vintage Baseball Today: Is There a Turf War?" This discussion has a unique New Jersey flavor as former Yankee Jim Bouton, the Newark native and now the commissioner of the Vintage Base Ball Federation, is part of the discussion group. Sports economist Evan Weiner and former baseball executive Bob Wirz spend an hour talking about the business of baseball and the different baseball commissioners they have observed and worked for.

As the conference moves into the afternoon, Brad Taylor, general manager of the Trenton Thunder, gives the audience his unique perspective on the operation of the Double-A affiliate of the New York Yankees. As Taylor presents, Newark Bears official and baseball historian Mike Collazo listens intently. Baseball authors Gene Carney, Stan Teitlebaum, and Dan Schlossberg participate in a lively discussion about their recent book projects. Finally, chapter members Cait Murphy, Mike Gimbel, and Roberta Newman enlighten the conference with presentations on their most recent historical research projects. Throughout the entire program, the attendees are treated to raffles and door prizes provided by individuals and the New Jersey ball clubs, including autographed balls, books, yearbooks provided by the Lakewood BlueClaws, and free tickets provided by the Camden Riversharks, Newark Bears, and Trenton Thunder. Joe Nardini's fine publication, *New Jersey Baseball Magazine*, is available to all as they enter the museum. Is it any wonder that I can now, with full authority, refer to this group as "the Community of New Jersey Baseball?" There was no conference like this in New Jersey just ten short years ago.

Leaving the conference and walking to my car outside of Yogi Berra Stadium, I do some quick math in my head and realize that in only thirty-two more days, the gates to the New Jersey ballparks will begin to open, one by one, for the new season.

It can't get here quickly enough!

Notes

One: Baseball's Early Roots in New Jersey

1. The definitive history of the game of baseball in New Jersey pre-1950 continues to be *The Jersey Game* by James M. DiClerico and Barry J. Pavelec (New Brunswick, NJ: Rutgers University Press, 1991). This informative book was written just as the modern era of minor-league baseball in New Jersey was about to take off. It serves as a complete historical guide to the early game in the state.

2. Unfortunately, "Cap" Anson is known as much for his blatant racism as he is for being a baseball pioneer. This topic is covered particularly well in *Baseball: An Illustrated History* by Ken Burns and Geoffrey C. Ward (New York: Alfred A. Knopf, 1994). This is the same work that resulted in the film documentary series *Baseball*, also by Ken Burns. Burns's book pays particular attention to the plight of blacks in baseball in the early twentieth century and is a very good source on black baseball in the United States.

3. Those interested in the history of baseball stadium construction should consult *Diamonds: The Evolution of the Ballpark, from Elysian Fields to Camden Yards*, by Michael Gershman (Boston: Houghton Mifflin, 1993). Gershman fully chronicles the development of the concrete-and-steel parks that dominated in the early twentieth century. Another great source for "all things ballpark" is *Green Cathedrals* by Philip J. Lowry (Reading, MA: Addison-Wesley, 1992).

4. Considerable information on the Newark Peppers and the construction of Harrison Field in 1915 can be found by viewing the microfilm of the *Newark Evening News* at the New Jersey Room of the Newark Public Library. My article, "Newark's Harrison Field," published in *The National Pastime* (Cleveland: Society for American Baseball Research, 1996), is a summary of the genesis of the Peppers and their home stadium in Harrison. For general information on the Federal League, Mark Okkonen's *The Federal League of 1914–1915: Baseball's Third Major League* (Cleveland: Society for American Baseball Research, 1989) remains a definitive work.

5. The rationale used and decisions made by the New York major-league clubs in the 1930s and 1940s concerning night baseball were researched by electronically searching the *New York Times* via the Proquest Historical Newspapers Database, available at many public and university libraries.

6. The effect of night baseball and television on minor-league attendance in the New York metropolitan area received much attention in the pages of the *New York Times* during the 1940s, and the topic of televising major-league games and its impact on the private business practices of baseball clubs was the subject of a U.S. Senate hearing in 1953 by the Subcommittee on Televising Baseball Games, Committee of Interstate and Foreign Commerce. Robert V. Bellamy Jr. and James R. Walker's study, "Did Televised Baseball Kill the Golden Age of the Minor Leagues?" appeared in the fall 2004 issue of *Nine* and is a comprehensive source of information on the impact of television on minor-league baseball.

7. Between 1978 and 1981, the baseball historian and author Randolph Linthurst published three volumes on the history of the original Newark Bears. His *Newark Bears: The Final Years* (West Trenton, NJ: self-published, 1981) details the struggle of the franchise in the late 1940s, resulting in its sale and relocation from Newark.

8. *Effa Manley and the Newark Eagles*, by James Overmyer (Metuchen, NJ: Scarecrow Press, 1993), is the definitive history of the legendary Newark Eagles of Abe and Effa Manley, and was used as a research source for details regarding the relationship of the Eagles club with the black community of Newark. It also gives valuable insight into the abilities of Effa Manley as a baseball owner, abilities that resulted in her becoming the first woman ever elected to the Baseball Hall of Fame.

9. Besides his work on the Newark Bears, Randolph Linthurst also provides a thorough history of the Trenton Giants in his publication *The 1947 Trenton Giants: A Factual Account of a Championship Team in the Bus Leagues that Flourished after World War II*. In it, he gives a detailed description of Dunn Field and talks about its inadequacies as a minor-league ballpark.

10. The history of the Havana Sugar Kings and the facts behind their abandonment of Havana for Jersey City in 1960 was researched by using the Jersey City clippings vertical files at the National Baseball Hall of Fame and Library in Cooperstown, New York, and by viewing microfilm reels of the *Jersey Journal* in the periodicals room of Alexander Library, Rutgers University, New Brunswick, NJ.

Two: The Reinvention of the Minor Leagues

1. Robert V. Bellamy Jr. and James R. Walker, "Did Televised Baseball Kill the Golden Age of the Minor Leagues?" *Nine*, Fall 2004.

2. For a comprehensive history of minor-league baseball prior to 1990, see Neil J. Sullivan, *The Minors* (New York: St. Martin's Press, 1990).

3. The story of how the demise of the Jersey City franchise in 1979 enabled minor-league baseball to return to Buffalo, New York is from the history section of the Buffalo Bisons' official Web site, http://www.minorleaguebaseball.com/app/about/page.jsp?ymd=20060119&content_id=38581&vkey=about_t422&fext=.jsp&sid=t422.

4. For more information on Robert Rich's skillful building of the Buffalo Bisons and Pilot Field into a minor-league success story, as well as his attempt to bring a major-league expansion franchise to Buffalo, see Irvin Muchnick, "Rich Makes His Pitch," *New York Times*, July 30, 1989.

5. Information on Miles Wolff's involvement with the Durham Bulls, as well as his pioneering role in the development of independent professional baseball in the 1990s is from Stefan Fatsis, *Wild and Outside: How a Renegade Minor League Revived the Spirit of Baseball in America's Heartland* (New York: Walker and Co., 1995).

6. The sports sociologist Dr. Rebecca S. Kraus, in her book *Minor League Baseball: Community Building through Hometown Sports* (New York: Haworth Press, 2003), describes the recent history and resurgence in minor-league and independent professional baseball from a social, community, psychological, and economic perspective. She also gives a detailed description of the fall and rise of the minor-league game and of the agreements with the major leagues that led to the growth of the minors in the 1990s to the present day. Readers who want to know more about the social aspects of the relationship between a community and its ball club will be interested in Kraus's book.

7. I used the following articles to research the modern condition of minor-league ownership, as well as personalities like Mike Veeck and Marvin Goldklang, and they are a rich source of information about the revitalization of minor-league baseball from 1990 on:

1. "Notebook: If You Do the Laundry, They Will Come," *Time*, August 30, 1999, p. 21.
2. Jerome Cramer, "So You Want to Own a Minor League Baseball Team," *Forbes*, Fall 2003, pp. 82–86.
3. Alan Schwarz, "Not Just Peanuts," *Newsweek*, May 9, 2005.
4. Ramesh Nagarajan, "Survival of the Minor Leagues," *Humanities*, September/October 2002, p. 45.
5. Alan Schwarz, "How I Did It," *Inc.*, April 2005, p. 116.

Three: Baseball Returns to New Jersey in 1994

1. Robert Mulcahy sat for an interview with me on August 24, 2006, and his recollections about the Meadowlands' efforts to bring the Yankees to New Jersey and build a major-league baseball stadium are taken from that interview.

2. Information regarding Cathedra Investment Corp.'s effort to build a minor-league ballpark in Jackson, as well as Freeholder Conover's attempt to bring a minor-league club to Atlantic City, was taken from articles in the *Newark Star-Ledger* and the *Press of Atlantic City* that appeared between 1988 and 1992.

3. Christopher T. Edwards, in his book *Filling in the Seams: The Story of Trenton Thunder Baseball* (Moorestown, NJ: Middle Atlantic Press, 1997), gives a detailed portrayal of the demographics of the Trenton area prior to the club's creation and the efforts made by Prunetti and others to make the Trenton Thunder baseball club a reality.

4. Christopher Edwards also describes the early organization of the Thunder front office in his above-mentioned book.

5. Tom McCarthy sat for an interview on August 9, 2006, during which he reminisced about the early days of the Trenton Thunder and his involvement with them. He still occasionally visits Waterfront Park when the Mets are playing in Philadelphia.

6. Ruth Bonapace, "After 16 Years, Minor League Baseball Returns," *New York Times*, June 19, 1994.

7. Rachelle Garbarine, "They're Not the Yankees, but Pro Baseball Is Coming," *New York Times*, October 31, 1993.

8. Richard Sandomir, "Field of Dreams Turns into Nightmare in New Jersey," *New York Times*, August 23, 1994.

9. Rod Allee, "Learning the Game," *Bergen Record*, August 31, 1994.

10. The continuous chaos that surrounded both Skylands Management Co. and Millennium Sports Management during the years of the New Jersey Cardinals is well documented in the *Newark Star-Ledger, Bergen Record, Morristown Daily Record*, and *New York Times*. The information contained in this chapter is mostly a result of researching these newspapers for information regarding Millennium Sports Management and Skylands Park. Also, I scanned the microfilm of the *New Jersey Herald* at the Sussex County Library, Newton branch, as part of my overall research.

Four: The Trenton Thunder

1. On September 4, 2006, Brad Taylor and the Trenton Thunder staff opened their offices to me and pretty much gave me the run of the place. I was able to shadow them as they went about their tasks of preparing for the day's game. Much of my material for this chapter is from this day.

2. From my August 9, 2006, interview with Tom McCarthy. See note 5 to chapter 3, above.

3. Dan Loney, the voice of the Trenton Thunder, sat for an interview on August 10, 2005, at Waterfront Park. He is one of the busiest people at the park before a game, gathering statistical information and game notes for the press box as well as preparing for the day's broadcast. He also is the basketball voice of the Princeton Tigers.

4. Nicole Sherry sat for an interview on October 25, 2006, right after it was announced that she was leaving the Trenton Thunder and returning to Baltimore to be the head groundskeeper for the Orioles.

5. This particular interview with Brad Taylor took place on June 15, 2006.

Five: A League of His Own

1. Doug Pappas, "Inside the Major League Rules," Society for American Baseball Research Business of Baseball Section, http://www.businessofbaseball.com/insidethemlbrules.htm.

2. Frank Boulton sat for an extensive interview with me on January 5, 2007, where he recounted the many events leading up to the founding of the Atlantic League. All quotations from Boulton in this chapter are from that interview.

3. Boulton made the comment to writer Bill LeConey in an article titled "New Jersey Baseball Subject of 'Summit,'" *Press of Atlantic City*, August 21, 1997.

4. See the Atlantic League Web page, http://www.atlanticleague.com/about.html.

5. From an interview with Bob Wirz at his Stratford, Connecticut, home on December 18, 2006. Wirz helped bring independent baseball to Waterbury, Connecticut, and is currently involved in the Can-Am League with the New Haven County Cutters.

6. From an interview with Joe Klein at the Atlantic League office in Camden, New Jersey, on August 23, 2005.

7. Source: Atlantic League Web site, http://www.atlanticleague.com. This information was included in an article commemorating the tenth anniversary of the league in 2007.

Six: The Somerset Patriots

1. Taken from the story "Patriots' Captain Escandon Retires," by Ryan Dunleavy and Jeff Weber, in the *Bridgewater Courier News*, October 3, 2005.

2. Taken from the Township of Bridgewater's Web site, http://www.bridgewaternj.gov/facts.htm.

3. Information concerning the American Cyanamid plant in Bridgewater was found on the Environmental Protection Agency's Web site, http://www.epa.gov/superfund/programs/recycle/success/1-pagers/amercyan.htm.

4. Denise Coyle is a Somerset County Freeholder, with a term expiring at the end of 2007. She was very instrumental in the financial planning that resulted in the Patriots' ballpark in Bridgewater. She sat with me for an interview on August 2, 2005, at the County Complex in Somerville, New Jersey.

5. Steve Kalafer sat with me for an interview on July 27, 2005, at Commerce Bank Ballpark during a Patriots game.

6. Professor Larry McCarthy granted me an interview on February 9, 2006 in his office at Seton Hall University, Stillman School of Business.

7. I laughed out loud the first time I saw Brian Traxler, with his big potbelly, take the field with the Patriots in 1999. The laughter ended when he cracked a huge home run. This man could hit! Traxler was remembered in an article in the Patriot's 2005 yearbook titled "In Memory of Brian Traxler."

8. Emiliano Escandon shared with me his views on his Patriots experiences and Sparky Lyle during an interview on July 25, 2005.

9. Adam Gladstone described his player-procurement strategy during an interview on January 29, 2006.

10. On July 25, 2005, I spent the afternoon and evening with the front-office staff at Commerce Bank Ballpark, observed their operation, and interviewed many

of their staff members as well as fans in the stands. Quotes from GM Patrick McVerry, shortstop Emiliano Escandon, broadcaster Brian Bender, and other members of the staff are as a result of interviews conducted on that day.

Seven: Newark and the Bears

1. From "Recalling the Mosque Theater and Building" by Nat Bodian, on the Virtual Newark Web site, http://www.virtualnewarknj.com/memories/dtheatre/bodianmosque.htm.
2. Dr. Clement Alexander Price of Rutgers–Newark sat for an interview with me on January 30, 2007. All of the quotes from Dr. Price come from that interview. The DVD of his documentary "The Once and Future Newark" can be obtained through the Rutgers–Newark Web site, www.newark.rutgers.edu/newark.
3. From a press release from the Rutgers–Newark Office of Communications, September 26, 2006.
4. Mike Collazo of the Newark Bears took me on a guided tour of the new historical room at Bears and Eagles Riverfront Stadium on November 6, 2006, and his comments are from that tour.
5. Rick Cerone gave me his thoughts on his years as owner of the Newark Bears in a personal interview on April 9, 2007.
6. From Ronald Smothers, "Newark Hails Baseball's Return, but the High Cost of a New Stadium Raises Doubts," *New York Times,* July 4, 1999.
7. I interviewed Jim Cerny at Bears and Eagles Riverfront Stadium on August 16, 2005.
8. Kim DaCosta Holton sat for an interview with me on October 11, 2006. Her walking tour of the Ironbound section of Newark, part of a course that she teaches at Rutgers–Newark, was featured in the fall 2006 issue of *Rutgers Magazine.*
9. Sportswriter Michael Ashmore, along with Scott Stanchak, publishes the Atlantic League Baseball News blog at http://albnews.blogspot.com. The quotes from John Brandt came from an interview that they conducted with Brandt for the blog on December 12, 2006.

Eight: Discovering Camden with the Riversharks

1. This information was taken from the history section of Camden's official Web site, http://www.ci.camden.nj.us/history/historymain.html.
2. From the Easterbrook Art and Drafting Pen page of the Vintage Nibs Web site, http://hans.presto.tripod.com/nibs/esterbrook.html#hist.
3. From the New York Shipbuilding Company historical site, http://members.aol.com/nyship/history.html.
4. From the Web site of the Victor Lofts, the new luxury condominiums that are now housed in the Victor Factory structure. This Web site gives the his-

tory of the building and the Victor and RCA companies at http://www.thevictor
lofts.com/history.html.

5. An excellent overview of the challenges faced by Camden since the 1950s
can be found in Peter Kerr's article, "Camden Forces Its Suburbs to Ask, What
If a City Dies?" *New York Times*, September 7, 1989.

6. Details of the Camden waterfront redevelopment are found on the Web site
of the American Planning Association, in their publication "The Commissioner,"
at http://www.planning.org/thecommissioner/19952003/winter03.htm.

7. Frank Boulton's comments appeared in Eileen Stilwell's article, "Stadium Not a One-Short Deal for Shilling," *Cherry Hill Courier-Post*, May 10, 2001.

8. Information regarding the community involvement of Rutgers–Camden
was taken primarily from Melanie Burney, "Rutgers–Camden Campus Turns
50—Once Known as Rutgers College of South Jersey, It Is Making a Name for
Itself in Academia and in the Surrounding Community," *Philadelphia Inquirer*,
December 26, 2000.

9. Additional information on Rutgers–Camden community initiatives can
be found on the university's Web page, http://www.camden.rutgers.edu/
community.htm.

10. An article detailing the Campbell's Soup Company's deal for naming
rights and sponsorship to the new ballpark in Camden appeared in the *Philadelphia Inquirer* on January 18, 2001, titled "Camden Stadium Will Restore Campbell's Name to Waterfront: The Soup Company Is Back—This Time with a
Plate," by Joseph A. Gambardello.

11. John Brandt sat for an interview at Campbell's Field on August 23,
2005, where he detailed to me the many challenges he encountered while running the Camden Riversharks in the club's first years.

12. This information is taken from an article that appeared in the *Cherry
Hill Courier-Post* on February 20, 2004, titled "Camden Riversharks Have Much
to Prove."

13. Details of the 2004 Atlantic League playoffs are from the *Cherry Hill
Courier-Post*, September 22–27, 2004.

Nine: The Atlantic City Surf

1. Frank Boulton shared his thoughts on his years as owner of the Atlantic
City Surf during an interview conducted on January 5, 2007.

2. On August 22, 2005, I spent the entire afternoon and evening at the
Sandcastle Stadium in Atlantic City. During the afternoon, I had lengthy conversations with front-office staff members about the operations of the Surf, from
which I quote in this chapter. Later, I attended the ball game that I describe in
this chapter, documenting the sights and sounds of the evening.

3. Pete Thompson, sports anchor for TV-40 in Atlantic City, sat with me
for an interview to discuss the Surf at the WMGM studios on January 19, 2006.
His comments are taken from this interview.

4. Chuck Betson is an ex–Atlantic City area newpaper reporter himself, and the former publicity director for the Atlantic City Surf.

5. Mark Schuster explained his hopes for the Atlantic City Surf in Lori Hoffman's article, "New Home Base," *Atlantic City Weekly,* April 27, 2006.

6. From the Bob Wirz personal interview cited above in chapter 5, note 5.

Ten: Youth Must Be Served

1. More information on the early Northeast League can be found at the Northeast Fan Web site, http://www.nefan.net/new_page_2.htm. The league's history on this Web page was written by Stephen Gates, as adapted from the Can-Am League's Web site in 2004.

2. All quotations from Bob Wirz in this chapter are from the personal interview cited above in chapter 5, note 5.

3. The history of Montclair State University was taken from the school's Web page, http://www.montclair.edu/welcome/history.html.

4. I did considerable research using the pages of the *Newark Star-Ledger* in gathering the events that led to the building of Yogi Berra Stadium in Little Falls, including Yogi Berra's involvement as well as Floyd Hall's securing of the Northeast League team to play in it. The years my research focused on were 1993 to 1999.

5. Dave Kaplan responded to some questions I had sent him pertaining to the origins of the Yogi Berra Museum and Learning Center via e-mail on December 27, 2006. His quotes are taken from that e-mail.

6. I interviewed Floyd Hall during a New Jersey Jackals game on August 1, 2005.

7. Statistical records of the New Jersey Jackals, as well as the noteworthy individual performance information, was taken from the New Jersey Jackals' Web page, http://www.jackals.com/history/yearbyyear.asp.

8. I interviewed Zach Smithlin on the field at Yogi Berra Stadium prior to the Jackals game on August 1, 2005.

9. I obtained information regarding the move of the Cardinals from Sussex County and the subsequent efforts to replace them at Skylands Park by researching the *New Jersey Herald* and the *Morristown Daily Record* between the end of the 2005 baseball season and the beginning of the 2006 season.

10. Josh Ury's baseball career and background from Morris County was well documented in both the *New Jersey Herald* and the *Morristown Daily Record* during the 2006 season.

Eleven: Nine Innings with the Lakewood BlueClaws

1. The baseball game described in this chapter was played on September 6, 2006. It was a South Atlantic League playoff game between the Lexington Legends and the Lakewood BlueClaws at FirstEnergy Park in Lakewood.

2. Details of the finances pertaining to the BlueClaws being in an urban enterprise zone were written about by Joe Adellizi in an article titled "Minor League Team Making a New Pitch" in the *Asbury Park Press*, February 9, 1999.

3. I conducted interviews with members of the BlueClaws front office, including general manager Geoff Brown, director of community relations Jim DeAngelis, and media and public relations manager Ben Wagner, at FirstEnergy Park on August 24, 2005.

4. From Wilford S. Shamlin, "BlueClaws Will Pay for Stadium Enhancements," *Asbury Park Press*, July 21, 2000.

5. Source: New Jersey Commerce, Economic Growth and Tourism Commission 2005 Tourism Economic Impact Study, http://www.state.nj.us/travel/pdf/2006–07-tourism-ecom-impact.pdf.

6. From Joe Delizzi, "Instincts Have Made Finley a Major Dealer in the Minors," *Asbury Park Press*, May 27, 2006.

Index

Bob Golon is assistant director of the Plainfield Public Library in Plainfield, New Jersey. Bob's father used to take him on Sunday drives to Newark's Ruppert Stadium and tell him stories about the old Bears. He is a lifelong devotee of baseball history and a self-described New Jersey baseball junkie.

A New Jersey native, Bob received his MLIS from Rutgers University in 2004 after spending the prior eighteen years in the technology industry as a sales engineer for the Hewlett-Packard Company. His articles have appeared in numerous magazines and Web sites, and he has appeared on television, most recently on "Yankeeography: Casey Stengel" on the YES Network. Bob also has made presentations at the National Baseball Hall of Fame and Museum in Cooperstown, New York, as well as various local libraries and associations. This is his first book.

Bob and his wife, Jill, live in South Plainfield, New Jersey. They have two grown children, son Jay and daughter Janet.